R. Gupta's®

MANIPUR
General Knowledge

A Treasure of Knowledge about the State
Covering All Important Details along with
Latest Who's Who & Current Affairs

by
RPH Editorial Board

2020
Thoroughly Revised and
Updated Edition

Ramesh Publishing House, New Delhi

Published by

O.P. Gupta *for* Ramesh Publishing House

Admin. Office

12-H, New Daryaganj Road, Opp. Officers' Mess,
New Delhi-110002 ℑ 23261567, 23275224, 23275124

✦ E-mail: info@rameshpublishinghouse.com

✦ Website: www.rameshpublishinghouse.com

Showroom

● Balaji Market, Nai Sarak, Delhi-6 ℑ 23253720, 23282525

● 4457, Nai Sarak, Delhi-6, ℑ 23918938

Book Code: R-1864

ISBN: 978-93-5012-899-2

HSN Code: 49011010

Contents

WHO'S WHO

N. Biren Singh

Governor : Dr. Najma A. Heptulla

Chief Minister : N. Biren Singh

MINISTERS

Si.No.	Name	Portfolio(s)
1.	N. Biren Singh	C.M., Home, Transport, Personnel, Planning, Minor Irrigation, Minority & OBC, General Administration, Sericulture, Tourism, IT, vigilance and other departments not specifically allocated to any other ministers.
2.	Y. Joykumar Singh	Deputy CM., Finance, Excise, Taxation, Science and Technology, Economics and Statistics and Civil Aviation
3.	T. Radheshyam Singh	Education, Labour and Employment
4.	Nemcha Kipgen	Social Welfare and Cooperation
5.	V. Hangkhalian	Agriculture, Veterinary and Animal Husbandry
6.	L. Jayantakumar Singh	Health, Family Welfare, Law and Legislative, Art and Culture, CADA
7.	Th Bishwajit Singh	Public works, Rural Development and Panchayati Raj, Information and Public Relations, Administrative Reforms, Commerce and Industries, Power
8.	Letpao Haokip	Youth Affairs, Sports, Irrigation and Flood Control
9.	Karam Shyam	PDS and Consumer Affairs, Weights and Measures, Revenue, Relief and Rehabilitation
10.	N. Kayishii	Tribal and Hill areas department and fisheries
11.	Th Shyamkumar	MAHUD, Forest and Environment, Horticulture, Soil Conservation and Town Planning
12.	Loshi Dikho	PHED, Printing and Stationary

N. Biren Singh (Honourable Chief Minister)

Nongthombam Biren Singh (born 1 January 1961) is the current Chief Minister of Manipur. He began his career as a footballer and got recruited in the Border Security Force (BSF) playing for its team in domestic competitions. He resigned from the BSF and turned to journalism. He began the vernacular daily *Naharolgi Thoudang* in 1992 and worked as the editor till 2001.

N. Biren Singh

Personal Information

Date of Birth	1 January, 1961, Luwangsangbam Mamang Leikai, Imphal East, Manipur, India
Political Party	BJP (2016-Present)
Other Political Affiliations	Indian National Congress (2003-2016), Democratic Revolutionary Peoples Party (2002-03)
Spouse(s)	Heiyainu Devi
Children	3
Alma mater	Manipur University

Politics

❏ In 2002, he was elected to the Legislative Assembly of Manipur, as the Democratic Revolutionary Peoples Party candidate in the constituency Heingang. He later joined the Indian National Congress.

❏ In May 2003, he was appointed Minister of State of Vigilance in the Manipur state government.

❏ In 2007, he retained his Assembly seat, contesting on behalf of the INC. He was later appointed as the Minister of Irrigation & Flood Control and Youth Affairs & Sports in the State Government.

❏ In 2012, he again retained his Assembly seat for the third consecutive term.

❏ In October 2016, Biren resigned from the Manipur Legislative Assembly and the Manipur Pradesh Congress Committee, this came after revolt against Chief Ministers of Manipur Okram Ibobi Singh.

❏ He formally joined the BJP on 17 October 2016 and later became the Spokesperson and Co-convener of the Election Management Committee of BJP Manipur Pradesh. He won the 2017 Manipur Legislative Assembly Election from Heingang Assembly Constituency.

❏ In March 2017, he was elected as leader of the BJP Legislature Party in Manipur and with a majority of MLAs having been presented to the Governor, he was sworn in as Chief Minister of Manipur on 15 March 2017. He is the first ever BJP Chief Minister in Manipur. ❏ ❏ ❏

MEMBERS OF THE MANIPUR LEGISLATIVE ASSEMBLY—ELECTIONS 2017

Name of Member	Constituency	Party
1. Thounaojam Shyamkumar*	Andro	INC
2. Konthoujam Govindas	Bishnupur	INC
3. Letpao Haokip	Chandel (ST)	NPP
4. Khashim Vashum	Chingai (ST)	NPF
5. V. Hangkhanlian	Churachandpur (ST)	BJP
6. Nongthombam Biren Singh	Heingang	BJP
7. Thokchom Radheshyam Singh	Heirok	BJP
8. T. Thangzalam Haokip	Henglep (ST)	BJP
9. Dr. Radheshyam Yumnam	Hiyanglam	BJP
10. Ashab Uddin	Jiribam	IND
11. Yengkhom Surchandra Singh*	Kakching	INC
12. Nemcha Kipgen	Kangpokpi	BJP
13. D. D. Thaisii	Karong (ST)	INC
14. Lourembam Rameshwor Meetei	Keirao	BJP
15. L. Jayantakumar Singh	Keishamthong	NPP
16. Surjakumar Okram	Khangabok	INC
17. Thokchom Lokeshwar Singh	Khundrakpam	INC
18. Leishangthem Susindro Meitei	Khurai	BJP
19. Dr. Sapam Ranjan Singh	Konthoujam	BJP
20. Nahakpam Indrajit Singh	Kshetrigao	BJP
21. Sanasam Bira Singh*	Kumbi	INC
22. Kshetrimayum Biren Singh	Lamlai	INC
23. Sorokhaibam Rajen Singh	Lamsang	BJP
24. Karam Shyam	Langthabal	LJP
25. Muhammad Abdul Nasir	Lilong	INC
26. Losii Dikho	Mao (ST)	NPF
27. Kongkham Robindro Singh	Mayang Imphal	BJP
28. Pukhrem Sharatchandra Singh	Moirang	BJP
29. Nameirakpam Loken Singh	Nambol	INC
30. Soibam Subhaschandra Singh	Naoriya Pakhanglakpa	BJP

Name of Member	Constituency	Party
31. Gaikhangam	Nungba (ST)	INC
32. Laishram Radhakishore Singh	Oinam	BJP
33. Akoijam Mirabai Devi	Patsoi	INC
34. K. Leishiyo	Phungyar (ST)	NPF
35. Rajkumar Imo Singh	Sagolband	INC
36. T. N. Haokip	Saikot (ST)	INC
37. Yamthong Haokip	Saikul (ST)	INC
38. Ngamthang Haokip*	Saitu (ST)	INC
39. Heikham Dingo Singh	Sekmai (SC)	BJP
40. Ginsuanhau*	Singhat (ST)	INC
41. Yumnam Khemchand Singh	Singjamei	BJP
42. Kangujam Ranjit Singh	Sugnu	INC
43. N. Kayisii	Tadubi (ST)	NPP
44. Awangbow Newmai	Tamei (ST)	NPF
45. Samuel Jendai Kamei	Tamenglong (ST)	BJP
46. D. Korungthang	Tengnoupal (ST)	INC
47. Tongbram Robindro Singh	Thanga	AITMC
48. Khumukcham Joykisan Singh	Thangmeiband	INC
49. Vungzagin Valte	Thanlon (ST)	BJP
50. Thongam Biswajit Singh	Thongju	BJP
51. Okram Ibobi Singh	Thoubal	INC
52. Dr. Chaltonlien Amo	Tipaimukh (ST)	INC
53. Alfred Kanngam Arthur	Ukhrul (ST)	INC
54. Yumnam Joykumar Singh	Uripok	NPP
55. Muhammad Fajur Rahim	Wabgai	INC
56. Paonam Brojen Singh	Wangjing Tentha	INC
57. Okram Henry Singh	Wangkhei	INC
58. Keisham Meghachandra Singh	Wangkhem	INC
59. Oinam Lukhoi Singh*	Wangoi	INC
60. Thokchom Satyabrata Singh	Yaiskul	BJP

* Elected on INC ticket but now in BJP.

GOVERNORS

Name	Period
Braj Kumar Nehru	21.01.1972 - 21.09.1973
Lallan Prasad Singh	21.09.1973 - 12.08.1981
Saiyid Muzaffar Hussain Burney	12.08.1981 - 02.06.1984
K.V. Krishna Rao	02.06.1984 - 01.07.1989
Chintamani Panigrahi	01.07.1989 - 20.03.1993
K.V. Raghunatha Reddy	20.03.1993 - 31.08.1993
V.K. Nayar	31.08.1993 - 23.12.1994
Oudh Narain Shrivastava	23.12.1994 - 02.12.1999
Ved Prakash Marwah	02.12.1999 - 12.06.2003
Arvind Dave	12.06.2003 - 02.08.2003
Shivinder Singh Siddhu	03.08.2003 - 23-07-2008
Gurbachan Singh Jagat	23.07.2008 - 22-07-2013
Ashwini Kumar (Add. Charge)	23.07.2013 - 31-12-2013
Vinod Kumar Duggal	31-12-2013 - 28-08-2014
K.K. Paul (Add. Charge)	29-08-2014 - 15-05-2015
Syed Ahmed	16-05-2015 - 27-09-2015
V. Shanmuganathan (Add. Charge)	28-09-2015 - 20-08-2016
Dr. Najma A. Heptulla	21-08-2016 - till date

CHIEF MINISTERS

Name	Period
Shri N. Biren Singh	15.03.2017 - till date
Shri Okram Ibobi Singh	07.03.2002 - 14.03.2017
Shri Radhabinod Koijam	15.02.2001 - 01.06.2001
Shri W. Nipamacha Singh	02.03.2000 - 14.02.2001
Shri W. Nipamacha Singh	16.12.1997 - 01.03.2000
Shri Rishang Keishing	25.02.1995 - 15.12.1997
Shri Rishang Keishing	14.12.1994 - 24.02.1995
Shri R.K. Dorendra Singh	09.04.1992 - 30.12.1993
Shri R.K. Ranbir Singh	23.02.1990 - 07.01.1992
Shri R.K. Jaichandra Singh	04.03.1988 - 17.02.1990
Shri Rishang Keishing	04.01.1985 - 04.03.1988
Shri Rishang Keishing	19.06.1981 - 04.01.1985
Shri Rishang Keishing	27.11.1980 - 28.02.1981
Shri R.K. Dorendra Singh	14.01.1980 - 26.11.1980
Shri Yangmasho Shaiza	29.06.1977 - 14.11.1979
Shri R.K. Dorendra Singh	23.07.1975 - 13.05.1977
Shri R.K. Dorendra Singh	06.12.1974 - 23.07.1975
Shri Yangmasho Shaiza	10.07.1974 - 05.12.1974
Md. Alimuddin	04.03.1974 - 08.07.1974
Md. Alimuddin	23.03.1972 - 28.03.1973
Shri M. Koireng Singh	19.02.1968 - 16.10.1969
Shri L. Thambou Singh	13.10.1967 - 25.10.1967
Shri M. Koireng Singh	20.03.1967 - 04.10.1967
Shri M. Koireng Singh	01.07.1963 - 12.01.1967
Shri M.K. Priyobrata Singh	14.08.1947 - 15.10.1949

SPEAKERS

Assembly	Name of Speaker	Period
I State Assembly (1948-49)	T.C.Tiankham	19.11.1948 to 15.10.1949
* I Territorial Council (1957-62)	1. H.Dwijamani Dev Sharma	Sept. 1957 to Oct.1958
	2. Sibo Larho	Oct. 1958 to 2.8.1962
* I Territorial Assembly (1962-67)	1. M.Koireng Singh	3.8.1962 to 21.7.1963
	2. Kh.Ibetombi Singh	23.7.1963 to 20.3.1967
*II Territorial Assembly (1967-69)	1. S.Tombi Singh	21.3.1967 to 24.10.1967
	2. Sibo Larho	5.3.1968 to 29.3.1972
I Manipur Legislative Assembly (1972-73)	1. Dr.L.Chandramani Singh	30.3.1972 to 8.3.1974
II Manipur Legislative Assembly (1974-79)	1. R.K. Dorendra Singh	26.3.1974 to 5.12.1974
	2. Md. Alimuddin	16.12.1974 to 4.9.1975
	3. Dr.L.Chandramani Singh	18.9.1975 to 21.10.1978
	4. R.K.Ranbir Singh	12.1.1979 to 18.2.1980
III Manipur Legislative Assembly (1980-85)	1. Y. Yaima Singh	18.2.1980 to 23.1.1985
IV Manipur Legislative Assembly (1985-90)	1. W. Angou Singh	24.1.1985 to 20.12.1988
	2. Th. Devendra Singh	20.12.1988 to 2.3.1990
V Manipur Legislative Assembly (1990-95)	1. Dr. H. Borbabu Singh	2.3.1990 to 9.1.1995
	2. E. Biramani Singh	9.1.1995 to 27.2.1995
VI Manipur Legislative Assembly (1995-2000)	1. W. Nipamacha Singh	22.3.1995 to 6.12.1997
	2. K. Babudhon Singh	29.12.1997 to 7.3.2000
VII Manipur Legislative Assembly (2000-02)	1. Dr. S. Dhananjoy Singh	13.3.2000 to 8.3.2002
VIII Manipur Legislative Assembly (2002-2007)	1. T.N.Haokip	12.3.2002 to 7.12.2005
	2. Maniruddin Sheikh	09.12.2005 to 15.3.2007
IX Manipur Legislative Assembly (2007- 2012)	1. Budhichandra Singh	16.3.2007 to 01.10.2010
	2. I. Hemochandra Singh	2-10-2010 to 19-03-2012
X Manipur Legislative Assembly (2012-2017)	1. Thokchom Lokeshore	19-03-2012 to 19-03-2017
XI Manipur Legislative Assembly (2017-)	1. Y. Khemchand Singh	20-03-2017 till date

* The nomenclature of the office of the Presiding Officer during the Territorial Council/ Territorial Assembly period is the 'Chairman'.

DEPUTY SPEAKERS

Assembly	*Name of Deputy Speaker*	*Period*
I State Assembly (1948-49)	T. Bokul Singh	19.11.1948 to 15.10.1949
I Territorial Council (1957-62)	—	—
I Territorial Assembly (1962-67)	1. L. Solomon 2. Md.Alimuddin	16.8.1963 to 15.11.1965 10.12.1965 to 12.1.1967
II Territorial Assembly (1967-69)	1. Kh.Chaoba 2. L.Ibomcha Singh	3.4.1967 to 24.10.1967 3.4.1968 to 20.10.1969
I Manipur Legislative Assembly (1972-73)	1. Atomba Ngairangbamcha	25.5.1972 to 26.3.1973
II Manipur Legislative Assembly (1974-79)	1. Th. Chaoba Singh 2. N. Paoheu 3. Ngurdinglien 4. O. Joy Singh	19.4.1974 to 30.7.1974 16.8.1974 to 10.3.1975 8.4.1975 to 16.7.1977 26.10.1977 to 14.11.1979
III Manipur Legislative Assembly (1980-85)	1. H. Lokhon Singh 2. W. Angou Singh	17.3.1980 to 14.12.1980 6.7.1981 to 4.1.1985
IV Manipur Legislative Assembly (1985-90)	1. H. Sanayaima Singh 2. M. Manihar Singh	19.2.1985 to 18.2.1990 21.3.1990 to 24.7.1990
V Manipur Legislative Assembly (1990-95)	1. N. Mangi Singh	25.9.1990 to 25.2.1995
VI Manipur Legislative Assembly (1995-00)	1. I. Hemochandra Singh 2. K. Babudhon Singh 3. Ksh. Biren Singh 4. T. T. Haokip	25.3.1995 to 28.3.1995 26.9.1995 to 27.12.1997 12.1.1998 to 7.4.1998 3.7.1998 to 1.3.2000
VII Manipur Legislative Assembly (2000-02)	1. K. Raina 2. Z. Mangaibou	6.4.2000 to 23.2.2001 23.3.2001 to 5.5.2001
VIII Manipur Legislative Assembly (2002-07)	1. K. Ranjit Singh 2. L. Lala Singh	21.3.2002 to 22.3.2002 10.7.2002 to 7.7.2004
IX Manipur Legislative Assembly (2007-2012)	1. Th. Shyam Kumar 2. Lokeshwar Singh	2-8-2007 to 18.4.2009 2009 to 18-03-2012
X Manipur Legislative Assembly (2012-2017)	1. M.K. Preshow	1-07-2013 to March 2017
XI Manipur Legislative Assembly (2017- ....)	1. K. Robindro	9-02-2018 to till date

CHAIRMEN OF HILL AREAS COMMITTEE (HAC)

Assembly	Name of Chairman	Period
I Manipur Legislative Assembly (1972-73)	1. S.P. Henry	18.10.1972 to 26.03.1973
II Manipur Legislative Assembly (1974-79)	1. Benjamin Banee 2. Saheni Adani	19.04.1974 to 03.01.1977 29.04.1977 to 13.01.1979
III Manipur Legislative Assembly (1980-85)	1. K. Huriang 2. L.S. John	17.03.1980 to 27.06.1980 11.07.1980 to 04.01.1985
IV Manipur Legislative Assembly (1985-90)	1. R.V. Mingthing 2. I.D. Dijuanang	15.03.1985 to 02.11.1988 15.11.1988 to
V Manipur Legislative Assembly (1990-95)	1. I.D. Dijuanang	24.02.1995
VI Manipur Legislative Assembly (1995-00)	1. Dr. M. Horam	02.05.1995 to 01.03.2000
VII Manipur Legislative Assembly (2000-02)	1. C. Doungel	04.04.2000 to 14.05.2001
VIII Manipur Legislative Assembly (2002-07)	1. Songchinkhup	9-4-2002 to 10-01-2007
IX Manipur Legislative Assembly (2007-2012)	Thangminlien Kipgen	13-4-2007 to 11-04-2012
X Manipur Legislative Assembly (2012-2017)	Dr. Chaltonlian Amo	12-4-2012 to 11-04-2017
XI Manipur Legislative Assembly (2017- ....)	Thangzalans Haokip	12-4-2017 till date

MEMBERS OF LOK SABHA FROM MANIPUR

Lok Sabha Term	Consti-tuency	Name	Party
• 1st Lok Sabha	(Inner) (Outer)	Shri Laisram Jugeswar Singh Shri Rishang Keishing	(Congress-I) (Socialist)
• 2nd Lok Sabha	(Inner) (Outer)	Shri Laisram Achaw Singh Shri Rungsung Suisa	(Socialist) (Congress-I)
• 3rd Lok Sabha	(Inner) (Outer)	Shri S. Tombi Singh Shri Rishang Keishing	(Congress-I) (Socialist)
• 4th Lok Sabha	(Inner) (Outer)	Shri M. Meghachandra Singh Shri Paokai Haokip	(CPI) (Independent)
• 5th Lok Sabha	(Inner) (Outer)	Shri N. Tombi Singh Shri Paokai Haokip	(Congress-I) (Congress-I)

Lok Sabha Term	Consti-tuency	Name	Party
• 6th Lok Sabha	(Inner)	Shri N. Tombi Singh	(Congress-I)
	(Outer)	Shri Yangmaso Shaiza	(INC)
	(Outer)	Shri Kaiho (By-Election)	(Manipur People's Party)
• 7th Lok Sabha	(Inner)	Shri Ngangom Mohendra Singh	(CPI)
	(Outer)	Shri N. Gouzagin	(Congress-I)
• 8th Lok Sabha	(Inner)	Shri N. Tombi Singh	(Cogress-I)
	(Outer)	Shri Meijinlung Kamson	(Congress-I)
• 9th Lok Sabha	(Inner)	Shri N. Tombi Singh	(Congress-I)
	(Outer)	Shri Meijinlung Kamson	(Congress-I)
• 10th Lok Sabha	(Inner)	Shri yumnam Yaima Singh	(Manipur People's Party)
	(Outer)	Prof. Meijinlung Kamson	(INC)
• 11th Lok Sabha	(Inner)	Shri Th. Chaoba Singh	(INC)
	(Outer)	Prof. Meijinlung Kamson	(INC)
• 12th Lok Sabha	(Inner)	Shri. Th. Chaoba Singh	(MSCP)
	(Outer)	Km. Kim Gangte	(CPI)
• 13th Lok Sabha	(Inner)	Shri Th. Chaoba Singh	(BJP)
	(Outer)	Shri Holkhomang Haokip	(NCP)
• 14th Lok Sabha	(Inner)	Dr. Thokchom Meinya	(INC)
	(Outer)	Shri Mani Charenamai	(Ind.)
• 15th Lok Sabha	(Inner)	Dr. Thokchom Meinya	(INC)
	(Outer)	Shri Thangso Baite	(INC)
• 16th Lok Sabha	(Inner)	Dr. Thokchom Meinya	(INC)
	(Outer)	Shri Thangso Baite	(INC)

MEMBERS OF RAJYA SABHA FROM MANIPUR

NAME	PARTY	TERM
❖ Shri Ng. Tompok Singh	INC	03.04.1954 — 02.04.1956
❖ Shri Laimayum Lalit Madhob Sharma	INC	01.12.1956 — 02.04.1960
❖ Shri Laimayum Lalit Madhob Sharma	INC	03.04.1960 — 02.11.1964
❖ Shri Sinam Krishnamohon Singh	INC	13.01.1965 — 02.04.1966
❖ Shri Sinam Krishnamohon Singh	INC	03.04.1966 — 02.04.1972
❖ Shri Salam Tombi Singh	MPP	10.04.1972 — 04.04.1974
❖ Shri Irengbam Tompok Singh	INC	18.06.1974 — 09.04.1978

NAME	PARTY	TERM
❖ Shri Ng. Tompok Singh	JAN	10.04.1978 — 09.04.1984
❖ Shri R.K. Jaichandra Singh	INC	10.04.1984 — 12.07.1988
❖ Shri R.K. Dorendra Singh	INC	20.09.1988 — 12.03.1990
❖ Shri B.D. Behring	JD	10.04.1990 — 10.04.1990*
❖ Shri W. Kulabidhu Singh	JD	13.06.1990 — 09.04.1996
❖ Shri W. Angou Singh	INC	10.04.1996 — 09.04.2002
❖ Shri Rishang Keishing	INC	10.04.2002 — 09.04.2008
❖ Shri Rishang Keishing	INC	10.04.2008 — 09.04.2014
❖ Shri Abdul Salam	INC	10.04.2014 — 28.02.2017
❖ Shri K. Bhabananda	BJP	25.05.2017 till date

* Resigned the same day without taking oath and seat.

PRESIDENT'S RULE IN MANIPUR

	During the Presidentship of	From	To
1st time	Dr S. Radhakrishnan	12 January 1967	20 March 1967
2nd time	Dr Zakir Hussain	25 October 1967	19 February 1968
3rd time	V.V. Giri	17 October 1969	23 March 1972
4th time	V.V. Giri	28 March 1973	04 March 1974
5th time	B.D. Jatti (Acting)	16 May 1977	29 June 1977
6th time	Neelam Sanjiva Reddy	14 November 1979	14 January 1980
7th time	Neelam Sanjiva Reddy	28 February 1981	19 June 1981
8th time	R. Venkatraman	07 January 1992	08 April 1992
9th time	Dr Shankar Dayal Sharma	31 December 1993	14 December 1994
10th time	K.R. Narayanan	02 January 2001	07 March 2002

CURRENT AFFAIRS

MANIPUR GOVT INKS MoU FOR SMART CITY PROJECT

The Manipur government on November 6, 2018 signed a memorandum of understanding (MoU) with IL&FS Township and Urban Assets Limited and Pricewaterhouse Coopers Pvt. Ltd. as a project management consultant for implementation of smart city project in Imphal. The project management consultant which was selected through a transparent e-tender, had assured to prepare a detail project report (DPR) in six months. The project is worth around ₹ 1,523 crore. The government, however, had requested the company to complete the DPR a bit earlier. Asserting that the signing of the MoU would pave way for opening a new chapter in urban development in the state, Chief Minister said that the project would include key infrastructure developments like sewerage system, Nambul and Imphal river rejuvenation, development of Kangla, transport service, pollution control and other beautification activities etc.

MARY KOM SCRIPTS HISTORY IN WORLD BOXING

MC Mary Kom's great stature touched a new high when she claimed her sixth title in the World women's boxing championships at Indira Gandhi Stadium Complex in New Delhi on November 24, 2018. The 35-year-old saw off Hanna Okhota of Ukraine with a 5-0 margin in the 48 kg final to take her first gold medal after eight years. This was her second Worlds crown on home soil and second in light flyweight. Her first four gold medals had come in pinweight. With six gold medals and a silver, the

Mary Kom

diminutive Mary now stands as the tallest woman boxer in the 17-year-old history of the event and equals legendary male boxer Cuban Felix Savon's World championships record. However, Sonia Chahal (57 kg), the other Indian in the finals, lost 4-1 to former World youth champion Ornelia Wahner of Germany and had to be satisfied with a silver medal. Overall, Indian boxers gave an improved performance as they secured four medals, including two bronze by Simranjit Kaur (64 kg) and Lovlina Borgohain (69 kg). In the previous edition, India had managed just one silver medal.

BUDGET 2018-19

Manipur's Deputy Chief Minister, Y. Joykumar Singh, who is in-charge of finance presented the budget estimates for 2018-19 fiscal on February 5, 2018 in Manipur legislative Assembly.

The finance minister said that the budget estimates for the year 2018-19 was with a total receipts estimated at ₹ 13,733.62 crore which includes revenue receipts of ₹ 12,648.94 crore and capital receipts of ₹ 1084.68 crore. The fiscal deficit is estimated at ₹ 612.41 crore. The total estimates of state's own tax and non-tax receipts assumed in the budget estimates are ₹ 1047.58 crore and ₹ 248.53 crore respectively. Stating that the government is not proposing any change in the existing tax rates, receipt from the state's share in central taxes and duties is expected to increase by 15 per cent over 2017-18 revised estimate and have been estimated at ₹ 4908.76 crore in the budget estimates.

Joykumar proposed the expenditure estimates for the year 2018-19 with a total gross expenditure of ₹ 13,731.04 crore out of the consolidated fund of the state, an increase of ₹ 3.68 percent over 2017-18 revised estimates of ₹ 13,243.67 crore. Out of the total gross expenditure, an amount of ₹ 1002.82 crore is charged expenditure and the remaining amount of ₹ 12,728.22 crore is voted expenditure and the total revenue expenditure is estimated at ₹ 11,123.82 crore. The finance minister further stated that capital outlay was estimated at ₹ 2252.89 crore. Though the capital outlay in budget estimates 2018-19 reduced vis-à-vis the revised estimates, it is still more than the budget estimates for the year 2017-18 of ₹ 2066.19 crore. Joykumar highlighted the likely fiscal position during the current year with an estimate of surplus revenue account. Fiscal deficit was estimated at (-) ₹ 612.41 crore. That is 2.32 percent of the GSDP and that is within the prescribed limit 3.5 per cent fixed as per the state fiscal responsibility and budget management act. The total outstanding debt is projected at 37.34% of the GSDP during 2018-19 against revised estimates of 38.25 %. Pertaining to revised estimates 2017-18, the finance minister said that the government had placed the total gross expenditure at ₹ 12,420.65 crore in the budget estimate. This has been revised to ₹ 13,243.67 crore showing an increase of ₹ 832.02 crores. Out of the revised estimates, an amount of ₹ 915.72 crore is charged expenditure under the consolidated fund of the state and the remaining amount of ₹ 12,327.95 crore is voted expenditure. The developmental outlay for 2017-18 budget estimates was ₹ 4972.07 crore and it has now been placed at ₹ 5388.82 crore in the revised estimates. Revenue receipts and capital receipts was estimated at ₹ 11,096.25 crore and ₹ 1414.35 crore respectively in budget estimates 2017-18. This has been revised to ₹ 12,025.33 crore and ₹ 1031.57 crore respectively. Including enhancement of transparency and efficiency in public procurement, the finance minister also highlighted the government's endeavour for an all round development of the state in different sectors/departments.

1901

MANIPUR
General Knowledge

CHAPTER 1

Manipur : At a Glance

The word "Manipur" which literally mean 'A Jewelled Land' or 'The Land of Jewels'. Here "Mani" means Jewel and "Pur" means Land or Place respectively.

Surrounded by blue hills with an oval shaped valley at the centre, rich in art and tradition and surcharged with nature's pristine glory, Manipur lies on a melting pot of culture. It is birth place of Polo.

Having a varied and proud history from the earliest times, Manipur came under the British Rule as a Princely State after the defeat in the Anglo-Manipuri War of 1891. After independence of India in 1947, the Princely State of Manipur was merged in the Indian Union on October 15,1949 and became a full-fledged State of India on the 21th January, 1972 with a Legislative Assembly of 60 seats of which 19 are reserved for Scheduled Tribe and one reserved for Scheduled Caste. The State is represented in the Lok Sabha by two members and by one member in the Rajya Sabha.

Manipur extends between 23°50' and 25°42' latitudes north and between 92°58' and 94°45' longitudes east. It covers an area of 22,327 square kilometers and is bounded on the north by Nagaland, on the west by Cachar of Assam, on the east by Burma (Myanmar) and on the south by Mizoram and Chin state of Burma.

MANIPUR : FACT FILE

- **Capital** : Imphal
- **Area** : 22327 sq.km.
- **Population (2011 Census)** : 28,55,794
  (*Males*: 14,38,586; *Females*: 14,17,208)
- **Decadal Growth Rate** : 24.50%
- **Density of Population** : 128 (per sq. km.)

+ **Literacy Rate** : 76.94%
+ **Sex Ratio** : 985 (Females per 1000 Males)
+ **Altitude** : 790 mtrs. above MSL (Imphal)
+ **Latitude** : 23°50'N to 25°42'N
+ **Longitude** : 92°58'E to 94°45'E
+ **Rainfall** : 1467.5 mm (Avg.)
+ **Rainy Season** : May to October
+ **Climate**
   Summer : 14°C to 32°C
   Winter : 0°C to 25°C
+ **State Language** : Manipuri
+ **State Emblem** : KanglaSha
+ **State Bird** : Nongyeen
+ **State Animal** : Sangai
+ **State Game** : Manipuri Polo
+ **State Flower** : Siroi Lily
+ **State Tree** : Uningthou
+ **Assembly Constituencies** : 60
+ **Parliamentary Constituencies** : 2 (One for Inner and One for Outer)
+ **Rajya Sabha Seat** : 1
+ **National Highways** : 3(NH-39-Indo-Myanmar road, NH-53-New Cachar Road, NH-150-Jessami-Tipaimukh Road)
+ **Districts** : 16-Senapati, Tamenglong, Thoubal, Ukhrul, Bishnupur, Chandel, Churachandpur, Imphal East, Imphal West, Jiribam, Kangpokpi, Kakching, Tengnoupal, Kamjong, Noney and Pherzawl
+ **Towns** : 51 *(Statutory towns 28, Census towns 23)*
+ **Small Town Committees** : 33
+ **Gram Panchayats** : 165

Nongin Bird

Siroi Lily

Sangai Deer

Uningthou

+ **Highly Populated District (2011)** : Imphal West
+ **Less Populated District** : Tamenglong
+ **Most Densily Populated District (2011)** : Imphal West (998 persons per sq. km.)
+ **Less populated District (2011)** : Tamenglong (32 persons per sq. km)
+ **Major Cities** : Imphal, Churachandpur, Kakching, Ukhrul, Andro, Bishnupur, Jiribam, Moirang, Moreh, Ningthoukhong, Thoubal, etc.
+ **Largest City** : Imphal
+ **Major Tourist Places** : Shaheed Minar, War Cemetery, Manipur Zoological Garden, Keibul Lamjao National Park, Kaina, Red Hill (Maibam Lok pa Ching), Loukoipat, Shree Shree Govindajee Temple, Phubala, Loktak Lake, Leimaram, Moreh, Tengnoupal, Andro, Khongjom, etc.
+ **Major Crops** : Wheat, Rice, Pulses, Paddy, Maize, Sugarcane, Potato, Mustard, etc.
+ **Major Fruits** : Pineapple, Banana, Papaya, Passion Fruit, Orange, Lemon, Mango etc.
+ **Major Vegetables** : Cabbage, Cauliflower, Peas, French Beans, Tomato, etc.
+ **Major Spices** : Green Chilli, Ginger, Turmeric, Corriander Seeds, etc.
+ **Major Forest Products** : Oak, Teak, Pine, Cane, Bamboo, Leihao, Uningthou, etc.
+ **Major Import Products** : Betel nut, Silk yarn, Pigs, Cotton thread, etc.
+ **Major Export Products** : Bamboo shoot products (orient food), ginger, pineapple, Maize, Mushrooms, etc.
+ **Chief Rivers** : Barak, Imphal, Khuga, Maklang, Ithai, Thoubal, Irang, Nambul, Chakpi, etc.
+ **Major Minerals** : Copper, Nickel, Chromite, Asbestos, Limestone, Lignite, etc.

MANIPUR ECONOMY

Agriculture

Agriculture is the backbone to the economy of Manipur. In fact, almost all of the businessmen in the state deal in crop growing. About 76% of the state's total working population is engaged in agriculture. And nearly 9.4% of the total geographical area is used for cultivation. Manipur produces considerable quantity of paddy, wheat, maize, pulses, and oilseeds, like mustard, groundnut, soybeans, and sunflower. Ginger, turmeric, and fruits & vegetables, like pineapple, lemon, banana, orange, papaya, plum, cauliflower, cabbage, tomato, peas, carrot, and pumpkin are also produced here.

Industries

Its industrial sector has not developed much, but still has a significant contribution in the economy. The State Government is making efforts to start industrialization. here over 7,700 small industrial units have been established. Also industries dealing in cement, drugs and pharmaceuticals, plastic, and steel have been set up. Above and beyond Moreh has emerged as an important business centre due to border trade with Myanmar.

Tourism

Owing to its geographical isolation, Manipur has not received much from the tourism sector. Moreover, its infrastructure is also not well developed. The hilly terrain is another weak point which makes communication difficult in the state.

Keibul Lamjao National Park, the only habitat of Brow Antered Deer, on the bank of Loktak lake, INA (Indian National Army) Memorial at Moirang, Siroi National Park at Ukhrul, Loktak lake, the biggest fresh water lake in the North-East of India, Khongjom War Memorial at Khongiom are the major tourist spots of the state.

Gross State Domestic Product (GSDP)

The money value of all the goods and services produced by the State during a specified period, generally one year before making any adjustment for Consumption of Fixed Capital (CFC) is known as GSDP. The GSDP of Manipur State in absolute terms is continuously increasing over years. The average annual exponential growth rates between 2011-12 to 2016-17 is worked out to be 10.68% and 5.27% for current and constant (2011-12) prices respectively.

Net State Domestic Product (NSDP)

NSDP is the value of all goods and services produced in the State during a specified period, after making adjustments for the Consumption of Fixed Capitals (CFC). The NSDP at current prices for the year 2016-17 is estimated at ₹ 19,824 crores as compared to ₹ 11,501 crores in 2011-12. The NSDP of Manipur at constant prices rose from ₹ 11,501 crores in 2011-12 to ₹ 15,015 crores in 2016-17 registering an annual exponential growth rate of 6.20%.

Per Capita Income

Per Capita Income (PCI) is generally considered as the most effective indicator for ascertaining the economic welfare of a state. It enables one to know the average size of the income and the standard of living of the people. It can be calculated for a country by dividing the country's national income by its population. The net PCI of Manipur at current and constant (2011-12) prices in 2016-17 are estimated to be ₹ 61,535 and ₹ 46,563 respectively showing an increase of 8.70% and 3.90% over the previous year.

Planning

Planning is the key to development for a developing country like India. India, the second largest country in terms of population, has its own significance of planning. Planning is generally taken to mean a State-planned economy. The Government prepares Plan in the field of economic, social and general services not only to raise the income of the economy but also for bringing about all-round development of an economy.

Five Year Plans

The Government of India set up the Planning Commission in 1950. The purpose of the Planning Commission was to assess carefully the human and physical resources of the state and to prepare plans for the effective use of these resources. The first five-year plan of India was presented to the Parliament of India on 8th December, 1951 by the first Indian Prime Minister, Jawaharlal Nehru. After the launching of the First Five Year Plan on 1st April, 1951, subsequent five-year plans followed. In between, there had been some annual plans.

With the launching of the First Five Year Plan in 1951 for India, the Process of Planned Economic Development also started in Manipur. The first five-year plan of the State was launched with a total outlay of ₹ 1.55 crores only. The outlay for the first three Five Year Plans for Manipur was only ₹ 20.68 crores. The Plan period beginning from the 1st April, 1966 and ending on 31st March, 1969 are known as the period of plan holiday or Annual plan. During this period, three annual plans were prepared with an investment of ₹ 10.14 crores. Fourth Five Year Plan began on 1st April, 1969 and lasted till

31st March, 1974 with an investment of ₹ 30.25 crores. During the 4th Five Year Plan period the process of most of the economic development in Manipur has been initiated. The Fifth Five Year Plan of the State started on 1st April, 1974. This plan was to continue till 31st March, 1979 but was terminated a year in advance by March, 1978. The Sixth Five Year Plan beginning on the 1st April, 1980 covered the five year period of 1980-85. The size of the Sixth Five Year Plan was quite big as compared to the previous plans with an allocation of ₹ 240 crores and that of the Seventh plan was again found to be bigger by about 1.79 times of the Sixth Plan, with ₹ 430 crores spreading over the period 1985-90.

There were 2 (two) annual plans such as 1990-91 and 1991-92 between the intervening periods of the 7th and the 8th plans. The 8th plan with an allocation of ₹ 979 crores was launched during the period 1992-97. The Ninth, Tenth, and Eleventh Five Year plan covered the period from 1997-98 to 2001-2002, 2002-2003 to 2006-2007 and 2007-2008 to 2011-2012 respectively with an outlay of ₹ 2426.69 crores, ₹ 2804.00 crores and ₹ 8154.00 crores.

Growth of Plan Outlay and Expenditure in respect of Manipur

(₹ in crore)

		Outlay		Expenditure	
Plan	Year	Total	Growth in percentage between plan period	Total	Growth in percentage between plan period
1	2	3	4	5	6
First Plan	1951-56	1.55	-	1.03	-
Second Plan	1956-61	6.25	303.22	5.97	479.61
Third Plan	1961-66	12.88	106.08	12.81	114.57
Three Annual Plans	1966-69	10.13	-	7.20	-
Fourth Plan	1969-74	30.25	134.86	31.00	142.00
Fifth Plan	1974-78	92.86	206.98	66.62	114.90
Annual Plan	1978-80	59.26	-	61.13	-
Sixth Plan	1980-85	240.00	158.45	262.93	294.67
Seventh Plan	1985-90	430.00	79.17	523.27	99.01
Annual Plan	1990-92	365.00	-	358.48	-
Eighth Plan	1992-97	979.00	127.67	1209.69	131.18
Ninth Plan	1997-02	2426.69	147.87	1848.65	52.82
Tenth Plan	2002-07	2804.00	15.55	2741.40	48.29
Eleventh Plan	2007-12	8154.00@	190.80	9218.94*	236.29
Twelfth Plan	2012-17	20457.91@	150.89	-	-

@ Project Outlay   * Anticipated Expenditure   **Source** : *Planning Department, Manipur*

12th Plan Proposals

(₹ crores)

Sector	Proposed Outlay 12th Plan	% of total
Agri & Allied Activities	630.95	3.08
Rural Development	929.17	4.54
Special Area Programme	332.24	1.62
Irrigation & Flood Control	3,159.41	15.44
Energy	1,533.75	7.50
Industries & Mineral	427.16	2.09
Transport	1,105.05	5.40
Science, Tec & Envn.	1,126.80	5.51
General Eco. Services	394.44	1.93
Social Services	10,554.25	51.59
General Services	264.67	1.29
Total	**20,457.91**	**100.00**

Banks

The total number of scheduled commercial banking offices in Manipur was 174 as on 31st March 2016 of which State Bank of India accounted for 33 offices. Manipur Rural Banks had the highest number of offices in the state with a total of 28 offices, followed by the UBI with 18.

A bank is an institution which deals mainly in credit by way of accepting deposits of money for the purpose of lending or investment, from the public repayable on demand or otherwise and withdrawable by cheque, draft, and order or otherwise. The need for a well- developed banking system in the economic life of the state can hardly be exaggerated. Growth of industry and trade has necessitated the development of banks and other financial institutions.

Scheduled Commercial Banks

Commercial Banks, an important segment of the banking organizations, accept deposits and provide short term loans and also discount bills of exchange and perform other subsidiary and general utility functions. In India, Scheduled Commercial Banks are categorized into five different groups according to their ownership and/or nature of operation namely (*i*) State Bank of India and its associates, (*ii*) Nationalised Banks, (*iii*) Regional Rural Banks, (*iv*) Foreign Banks and (*v*) Other Indian Scheduled Commercial Banks (in the private sector).

AWARDS

Padma Bhushan Awards

Recipient	Year	Field
• M. Chungneijang Mary Kom	2013	Sports
• Heisnam Kanhailala	2016	Arts

Padma Shri Awards

Recipient	Year	Field
• Atombapu Sharma	—	Literature
• Major Ralengnao Kathing	1957	Public Affairs
• Maisnam Amubi Singh	1970	Arts
• Ch. Kalachand Shastri	1971	Literature and Education
• T.A. Mudon Sharma	1972	Dance
• Smt. Lhingioneng Gangte	1975	Social Service
• G.C. Tongbra	1975	Literature
• M.K. Binodini Devi	1976	Literature and Education
• Shri L. Damu Singh	1983	Sports
• Dharamchand Patni	1984	Social Work
• A. Minaketan Singh	1985	Literature
• Th. Haridas	1985	Social Service
• N. Khelchandra Ongjam	1987	Literature
• Ratan Thiyam	1989	Drama (Arts)
• G. Surchand Sharma	1990	Literature & Social Service
• M. Kirti Singh	1992	Literature & Social Service
• Shri K. Ibomcha Sharma	1998	Arts
• R.K. Jhalajit Singh	1999	Literature
• E. Nilakanta Singh	2000	Literature
• Shri L. Nabakishore Singh	2001	Herbal Medicine
• Smt. K.O. Thouranisabi Devi	2003	Arts
• Smt. Gurumayum Devi	2004	Sports
• Shri Heisnam Kanhailal	2004	Arts

M. Chungneijang
Mary Kom

Kunjarani
Devi

Elam Endira
Devi

Heisnam
Kanhailala

N. Dingko
Singh

S. Bimola
Kumari Devi

Recipient	Year	Field
• Shri Sougaijam Thanil Singh	2005	Arts
• Smt Y. Gambhini Devi	2005	Arts
• Aribam Shyam Sharma	2006	Arts
• Mangte C. Mary Kom	2006	Sports
• T. Babu Singh	2007	Arts
• Neelmani Devi	2007	Arts
• Sabitri Heisnam	2008	Arts
• A. Jayanta Kumar Singh	2008	Medicine
• Gurumayum Gourakishor Sharma	2009	Arts
• Haobam Angbi Naganbi Devi	2010	Arts
• Raj Kumar Achauba Singh	2010	Arts
• Aekpam Tom Muti	2010	Social Science
• Kunjarani Devi	2011	Sports
• Khangembam Mangi Singh	2011	Arts
• N.I. Devi	2012	Arts
• N. Dingko Singh	2013	Sports
• Elam Endira Devi	2014	Arts
• Dr. Waikhom Gojen Meeitei	2014	Literature & Education
• Dr. S. Bimola Kumari Devi	2015	Medicine
• Laishram Birendra Kumar	2017	Art-Music
• Wareppa Naba Nil	2017	Art-Theatre
• Saikhom Mirabai Chanu	2018	Sports
• L. Subadani Devi	2018	Weavine-Art

Rajiv Gandhi Khel Ratna Awards

Year	Sports	Winners
• 1996	Weightlifting	N. Kunjarani Devi
• 2008-09	Boxing	M.C. Mary Kom
• 2018	Weightlifting	Saikhom Mirabai Chanu

Arjuna Awards

Year	Sports	Winners
• 1990	Weightlifting	N. Kunjarani Devi
• 1998	Boxing	Shri Ng. Dingko Singh
• 2000	Hockey	Ms. Tingonleima Chanu
	Weightlifting	Ms. Sanamacha Chanu Thingbaijam
• 2003	Boxing	M.C. Mary Kom
	Hockey	Suraj Lata Devi
• 2004	Judo	Angom Anita Chanu
• 2007	Judo	Tombi Devi
• 2008	Boxing	L. Sarita Devi
• 2011	Boxing	Suranjoy Singh
• 2011	Wushu	Sandhya Rani
• 2012	Archery	L. Bombayla Devi

Year	Sports	Winners
● 2012	Weightlifting	Ng. Sonia Chanu
● 2012	Wushu	M. Bimoljit Singh
● 2014	Weightlifting	Y. Renubala Chanu
● 2015	Wushu	Y. Sanathoi Devi
● 2017	Boxing	Devendro Singh Laishram
● 2017	Football	Oinam Bembem Devi

Sahitya Akademi Awards

Authors	Year	Books
● Pacha Meitei	1973	Imphal Amasung Magee Isingnung-shitkiphibam (Novel)
● N Kunjamohon	1974	Elisha Amagi Mahac (Short Stories)
● L Somendro	1976	Mamang Leikai thambal Saatle (Poetry)
● A Minaketan	1977	Asheibagi Nityapad (Poetry)
● GC Tongbra	1978	Ngabong Khao (Play)
● MK Binodeni	1979	Boro Saheb Ongbi Sanatombi (Novel)
● E Rajanikanta	1981	Kalenthagi Leibaklei (Short Stories)
● E Dinamani	1982	Pistol Ama Kundalei Ama (Short Stories)
● N Ibobi	1983	Kamagi Mama Amasung Magi Aroiba Yaheep (Play)
● L Biramani	1985	Chekla Paikharabada (Short Stories)
● Hijam Guno	1985	Bir Tikendrajit road (Novel)
● Kh. Prakash	1986	Munggi Eshei (Short Stories)
● E Nilakanta	1987	Tirtha Jatra (Poetry)
● E Sonamani	1988	Mamangthong Lolabadi Maningthongda lak Una (Short Stories)
● Nilbir Shastri	1989	Tatkhraba Punshi Leipun (Short Stories)
● Shree Biren	1990	Mapan Naidrabasida (Poetry)
● Y Ibomcha	1991	Numittee Asum Thengillakli (Short Stories)
● A Chiteswar	1992	Tharo Sangbi (Novel)
● Arambam Biren	1993	Punshigi Marudhyan (Novel)
● RK Mani	1994	Mayai Karaba Shamu (Short Stories)
● A Samarendra	1995	leibaklei (Play)
● RK Madhubir	1996	Praloigi Meiriraktagi (Poetry)
● Thangjam Ibopishak Singh	1997	Bhut Amasung Maikhum (Poetry)
● Krisham Priyokumar	1998	Nongdi Tarak-Khidare (Short Stories)
● Sagolsem Lanchenba Meitei	1999	Hi Nang bu-Hondeda (Poetry)
● L. Premchand Singh	2000	Eemagi Phanek Machet (Short Stories)
● Ningombam Sunita	2001	Khongji Makhal (Short Stories)
● Rajkumar Bhubonsana	2002	Mei Mamgera Budhi Mamgera (Poetry)
● Sudhir Naoroibam	2003	Leiyee Khara Punsi Khara (Short Stories)
● Birendrajit Naorem	2004	Lanthengndriba Lanmee (Poetry)
● M. Nabakishore Singh	2005	Pangal Shambu Eishe Adom geeni (Short Stories)
● Saratchand Thiyam	2006	Noongshibi Gris
● B.N. Maisanamba	2007	Imasi Nurabee (Novel)

Authors	Year	Books
• A.O. Memchoubi	2008	Idu Nidthoo (Poetry)
• Raghu Leishangthem	2009	Khungangi Chithi (Poetry)
• M. Borkanya	2010	Leikangla (Novel)
• Kshetri Bira	2011	Nangabu Dagaibada (Novel)
• Jodha C. Sansam	2012	Mathou Kanba DNA (Novel)
• Makhonmani Mongasaba	2013	Chinglon Amadagi Amada (Travelogues)
• Naorem Bidyasagar Singh	2014	Khung-gang Amasung Refugee (Poetry)
• Kshetri Rajen	2015	Ahingna Yekshilliba Mang (Poetry)
• Moirangthem Rajen	2016	Cheptharaba Eshing Pun (Short Stories)
• Rajen Taijamba	2017	Chahi Taret Khuntakpa (Play)
• Budhichandra Heisnamba	2018	Ngamkheigee Wangmada (Short Stories)

(No Awards has given in 1975 and 1980)

National Awardees for Films From Manipur

Film	Year	Award	Director
• Matamgi Manipur	1972	President's Medal	Debkumar Bose
• Saphabee	1976	Best Regional Film	Aribam Shyam Sharma
• Khutthang Lamjel	1980	Best Regional Film	—
• Sanakeithel	1984	Best Regional Film	M.A. Singh
• The Deer of Manipur	1990	Best Environment/ Conservation/ Preservation Film	Aribam Shyam Sharma
• Ishanou	1991	Best Regional Film	Aribam Shyam Sharma
• Indigenous Games of Manipur	1991	Best Exploration/ Adventure Film	Aribam Shyam Sharma
• Meitei Pung	1992	Special Jury Award	Aribam Shyam Sharma
• Sambal Wangma	1993	Best Regional Film	K. Ibohal Sharma
• Orchids of Manipur	1994	Best Environment/ conservation/preser- vation Film	Aribam Shyam Sharma
• Moyophygee Macha	1995	Best Regional Film	Oken Amakcham
• Sanabi	1996	Best Regional Film	Aribam Shyam Sharma
• Yellhou Jagoi	1996	Best Anthropological and Enthnographical Film	Aribam Shyam Sharma
• Chatledo Eidi	2001	Best Regional Film	Makhonmani Mongsaba
• AFSPA 1958	2008	Best Non-Feature Film	Haobam Paban Kumar
• Phijigee Mani	2011	Best Regional Film	Oinam Gautam
• Loktak Lairembee	2017	Best Film on Environment	Haobam Paban Kumar

SUPERLATIVES OF MANIPUR

First in Manipur

• Teacher	M.Purna Singh
• Governor	B.K. Nehru
• First Lieutenant Governor	Baleswar Prasad
• First Union Minister	R.K. Jaichandra
• Speaker of Manipur Legislative Assembly	T.C. Tiankham
• First MP of Rajya Sabha	N.G. Tompok
• Mr. Manipur	Irom Leikhendra
• First Mr. India	N. Maipak
• Recipient of Padma Shree Award	Atombapu Sharma
• Recipient of Sahitya Akademi Award	Pacha Meitei
• Recipient of Sangeet Natak Akademi Award	M. Amubi Singh
• Recipient of Arjun Award	N. Kunjarani Devi
• Recipient of Rajiv Khel Award	N. Kunjarani Devi
• Recipient of Gold Medal in Asian Games	Dingko Singh
• Olympian	P. Neelkomal
• Graduate	S. Somerendra Singh
• Woman MLA	Mrs. Hangmila Saiza
• Woman MP	Kim Gangte
• Woman Minister	K. Apabi Devi
• Woman Doctor	T.O. Bedamani Devi
• Chief Commissioner	Maj. Gen. Rawal Amar Singh
• First Manipuri D.G.P.	L. Jugeswor
• British Political Agent	Captain Gardon
• Feature Film	Matamgee Manipur
• Newspaper	Dainik Manipur Patrika
• Journal	Meetei Chanu
• Health Journal	Meetei Maiba
• English Journal	Meetei Leirang
• University	Manipur University (Estd. 1980), Canchipur
• Railway Station	Jiribam (Estd. 1990)

FESTIVALS OF MANIPUR

Festivals	Celebrated by	Festivals	Celebrated by
• Lai Haraoba	Meiteis	• Gan Ngai	Kabui Nagas
• Rath Yatra	Hindus	• Heikru Hitongba	Meiteis
• Yaoshang (Dol Jatra)	Hindus	• Kwak Yatra (Durga Puja)	Hindus
• Christmas	Christians		
• Mahavir Jayanti	Jains	• Kut	Kuki Chin Mizos
• Depawali	Hindus	• Lui-Ngai-Ni	Nagas
• Cheiraoba	Meiteis	• Mera Nongma Panba	Meiteis
• Chumpha	Tangkhul Nagas	• Ningol Chakkouba	Meiteis

• • •

History

As per the Manipur State Archives, Manipur was ruled by 76 kings since 33 A.D. The development of the political power of the Meiteis was related to the control and organization of resources around the central loci of Imphal, and the entire valley and hills. The Kingdom was later governed based on the written constitution "Loyumba Shinyen". This decree was issued by King Loiyumba in 1110 A.D and was based on the earlier codes and conventions. The Loyumba Shinyen was further expanded by the later kings like Kiyamba (1467-1508), Khagemba (1597-1652), Garibniwaj (1709-1748), Bhagyachandra (1763-1798) and Chourjit (1803-1813). The latter additions make the decree a complete code on the duties to be rendered by the hill tribes and other communities in the Kingdom (Kabui 2003). Oinam Bogeshwar, the renowned Meitei historian and scholar observed that there was a centralized constitutional Government since A.D 429 (CORE 2007).

Not only have the Meiteis possessed a distinct political and territorial status for centuries, they can also legitimately boast of a highly literate and developed culture , an advanced literary tradition which stretches back a thousand years, and a distinctive linguistic tradition. Various ethnic groups belonging to southern-Mongoloid groups, the Tibeto-Burman, the Indo-Aryans and a sizeable section of Tai (Shans) came to Manipur from pre-historic times down to the present day. The present ethnic groups of Manipur, viz the Meiteis, the Naga tribes, the Kuki Chin tribes and other Indian communities are the descendants of those migrating people. And Manipur and its central valley provided the ecological setting for building up a civilization. These migrating people brought with them varying degrees of technology ranging from the Old-Stone Age, rough-stone tools to more refined Neolithic potters. With the coming of metal tools mostly bronze, cooper and tin during the historical period from Thailand and Upper Burma cultural zone, the metal civilization of Manipur was developed mostly through trades. The trade between the Burma and Manipur was terminated because of the emerging antagonistic relationship between the two powers.

PREHISTORY

Manipur being one of the oldest civilizations, the evolution process of the state goes back to prehistory. In Manipur prehistoric cultured objects have been discovered. Though archaeological research in the area is still not fully developed, there are evidences of the Old Stone Age, New Stone Age, Bronze Age, Iron Age cultures in Manipur. Further, there are a number of caves and rocks shelters in the hills of Manipur which once provided shelters to the prehistoric men, while the evidence of the Old Stone Age is confined to the hills, the New Stone Age relics are spread over the hills and the valley. It has been stated that Imphal valley may be an important zone of copper-bronze age culture which is a cultural phase of great significance in human history, but still unknown in the entire Northeast India. Manipur appears to have received Bronze Age Culture traits from Thailand and Upper Burma where indigenous early metal age culture developed at a comparatively early date around 4000 B.C. Post 1970 Manipur evacuations have led to the interference that Hoanbinhian culture also existed in Manipur sites. The archaeological linkage of pre-historic culture also existed in Manipur with the cradle of mankind on the one hand and with the South East Asian pre-history on the hand has been fairly established.

MEITEIS

The ethnic group Meiteis, as we find it today was formed by the amalgamation of the seven different but close knit and allied principalities, once settled in different parts of Manipur, each independent of each other. The components of Meitei confederacy were: the Meiteis, Khaba-Ngamba, and Chenglei, Angom, Khuman, Luwang, Moirang. Besides these, there exist several other tribes, such as Mangang, Mangding, Chiren, khende, Heiren Khunju etc., all of whom were in course of time, merged into one or the other seven other principalities.

During the historical period, there were seven clan of the Meiteis but there were five principalities ruled by five clan chieftains who were also both social and political head of their respective clans. The foremost among them was the Kingdom of Kangla established by Pahangba whose dynasty was the Ningthouja which, though the name was coined later on becomes the name of the clan; the Luwang principality, the principality of Angom, the Khuman principality, and the Kingdom of Moirang. The Khaba who once ruled at Kangla and put up a strong challenge to Pakhangba were already destroyed by Ningthouja dynasty, and Nganba had already ceased to be a political power. During the same period, the Chengleis, the Sarang Leishangthem, The Heiren Khunjan, the Chakpas and the Mangangs had village level chiefdoms. Pakhangba consolidated the seven clans with one pibas of each clan. After five days of coronation ceremony, He established villages in different part of his kingdom for easy administration but in course of time, the clans group became stronger with the growth of population, economic prosperity, conquering small weaker groups and addition of captives and newly migrant groups. With the growth of power they became independent groups and made frequent disturbance within the Kangla principality. But Pakhangba controlled the rising power diplomatically by introducing the clan system.

The emergence and sophisticated Meitei State under the leadership of the Ningthouja chiefs was a significant development in the history of Manipur in pre-colonial period. The state formation occurred in the valley, and the kings subsequently established their control over the hills and also to other kingdoms that lay beyond the hills. Their power was recognized by foreign nations especially the Shan principality of Burma in the 15th century and later by the British and many Kingdoms in South East Asia and South Asia.

The recorded history of Manipur begins with the coronation of the first Meitei King, *Nongda Lairen Pakhangba* in 33 A.D. The historical capital and focal centre of the state was Kangla, the control of which lay at the roots of all political and religious power. The legendary 'Kangla' complex had been the capital of Manipur from the very ancient times down to 1891. Topographically, Kangla incorporated adjoining stretches of land from the traditional four divisions or Panas of the state, namely *Laipham, Khapham, Ahallup and Naharup,* with Imphal forming a separate administrative territorial unit inclusive of the capital Kangla. Kangla was earlier a vast piece of sprawling land, originally a mound or hill east of the Nambul River.

The act of accession to the throne of the Meitei king, like its counterparts in Southern-Mongoloids South-East Asian Kingdoms, was not simply a political act of affirming the ruler's right to get obeisance from the ruled. It was to be a serious invocation to the ancestral spirits to help secure the life power for affecting the welfare and prosperity of the realm. The entire rituals were built up on traditional cosmogonies, embellished by the cult of veneration of ancestors and belief in the fertility principle. The cult of the placenta was also deeply embedded into this principle.

NINGTHOUJA DYNASTY

With the foundation of the Ningthouja dynasty, the social and political development of the Meitei's was centered around the ruling dynasty. Monarchy was the prevalent form of government. Gangumei observes that the state emerge as a result of the gradual growth of human civilization with development of economic organization, social order and steady livelihood. The King was the head of the state and all veto powers were vested to him. However there was no evidence of centralized king's power. The autocratic rule of the king and his power was controlled and limited by the Ninghou Pongba Tara, Nine Khunpangthous, Sixty four Phandous and Clan Pibas. The Angom Ningthou was the most powerful. He was the head of the 64 Phamdous. He was always on the advice of the Maichous (Pandits). Both the King and Council of Minister controlled each other. There were some traces of democratic elements. Even if, the King was the head of the state, public opinion was an important factor that restrained the power of the King and the State. However with the increase of King's power, the monarchy form was strengthened. It also depends on the power of the Council of Minister. If the Angom Ningthou and other members were weak, the King could use his autocratic power.

Prior to the 8th Century very little information is available about the history of Manipur. The Puranas refer to the names of only ten rulers of that period. But no definite information is available regarding their reigns and places of residence. From the 8th century till the succession of Gharib Niwaz (1714 A.D.) we get the names of 36 rulers, each of whom might have ruled on the average for 28 years. At about 700 A.D. ***King Konthouba*** was the ruler of Manipur. He enjoyed undisturbed rule for five years.

Konthouba was succeeded by ***Naothingkhong*** in 750 A.D. The most important incident of his reign is the fight against a Naga community called Angom.

Naothingkhong was succeeded by ***Khongtekcha***. One copper plate issued by him has been discovered. Some religious changes are indicated in the context of that copper plate. It mentions the existence of 363 gods; of them Hari is the supreme. Special stress is laid on the worship of Shiva and Durga. But in the old manuscripts of Manipur there is reference to only 9 gods. Such increase in the number of Gods must have been due to the influence of the Hindu mythology. Changes are noticed also in the materials as well as in the incantations for worhip. His swords were made of gold and silver and on his head he used to put on a nine-storied umbrella. His 'doolie' was named 'pushpamahamanik'. Vassal kings paid him tribute.

After Khongtekcha we find the names of two rulers Keiremba (880 A.D.) and Yaraba (949 A.D.). During the period of Yaraba (949 A.D.) the Khuman chief grew very powerful and occupied a considerable portion of Manipur. For some time Yaraba's authority remained totally eclipsed. The Khuman chief established his headquarters at Mayang Imphal. Till that time the Khumans had the custom of human sacrifice.

After Yaraba the following names are found in the list of the ruling chiefs of Manipur. Ayangba (968 A.D.), Ningthoucheng (987 A.D.), Chengloipam Lanthaba (1007 A.D.), Yunglaw Keiphaba (1027 A.D.), Irengba (1107 A.D.), Loyamba (1127 A.D.), Loitongba (1154 A.D.), Hematowi Wanthaba (1170 A.D.). There is no mention of any notable incident during the period of their reigns. After these eight rulers we come across the name of **Thawan Thaba** (1199 A.D.). During his reign a naval battle took place with the Khumans in the Loktak Lake. The Manipuri festival Hiyanghirel or boat-race bears the memory of that battle even today.

Thawanthaba was followed by Chingthang Lanthaba (1211 A.D.), Puranthaba (1226 A.D.) and Khumbomba (1236 A.D.). No important incident is found during this period except the invasion of Manipur by the ruler of Pong in 1220 A.D.

Colonel Johnstone has made a reference to the invasion of Manipur by a Chinese force and their defeat in 1250 A.D. by the ruler of Manipur. The Chinese prisoners were allowed to settle at a place called Susa Kameng. Their descendants are still living as a Loi community, in the Kameng village, 9 miles away from Imphal by the side of the Dimapur road. These Chinese prisoners for the first time introduced silk-wearing and brick-laying in Manipur. Once 'Kamen Chatpa dhoti', a kind of white silk 'dhoti' with purple patterns and scrolls stamped on it by means of wooden blocks made by the people of that Kameng village was very popular in Manipur.

According to Hodson, the Chinese army entered Manipur during the reign of Khagemba at about 1630 A.D. Khagemba was succeded by **Marangba**. He struck a kind of small and round coin. The names of persons who ruled in Manipur during the 14th century are stated to be Thangbi Lanthaba, Kongyamba, Telheiba, Tabungba and Nigthou Khomba. **Ningthou Khomba's** reign extended up to the beginning of the 15th century. Once he proceeded to the east to resist an invading Burmese force. In his absence the Tangkhuls came down from the hills and attacked the unprotected capital. Queen Linthoi-Ngambi with other women heroically fought against them and eventually succeeded in driving them away. Ningthou Khomba was succeeded by **Kyamba**. He also struck coins. After ascending the throne he went out for conquests. It is said that he subjugated the entire land from Moran to Lushai hills. For the purpose of administration he divided the Manipur Valley into 4 panas, viz., Ahallup, Naharup, Khabam and Laipham. Rest of India was then under Muslim rule. Many Brahmins of the neighbouring Muslim state entered into Manipur at that time. Ancestors of Adhikarimayum, Laihaothabam, Sijagurumayum, Kakchingtabam, Phurailatpam and Aribam families came to Manipur in that period. Kyamba introduced the festival of Cheiraoba at about 1485 A.D.

At about 1475 A.D. the strength and influence of Manipur state increased to a considerable extent. The ruler of Pong proposed to marry a daughter of the king of Manipur. On her way to Pong she was carried off by the Raja of Khumbat but he was promptly attacked and conquered by the combined forces of Pong and Manipur.

In the 16th century we come across the following list of rulers vis— Keirengba, Langaingmba, Ngaiphaba, Kahomba, Atongjamba, Chalamba and Mungyamba. Mungyamba has been discussed in connection with the Chinese invasion. In the history of Cooch-Bihar it is found that the Koch King Nara Narayan after defeating the rulers of Assam and Cachar in 1562 demanded tribute from the ruler of Manipur. The ruler of Manipur had not at that time the sufficient strength to defy the victorious Koch King. He submitted without any protest and offered ₹ 20,000,300 gold coins and 10 elephants.

According to the calculation of Bijoy Panchali the reign of Khagemba falls in the beginning of the 17th century. He divided his kingdom into 8 divisions. He made the system of measuring lands and weighing goods.

After Khagemba, these kings, Khunjaoba, Paikhomba and Charairongba ruled successively. Coins struck by Paikhomba and Charairongba respectively have been found. The son of Charairongba is Pambeiba, alias Gharib Niwaz, the most powerful ruler of Manipur who effected a great religious reformation in the country.

The beginning of the 18th Century saw the dawn of a new era in the history of Manipur. It was at this time that ***Gharib Niwaz Pamheiba*** with a revolutionary outlook and the zeal of a conqueror, comparable to that of Emperor Harshabardhana, assumed the political leadership of Manipur. In one hand he carried his victorious arms to the imperial city of Ava and in the other he effected a religious revolution within his own country. His activities paved the way to rapid cultural integration of Manipur with the rest of India.

In the year 1725 Gharib Niwaz was able to make the first of his series of raids against the kingdom of Burma. He attacked and defeated a Burmese force at the mouth of the Haglung river. In the following year the Burmese tried to retaliate. An army of 30,000 men penetrated into the valley, but were finally repulsed. Three entire divisions were captured by the forces of Manipur.

As a king Gharib Niwaz's energy was not completely used up in the expeditions against Burma. The images of Ramji and Hanumanji were installed by him in two separate temples of which that of Hanumanji was made of brick. Of his other philanthropic acts, mention may be made of the construction of the Ningthem Pukhari (tank) at Wangkhei Leikai. The size of the tank reflect to some extent the greatness of the king. Among the literary activities it is mentioned that Bijoy Panchali was rewritten by Dwija Sita Ram Sarma, a chronicler in the court of Gharib Niwaz.

Almost all the accounts of Manipur refer to the spread of Brahmanical Vaishnavism on a wide scale in Manipur under the royal patronage of Gharib Niwaz. Baptized by the Vaishnava missionary, Shantidas Adhikary, he declared Vaishnavism as the state religion and advised his subjects to accept it.

Garibniwaz, the reigning king of Manipur, and his eldest son, Sham Sai, were murdered in 1751, on their return from Burma, by the emissaries of Ajit Sai, the second son of Garibniwaz. On the death of the reigning king and his eldest son, the next heir to the throne, *Ajit Sai* succeeded to the throne of Manipur. After some years of his reign it came to light that Ajit Sai was implicated in the murder of his father and his brother. The people, therefore, became averse to the rule of Ajit Sai.

Bhorot Sai, the brother of Ajit Sai, taking advantage of the situation, gathered his men and forced Ajit Sai to abdicate the throne. Ajit Sai fled and took shelter at Tippera (now Tripura). Bhorot Sai ascended the throne.

Ananta Sai, with the consent of the nobles and the people, made Sham Sai's eldest son, Gourasham, King and the younger son, Jai Singh, Yuvaraja in 1753. As Ananta Sai had arranged for alternate kingship for the two brothers for a period of five years each, Jai Singh became king and Gourasham Yuvaraja in 1759.

In 1762 Ajit Sai, the deposed king who was taking refuge at Tippera, complained to the British authorities saying that he had been forcibly expelled from the state; and he sought British assistance for regaining the throne of the state.

Having learnt of the situation, Jai Singh sent his Vakil. Haridas Gossain, to Mr. Verelhst, the Chief of the Chittagong factory, (who had been requested by Ajit Sai for support) to convince of the deceitfulness and the guilt of Ajit Sai. Besides, Haridas Gossain also requested for British assistance in getting redress of the grievances the state had suffered in the hands of the Burmese. The Vakil, in his anxiety to secure British favour, also held out that there could be an extensive British trade from India to China through Manipur and Burma when the two states were on good terms. To serve both ends, the Vakil proposed a trade and defensive alliance between the British and Manipur State.

The above treaty was confirmed by Gourasham in 1763 it self after he became king; but it was of no avail till 1823-24. In that year the Burmese forces dominated over Assam and Manipur and sent their army to Cachar, thereby threatening the British frontier of Sylhet. This afforded a chance to revive the old tie between the British and Manipur State. It was, to be true, the combined effort of the two that succeeded in repelling the Burmese from Assam and Manipur by defeating the Burmese in the first Anglo-Burmese War, 1824-26.

GOVERNANCE

The governance of the country was based on the written constitution "Loyumba Shinyen". Prof Kabui observed that it is a royal edict (Constitution) on the social distribution of economic and administrative functions proclaimed by King Loiyumba of Manipur (1074-1112 A.D).

This decree was issued by Loiyumba in 1110 A.D. The decree was based on the earlier codes and conventions during the previous resign as there are references to them in the text. The Loyumba was further expanded by later kings like Kyamba (1467-1508), Khagemba (1597-1652), Garibniwaz or Pamheiba (1709-1748), Bhagyachandra (1763-1798) and Chourjit (1803-1813).

The decree of Loiyumba deals with the distribution of occupation according to Yumnaks (families), assignment of duties to priests and priestesses, assignment of the works of maintenance of abode of village deities (Umanglais), creation of administrative department (Loishang), duties and function of the kings and queens, royal etiquette, titles and decorations awarded to the nobles, administration of justice, keeping of standard time and many other things.

The constitutional framework-in its early pattern, with little sophisticated-was found during the period of *king Neophangba in 429 A.D.* and the administration of the Meiteileipak was done by 10 cabinet ministers, known as "Pongba Tara" viz Nongthongba, Khwairakpa, Yaiskul Lakpa, Naharus Lakpa, Ahallup Lakpa, Hiyangloi, Wangkhei Louremba, Khurai Angouba, Pukhangba, and Chonghanba, over and above 64 high lords representing 32 administrative units.

The Council of Minister *(Ningthou Pongba Tara)* was regarded as a vital organ for the administration of the country. Their importance lay in the fact that the king feels that he should have diverse views in dealing with his people and the country. The king should enlist the competent person as minister. It is not hereditary. The members of the council can be represented by any person who is considered of marked ability and loyalty to the throne. Earlier without the approval and co-operation of the Council of Ministers the King does not act on any issue of national importance. But during the period of Pamheiba, he overrules his Council of Minister and adopts Vaishnavism. This depends upon the personality of the King. The strength of the council of Ministers varied from time to time. Out of the sixty four Phamdous, ten were selected and known as *"Ningthou Pongba Tara"*. Therefore generally the strength of Council of Minister was 10 till the time of King Loyumba (1074 A.D). Afterward the strength was reduced to nine and during the period of King Garib Niwaz, the number was again increased to twelve including his Chief Queen. The post of Chief Queen was replaced by *Awa Purel* (foreign Minister) during the time of King Chandrakiti. The *Awa Purel* was associated with the military rather than the civil organization. The *Pandit Achouba* (Chief Pandit) was also treated as member of the council during emergencies.

In the post-independence period, the representatives of the hill tribes were appointed as Ministers of the State which had never occurred in the history of Manipur. In the election of 1948, 18 seats were reserved for the hills but not on the basis of tribes, the remaining seats were for the valley including Mohammedans. Democracy had provided the opportunity for participation in the governance of the State either as Ministers or members of the Assembly. Every community was represented except the Mao as there was no election due to political agitation. The election of 1948 was the endorsement of the State by the people of Manipur in a democratic way. There were 8 Naga MLAs - 5 Tangkhuls, 2 Zeliangrongs and one Monshang, the other 9 were Kuki-Chins including Kom and Paite. In this short-lived experiment in constitutional monarchy, the tribal people accepted the primal position of the Maharaja as the head of the kingdom and leadership of the Meiteis in the democratic set-up as the Chief Minister was a prince appointed by the Maharaja. The hill people accepted the Maharaja as the symbol of unity of the kingdom. This symbol was destroyed when the State was merged with the Dominion of India in October 1949. The Merger destroyed both autonomy and democracy of Manipur and brought a bureaucratic Central rule under a Chief Commissioner.

JUDICIAL SYSTEM

The efficiency of government means the efficiency of the judiciary. In early societies the administration of justice was a private affair but sometimes it was administered with the help of the community. The punishment for breaking the community law was given before the whole people of the community so as to prevent others from breaking the community law particularly customary law. Such type of administration of system was prevalent in the early Manipur. The criminal law of the early Manipur was very simple. When a complaint was received, Dolaipada (Police) was sent to arrest the accused. When the accused was produced before the court, trail was at once commenced by giving punishment or oral examination.

The Royal Edicts are the earliest materials sources for criminal law, and the most important among them was the Edict of *Meidingu Naophangba* (429 A.D). The Edict of Meidingu Naophangba chalked out a brief account of crimes and punishments of ancients Manipur.

Before 1709, the kings of Manipur sat in the Cheirap Court (Highest Court) and disposed all the cases in consultation with the sixty four phamdous. He took active parts in day to day administration of justice. But in 1715, during the Garib Niwaz (Pamheiba) a reform was introduced. The administration was handed over his nobles but the king remained the highest appellate authority. In Manipur there used to have four kinds of court over and above the king court *(Kuchu)* which is the highest. The courts were: (i) Courts concerning religious matters, (ii) Court concerning secular matters, (iii) Court for females, (iv) Military courts. The court can be divided into Cheirap Court (Similar to Supreme Court) which has both original and appellate jurisdictions and Village court that tried small cases.

The Kuchu was instituted during the reign of the kind Nongda Lairem Pakahngba (33 A.D-154 A.D). It was the highest court having comprehensive jurisdiction of the state. In the court the king and his nobles tried serious cases. The king presided over the hearing.

At the village level the delivery of justice was done by the village headman and elders of the village. Appeals against the decisions of the village court could be taken to Cheirap. It was usually conducted at the house of the village headman or at the village Mandop (community hall). In 1892-93, for the purpose of administration of the judicial system, the valley was divided into eleven circles with a panchayat court in each circle. Each circle contained about one thousand houses. The strength of the panchayat court was five including the village headman. Similar to the village justice system, the hill areas were tried by the village council which consists of Khullakpa (headman), Luplakpa, Khunpu and Yu Phalba and some village elders. Oath taking was very common among the hills for delivering justice.

Punishment in early Manipur society is of various kinds. Women and Brahmins were exempted from death sentence and imprisonment. Treason or conspiracy against the king was the highest offence in the state. The highest punishment to be inflicted on the accused was death sentence.

Offence of Murder was also awarded death sentence. Such punishments were given to all the people involved in the activities. Mutilation of Limbs was given to offender of stealing, theft, robbery etc. Kidnapping and murder were punished by blinding the offenders.

Cases of assault and petty offences were punished by flogging with a cane on the shoulder of the accused. Sometimes the culprit was severely beaten and exposed in the bazaar for the said offences. Another feature of corporal punishment was *Phaouba* (exposed in the sun). Banishment means sending away to Loi village was very common form of punishment. Imprisonment was given to the offender as it gives sufficient time to the accused to change his law breaking behaviour.

MANIPUR LEVY

In the year 1819 the Burmese forces, as mentioned above, dominated over Manipur and the Manipuri. Princes fled for shelter to Cachar and Sylhet. But later on, the three Manipuri Princes, Chourajit Singh, Marjit Singh and Gambhir Singh, had usurped power in Cachar by defeating and deposing Govindachandra, the ruler of Cachar. Meanwhile, they also tried their best to regain Manipur from the Burmese.

With this British assistance Gambhir Singh raised his troops consisting of purely Manipuris and Cacharis of 500 strong; it was called the Manipur Levy. The British, thus, made full use of the advantage in hand by making friendship with the enemy's enemy which had proved its worth in the days of need. The Manipur Levy had played a great role in driving away the Burmese from Assam and Manipur in the first Anglo-Burmese War.

ANGLO-MANIPURI RELATIONS (1826-1891)

The political situation of the states in north-eastern India like, Assam, Cachar and Manipur, show vividly the developments in these areas consequent upon the British policy of non-interference. Badanchandra, disappointed with the British response, turned to the Burmese for help. The Burmese sent a large army to Assam and occupied it. Govindachandra, the Raja of Cachar, failing to get British support, requested for Burmese assistance. The Burmese army was sent to Cachar also. The result was physical confrontation between the British and the Burmese forces leading eventually to the first Anglo-Burmese War of 1824-26.

Treaty of Yandaboo

The Treaty of Yandaboo was signed between the British East India Company Government and the Burmese Government in February 1826. Manipur was not a party to the treaty. However, the treaty made a reference to the political status of Manipur by inserting an article.

Jiri Treaty of 1833

In 1833 Raja Gambhir Singh signed a treaty with the British Government known as the Jiri Treaty. The Treaty provided for :

(a) Transfer of Jiribam (Jiri in short) a portion of British territory in Cachar, to Manipur;

(b) Withdrawal of Raja Gambhir Singh's thana from Chandrapur in Cachar;

(c) Supply of porters by the Raja for the British troops going through Manipur (either for the protection of Manipur or a war with Burma);

(d) No obstruction by the Raja to the British trade and no imposition of heavy duties and no monopoly with any article;

(e) Repairing of the Cachar-Manipur briddle path by the Raja;

(f) Assistance by the Raja with his troops in case of disturbances in the eastern frontier of British India; and

(g) The Raja would be responsible for the arms and ammunitions received from the Government of India.

The Jiri Treaty, thus, represented an instrument for exchange of Jiribam with Chandrapur, and side by side with this, a trade and defensive alliance between the two governments. However, the clause on arms and ammunitions became virtually nullified owing to the withdrawal of British support to Manipur in 1835.

Kabo Valley Treaty of 1834

Kabo Valley, a small valley between Burma and Manipur, became a part of Manipur State after the epochal year, 1826 by right of conquest as Gambhir Singh succeeded in driving away the Burmese from Manipur and beyond the Ningthee river (Chindwin) in Burma. Kabo Valley had been a bone of contention between Burma and Manipur. The Burmese had nursed her desire to possess the Kabo Valley even after her defeat in 1826 and did not stop the pursuit.

The British East India Company Government wanted to make the eastern frontier of British India and the British ports of Pegu and Shahpuree in Burma safe from Burmese belligerency. In 1833-34, therefore, the British thought of restoring the Kabo Valley to Burma as a distinct act of appeasing the Burmese. The Governor-General in Council, under the influence of Colonel Burney, the British Commissioner at Ava, decided on handing over Kabo Valley to Burma as a mark of "expediency and gratification" The Government of Manipur was to be given, as a consolation for the loss, a compensation of 500 rupees per month.

Opening of Political Agency

In 1835 Lord William Bentinck decided to withdraw British support to Manipur. Though the British officers in the north-eastern India resented such a decision in appreciation of the dangers to British interests in the region, all were in vain. But the British authority did not entirely withdraw from the state in the sense that a Political Agency was established to protect Imperial interests in the region, and a Political Agent in Manipur was appointed.

The Political Agent in Manipur was to serve as a communicating link between the Government of Manipur and the Government of Burma. It was also his business to prevent all border feuds between the two states. Thus, the Political Agency in Manipur was established in 1835 during the reign of Maharaja Chandrakirti Singh. Major Gordon was appointed the first Political Agent in Manipur State.

MANIPUR : A PROTECTORATE

Gambhir Singh's infant son, Chandrakirti Singh, ascended the throne as a minor Raja in 1834. Nara Singh, a cousin brother of Gambhir Singh, was made the Regent. In 1844 Nara Singh was seriously injured following an attempt to murder him. by one Nobin Singh, a servant of the widow, Maharani Kumudini. The murder attempt having failed and apprehending danger, Kumudini left the state for Cachar along with her infant son, Chandrakirti, the reigning king.

Nara Singh, in the absence of Chandrakirti Singh, became the Raja. The British Government recognised him as the Raja. On the death of Nara Singh in 1850, his brother, Devendra, succeeded Nara Singh as the Raja. This time also the British Government, recognised Devendra as the Raja. But, before the Political Agent in Manipur could announce the decision of recognising Devendra Singh, an abnormal political situation developed.

The ex-Raja, Chandrakirti Singh, attaining majority by that time, appeared in Manipur and claimed the throne. The British Government, on the recommendation of the Political Agent, Colonel McCullock, removed Chandrakirti Singh ond his mother to Dacca (now capital of Bangladesh). But they managed to escape somehow. Chandrakirti Singh came again to Manipur and claimed the throne. But, he came this time with a force. The Manipuri soldiers showed their loyalty to Chandrakirti Singh as the ex-Raja happened to be the rightful heir to the throne. Thus, the supporters of Chandrakirti mustered strength while that of Devendra dwindled. Chandrakirti defeated Devendra and became the Raja.

The fact was that the British Government was afraid lest the Burmese should exert greater influence on Manipur and thus threaten British interests in eastern India. Therefore, the declaration of the British making Manipur as a protectorate state was solely motivated by imperialist interests.

After a long period of friendly and cordial relations between the two Governments till 1890, unhappy events came to pass. In September 1890 a fight took place between two groups of the Manipuri princes. Mr.Grimwood, the Political Agent tried to bring about a compromise; but failed. The ruling Raja, Surchandra Singh, abdicated the throne in favour of his brother Kulachandra Singh, Yuvaraja, and eldest in the line from the other group. Tikendrajit Singh, Kulachandra's brother in the same group and leader of the revolt, was appointed Yuvaraja.

The ruling Raja, Kulachandra, was recognised as the Raja; while Tikendrajit, the Yubaraja was to be deported by the Britishers. The Government of Manipur took such British action as an unwarranted interference in the administration of the state. The British attempt to forcibly arrest Tikendrajit by attacking the palace was a severe provocation. Therefore, the Manipuri troops resisted the British. As a result the Anglo-Manipuri War of 1891 broke out. Three British columns from Kohima, Silchar and Tamu advanced to Manipur; defeated the state forces and took over Manipur administration in April 1891.

Consequences of Anglo-Manipuri War of 1891

The 1891 war came to an end with the defeat of the Manipuris. The British troops occupied the Manipur palace on 27 April 1891. The Government of India adopted various punitive measures against the State and her people in retaliation of the loss of British lives and property in Manipur as a result of the war.

Brigadier General H.Collett, the General Officer Commanding, took up a number of steps to punish the State and the persons actively involved in the revolt of 1891 and the murder of the British officers in Manipur. The steps included:

(a) The General Officer Commanding, by a public announcement, declared that the State of Manipur was guilty of rebellion against the Government of India. By a proclamation dated 19 April 1891 it was made clear that the reign of Kulachandra Singh, the Raja of Manipur, had come to an end and that the general administration of the state had been taken over by the Commander of the British forces in Manipuri.

(b) To remove all doubts regarding the subordination of Manipur State to the British all previous treaties were repudiated;

(c) Manipur State was to pay to the British Government a tribute of 50,000 rupees per year;

(d) A pecuniary penalty of 2,50,000 rupees was imposed on the Manipur State subjects, however, the incidence of paying the fine was later shifted to the state;

(e) The lineage of the Manipuri kings before 1891 was precluded from their right to reign the state and the use of the word 'Royal' in regard to the family of the Maharajas of Manipur was also dropped.

The war of 1891 was significant in the history of Manipur because the sovereign status of Manipur terminated with it; Manipur became a state subordinate to the British. The subjects of the state suffered great hardships after the war.

In addition to the sufferings on account of the punishments stated above, the people had to live a difficult life owing to scarcity of food and increasing prices of the essential commodities. They had to face a reign of terror at the hands of the British troops who made it a point to look, down upon the common people.

THE REGENCY RULE

The proposal from the Local Government (Government of Assam) regarding Regency rule in Manipur was accepted by the Government of India. Churachand Singh, a minor from a collateral branch of the Manipuri kings was appointed Raja of Manipur under a Sanad to be honoured with 11 Salute Guns.

The British policy had the following implications:

(i) Lapse of the administrative authority of the British political Officer;

(ii) appointment of a Political Agent to represent the British authorities; and

(iii) appointment of a Regent to the minor Raja to run the administration in his behalf.

A fresh arrangement was made to fulfil the above condition. The designation of the Chief Political Officer of Manipur was changed to that of the Political Agent in Manipur. A special designation of Superintendent of State was added to that of the Political Agent so as to enable the Political Agent to administer the affairs of the state. Thus, Major Maxwell, the former Chief Political Officer of Manipur, combined the two posts and became the real administrator of the state.

Installation of Raja Churachand Singh

The Regency Rule in Manipur was nearing its end as the minor Raja attained majority in April 1906. Therefore, the question of placing Raja Churachand Singh in direct charge of the state administration was discussed by the British authorities since 1905.

In 1907 Major Shakespear reported to the Government that it would be expedient to hand over the state administration to the Raja as he had already attained majority. The Government of India approved the proposal. Accordingly, Major Shakespear handed over the charge of the state administration to the Raja on 15 May 1907.

MANIPUR STATE ADMINISTRATION RULES, 1907

It had been a constant British policy that the Government should pay close attention to the Raja until his rule in the state was firmly established. Side by side with this, the rule of the Raja had to be popularised without losing any control of the Government over the state administration.

Influenced by these ideas, the Government of India, on the recommendation of the Local Government, enforced a set of rules called the Manipur State Administration Rules, 1907, with the following provisions:

(a) The administration of Manipur was vested in the Raja assisted by a Darbar of which the Raja was to be the ex-officio President.

(b) A State Darbar was to be formed consisting of, in addition to the Raja, one Vice-President, three Ordinary Manipuri members and three Additional Manipuri members. The Vice-President was to be selected and appointed by the local Government from amongst the members of the Assam Provincial. Service Cadre; while the Ordinary and the Additional Manipuri members were to be appointed by the Local Government or the recommendation of the Political Agent in Manipur.

(c) The Vice-President of the Darbar was vested with the charge of the hill affairs, finance and revenue of the state. He was to prepare the state budget.

(d) The Political Agent in Manipur was responsible for the administration of the British Reserve and the British. Indian subjects in Manipur. All cases arising within the British Reserve and involving British subjects were to be settled by the Political Agent.

(e) The State funds were to be deposited in the State Treasury. The Accountant General of the Eastern Bengal and Assam was to act as the auditor.

REVISED RULES FOR ADMINISTRATION OF MANIPUR STATE

In 1910, as the Raja's performance during the probationary period was found satisfactory, the Manipur Administration Rule was amended. Under the new arrangement there was no drastic change in the relationship between the Government and the Raja or the Darbar. However, there was a change in the relative powers of the Raja and the Darbar. The Raja was made more responsible for the executive functions. The powers and authority of the Darbar were reduced to the position of a simple committee. As a rule, the Darbar had to submit a copy of the proceedings to the Raja who had the power either to approve of it; or send it back for reconsideration; or even veto the resolution of the Darbar. However, the powers of the Darbar to act as the highest Court of Appeal in cases involving only the Manipuris were still retained.

The second revision of 1916, initiated by the Raja, had sought further increase of the Raja's powers. It had been contended by the Raja that even in the absence of the Darbar he could run an equally efficient government. A subsequent revision prepared by the Political Agent in consultation with the Chief Secretary to the Government of Assam and the Vice President of the Manipur State Darbar and approved by the Government of India was introduced.

In 1928 the Indian States Committee, popularly known as the Butler Committee was formed to review the relations if the Government of India with the Native States. It was taken as an opportunity for the Maharaja and the Darbar to make a representation seeking extension of more powers and authority to them in the administration of the state. Thus, the Darbar, in consultation with the Maharaja, adopted the resolutions covering the following points:

(a) Handing over of the entire hill administration to the Maharaja;

(b) bestowing of more powers and authority to the Manipur State Darbar enabling the Darbar to select and appoint a permanent President of the Darbar;

(c) decisions of the Maharaja should not be subject to the approval of the Political Agent.

THE MANIPUR HILL PEOPLES' (ADMINISTRATION) REGULATION, 1947

The British Government, made a separate rule for the administration of the hills known as the Manipur State Hill Peoples (Administration) Regulation, 1947. It was enforced from 10 August 1947. It was considered that the enforcement, of such a rule for the hills was necessary in view, of the impending amalgamation of the Hills and the Valley administrations.

The Regulation for the hills provided that:

(i) the responsibility for administration of the hill people would be vested in the Maharaja in Council.

(ii) appointment to all the executive posts in the hill administration should be made in accordance with the rules for the Manipur State Appointment Board;

(iii) there would be three levels of local authorities in the hills : the Village Authority, the Circle Authority and the Sub-Divisional Authority.

(iv) administrative powers would be divided between the local authorities in the hills and the State Government, specially, in matters of Education, Public Works, Medical, Revenue, Forest and maintenance of public law and order.

The Manipur State Hill Peoples (Administration) Regulation, 1947, was a safeguard for the hill tribes following the unification of the hills and the valley administrations. In the exercise of executive, financial and judicial matters the local authorities played an important role. However, the hill budget was passed by the State Council; and the Chief Court at Imphal was given the power to review cases already disposed of by the Hill Bench.

HILL ADMINISTRATION UNDER THE STATE CONSTITUTION

After the Manipur State Constitution came into force, there was provision for appointing two Ministers from the hillmen out of a total of six, excluding the Chief Minister. In the State Legislative Assembly there were 18 seats for the hill people; while there were 30 for the valley and 3 for the Muhamadans, While administering the hill affairs, strict adherence to the State Constitution, the Hill Peoples' Regulation, the Manipur State Courts' Act, 1947 and the rules governing the Manipur State Appointment Board, 1947, etc., was ensured. Under the provisions of a cluster of these Acts and Rules, the executive and the judicial authorities of the local units in the hills were guaranteed complete autonomy within their jurisdictions.

Chronology of the Rulers (Kings) of Manipur

Sl. No.	Name of King/Ruler	Tenure
1.	Meidingu Nongda Lairen Pakhangba	33-154 A.D.
2.	Khuiyol Tompok	154-264 A.D.
3.	Taothing-Mang	264-364 A.D.
4.	Khui Ningomba	364-379 A.D.

Sl. No.	Name of King/Ruler	Tenure
5.	Pengshiba	379-394 A.D.
6.	Kaokhangba	394-411 A.D.
7.	Nao-Khamba	411-428 A.D.
8.	Nao-Phangba	428-518 A.D.
9.	Sameirang	518-568 A.D.
10.	Ura-Khonthouba	568-658 A.D.
11.	Naothingkhong	663-763 A.D.
12.	Khongtekcha[#]	763-773 A.D.
13.	Keirencha	784-799 A.D.
14.	Yaraba	799-821 A.D.
15.	Ayangba	821-910 A.D.
16.	Ningthoucheng	910-949 A.D.
17.	Chenglei Ipan-Lanthaba	949-969 A.D.
18.	Yanglou Keiphaba	969-984 A.D.
19.	Irengba	984-1074 A.D.
20.	Loiyumba	1074-1122 A.D.
21.	Loitongba	1122-1150 A.D.
22.	Atom Yoiremba	1150-1163 A.D.
23.	Iwanthaba	1163-1195 A.D.
24.	Thawanthaba	1195-1231 A.D.
25.	Chingthang Lanthaba	1231-1242 A.D.
26.	Thingbai Shelhongba	1242-1247 A.D.
27.	Puranthaba	1247-1263 A.D.
28.	Khumomba	1263-1278 A.D.
29.	Moiramba	1278-1302 A.D.
30.	Thangbi Lanhaba	1302-1324 A.D.
31.	Kongyamba	1324-1335 A.D.
32.	Telheiba	1335-1355 A.D.
33.	Tonaba	1355-1359 A.D.
34.	Tabungba	1359-1394 A.D.
35.	Lairenba	1394-1399 A.D.
36.	Punshiba	1404-1432 A.D.
37.	Ningthoukhomba	1432-1467 A.D.
38.	Kyamba	1467-1508 A.D.
39.	Koiremba	1508-1512 A.D.
40.	Lamkyamba	1512-1523 A.D.
41.	Nonginphaba	1523-1524 A.D.
42.	Kabomba	1524-1542 A.D.
43.	Tangiamba	1542-1545 A.D.
44.	Chalamba	1545-1562 A.D.
45.	Mungyamba	1562-1597 A.D.
46.	Khagemba	1597-1652 A.D.
47.	Khunjaoba	1652-1666 A.D.
48.	Paikhomba	1666-1697 A.D.
49.	Charairongba	1697-1709 A.D.
50.	Pamheiba (Garibniwaj)	1709-1748 A.D.

As per Cheitharol Kumpaba there is a gap after Meidingu Khongtekcha for 11 years.

Sl. No.	Name of King/Ruler	Tenure
51.	Chitshai	1748-1752 A.D.
52.	Bharatshai	1752-1753 A.D.
53.	Gourashyam (Maramba)	1753-1759 A.D.
54.	Bheigyachandra	1759-1762 A.D.
55.	Gourashyam (Maramba)	1762-1763 A.D.
56.	Bheigyachandra	1763-1798 A.D.
57.	Labeinyachandra	1798-1801 A.D.
58.	Madhuchandra	1801-1803 A.D.
59.	Chourajit	1803-1813 A.D.
60.	Marjit	1813-1819 A.D.
61.	Herachandra*	1820 A.D.
62.	Sana Yumjaotaba	1821 A.D.
63.	Gambhir Singh	1821 A.D.
64.	Jay Singh (Jai Singh)	1821-1822 A.D.
65.	Jadu Singh, Nongpok Chinglenkhomba	1822-1823 A.D.
66.	Raghop Singh	1823-1824 A.D.
67.	Bhadra Singh (Nongchup Lamgai Ngamba)*	1824-1825 A.D.
68.	Gambhir Singh (Chinglen Nongdren Khomba)	1825-1834 A.D.
69.	Chandrakriti (Ningthempishak)	1834-1844 A.D.
70.	Nar Singh	1844-1850 A.D.
71.	Devendra Singh	1850 A.D.
72.	Chandrakriti (K.C.S.I.)	1850-1886 A.D.
73.	Surchandra	1886-1890 A.D.
74.	Kulachandra	1890-1891 A.D.
75.	Churachand	1891-1941 A.D.
76.	Budhachandra	1941-1955 A.D.
77.	Okendrajit (Pareihanba)@	1955-1966 A.D.

* *As per Cheitharol Kumpaba Sl.No. 61 to 67 was the period of 7 years devastation (1819-1826). The Burmese occupation which is generally known the Seven Years' desertion was the darkest period in the History of Manipur.*

@ *By an orders of the President of India dated 2-2-1956 Shri Okendrajit (Pareihanba) was recognized as king of Manipur w.e.f. 9-12-1955.*

Source: *Directorate of Economics & Statistics Govt of Manipur.*

PRESENT MANIPUR

On 21 January 1972, Manipur was granted Statehood after several years of demand by All Manipur Students Union and several political organisations. The ceremony was performed at the Palace Polo ground in Imphal. In 1992, Meitei-lon (Manipuri) was included in the Eighth Schedule as one of the 22 official languages of India. Manipur has yet to see a proper road connection to the rest of India. Air transportations are provided from Kolkata, New Delhi, Gauhati and Silchar but much beyond the reach of commoners.

● ● ●

Physiography

The geological framework of Manipur including Indo-Burma range along its eastern frontier is closely linked up with the evolution of Neogene Surma basin, Inner Palaeogene fold belt and Ophiolite suture zone. The ophiolite belt occurring along Indo-Myanmar border in Manipur, forms a part of Naga-Arakan Yoma flysch trough of Upper Cretaceous-Middle Miocene age. Geological data collected so far mainly relates to Ophiolite zone and adjoining terrain. A large part of the state is yet to be covered by systematic geological mapping. These are the main mineral-bearing areas which have already been covered. The study of the rock formations in and around ophiolite belt elucidates and helps in understanding the broad stratigraphy and structure of the whole terrain. Available information brings forth a geological picture depicting the spread of Tertiary rocks over the entire state with small patches of Quaternary sediments in the central part (e.g. Imphal valley) and a long narrow N-S trending ophiolite belt towards the eastern margin of the state. It, thus, emerges that geotectonically three distinct domains exist which are: (1) Neogene Surma basin, (2) Inner Palaeogene fold belt and (3) Ophiolite zone associated with Late Mesozoic-Tertiary sediments.

Manipur is an isolated hill girt in the North Eastern Corner of India along the Indo-Myanmar border with Imphal, a flower on the Lofty heights, as the state capital.

Manipur has a multi-topographic characteristic. The eastern wing of the Himalayas especially its lower hills, constitute an important feature of the Landscape of Manipur.

GEOLOGY

According to Dayal and Duara (1963) the classification of rocks in Manipur is more or less in the line with that of Oldham (1883) with some modified views of Pascoe (1929) and Evans (1932).

According to them the geologic succession is:

Age	Rock Type
Recent to sub-recent	Alluvium
Oligocene	Barails
Intrusive rocks	Disang Series
Intrusive rocks (Cretaceous to early Ecocene)	Surpentinities
Cretaceous	Axials

Tectonically, the whole of Manipur forms a part of the great geosynclines that apparently had original basin topography of ridges and furrows. Sediments started depositing in the geosynclines, argillaceous sediments deposited in the furrows and arenaceous and calcarious sediments in the ridges.

The structural zones within the broad eugeosyncline as classified by Aubuoin (1965), from West to East are:
- Assam-Arakan trough (Eugeosynclinal furrow)
- Arakan Yoma Eugeosynclinal ridge
- West Burmese trough (Eugeosynclinal furrow)
- Pegu Yoma (Eugeosynclinal ridge) and
- East Burmese trough (Eugeosynclinal furrow)

Physiographically Manipur may be characterised in two distinct physical regions – an outlying area of rugged hills and narrow valleys, and the inner area of flat plain, with all associated land forms. These two areas are not only distinct in respect of physical features but are also conspicuous with regard to various flora and fauna. The valley region would have been a monotonous, featureless plain but for a number of hills and mounds rising above the flat surface. The Loktak Lake is an important feature of the central plain. The total area occupied by all the lakes is about 600 km². The altitude ranges from 40 m at Jiribam to 2,994 m at Mt.Iso Peak near Mao Songsong.

Major portion of the state is covered by hill ranges. Topographically the state is divided into three major regions: a) Hills, b) Imphal Valley and c). Barak Basin. The Imphal valley which is around 48.3 km in length and 32.2 km in breadth lies in the centre of the state. Several hill ranges dotted the valley, the biggest being the Langol Hill Range. The hills are generally irregular serrated ridges, occasionally rising into conical peaks and flattened cliffs.

The major rivers of Manipur are Barak river and the Turela Achonba river which is also known as Imphal or Manipur river. Imphal River is the longest river and it also collects excess water from the Loktak Lake and flows to join the streams of Ningthee and chindwin river of Myanmar. The other major rivers of Manipur are Thoubal, Fril, Sekmai, Kongba, Chakpi, Khuga and Nambol. Many small streams also flow in the hill.

● ● ●

Drainage and River System

The National Wetland Inventory and Assessment published by the Space Application Centre reported that Manipur has 15 major rivers/streams having 166.77 sq. km. of total area *i.e.* about 0.75% of the total geographical area of the state.

The state is drained by various streams, which belong to three river systems.

The **Manipur River basin** in the central Manipur, with a far less discharge capacity of 0.5192 Million ha. meter in a catchment area of 6332 sq. km. on the other hand, is the most important as it passes through thickly populated areas and covers the whole of Manipur valley consisting of the four valley districts. It also covers most of the habitations of Senapati district, the western portion of Ukhrul and Chandel districts and also the more populated eastern one-third of Churachandpur district.

The **Chindwin Drainage System** consists of the Imphal River and its tributaries, the lakes and marshes lying in the valley and the hill streams of Ukhrul and Chandel districts which drain into the Chindwin River of Myanmar or into the Yu river, a tributary of Chindwin in Myanmar. The Imphal River, also known as Manipur River originates from the north of Kangpokpi and flows southward to the eastern side of the Loktak lake. The principal tributaries of the river in the valley are the Iril, Thoubal, Nambul and Nambol. The Barak River basin is the largest in terms of the area drained in the state *i.e.*, 9041 sq. km and 68% yield.

BARAK RIVER

The Barak River is the biggest and the most important of the rivers in the Manipur hill territory. It is considered a legendary river in Manipur. It is part of the Surma-Meghna River System.

The major tributaries of the Barak River are the Jiri, Dhaleshwari, the Singla, the Longai, the Madhura, the Sonai, the Rukni and the Katakhal.

The Barak River originates from the Manipur hill territory, near Mao Songsang. At ite source it is known as 'Sanglook'. At the source there are a lot of hill stream namely Gumti, Howrah, Kagni, Senai Buri and Durduria.

The Barak river is the western part of the state with a number of its tributries, like the Jiri, the Makru, the Irang, the Tuivai and their associated streams, which drain in the northern and western hill areas, have a catchment of 1,042 sq. kms. covers about 40.5 per cent area of the entire region.

River Basin	Catchment area (km^2)
Barak River Basin	
Barak	6,865
Tuvai River	1,860
Jiri River	316
Total	**9,041**
Manipur River Basin	
Manipur River (upto Ithai Barrage)	5,109
Manipur River (beyond Ithai Barrage)	1,223
Total	**6,332**

IMPHAL RIVER

The Imphal River is one of the important rivers of Manipur. It is a tributary of the Manipur River. The river joins the Manipur River in Thoubal district. The river flows past the Loktak Lake and the city of Imphal. It joins the Lilong River, 10 km to the south.

The Imphal River rises in the hills of the Senapati. The river has an elevation of 2300 metres. It flows west through Manipur, then southwest leaving Manipur and enters the state of Mizoram.

Geologically Barak valley lies on ancient alluvial sediments. Barak River is proposed to be declared as National Waterway-6 by the Government of India.

IRIL RIVER

The Iril River runs through the eastern suburbs of Imphal. The name of the river is derived from two words 'ee' and 'ree'. In Manipuri language 'ee' means blood and 'ree' means river. Hence, it becomes Blood River.

The river originates from Sirong. It flows through Ngamju village. The river then runs through Sagolmang and flows through Lamlai, Top, Naharup, Pangong and Irilbung and finally joins the Imphal River. The river has endangered indigenous fish species called Ngaton Meitei Sareng.

THOUBAL RIVER

Thoubal river starts from Huimi hills of Ukhrul and flow westward upto Yaingangpokpi and turning southwards, joins the Imphal river at Irong Ichin.

LAKES

The state of Manipur is characterised by numerous lakes. Many of them are also known for its scenic and aesthetic beauty. Loktak lake, the biggest of North East India, is also a part of Manipur. It is also famous for its great beauty.

Lakes in Hill Areas

There are two major lakes in hilly areas of Manipur. These are Kachouphung Lake in Ukhrul district and Zailad Lake in Tamenglong district.

Main Lakes : At a Glance

Lakes	District	Lakes	District
❖ Loktak Lake	Bishnupur	❖ Kharung Pat	Bishnupur
❖ Heingang Pat	Imphal East	❖ Kachouphung Lake	Ukhrul
❖ Waithou Pat	Thoubal	❖ Pumlen Pat	Thoubal
❖ Utra Pat	Bishnupur	❖ Zailad Lake	Tamenglong
❖ Loushi Pat	Bishnupur	❖ Ikop Pat	Thoubal
❖ Ishok Pat	Bishnupur	❖ Sana Pat	Bishnupur
❖ Loukoi Pat	Bishnupur		

Waterfalls

Waterfalls	District	Waterfalls	District
❖ Barak Waterfalls	Tamenglong	❖ Sadu Chiru Waterfalls	Bishnupur
❖ Khayang Waterfalls	Ukhrul	❖ Leimram Waterfalls	Bishnupur
❖ Dilily Waterfalls	Ukhrul		

UNDERGROUND WATER RESOURCES

Groundwater in the state is mostly exploited through open wells. As per reported by the Central Ground Water Board (CGWB), ground water in the deeper aquifers occurs under sub-artesian and artesian conditions. Granular zones are encountered at a depth of about 150 m in Imphal valley and at about 220 m in Jiribam valley. Tube wells have been installed at various places of the valley areas with the yields ranging from 0.6 to 4 cu.m/hr. On the basis of the monitoring of water level in key/dug wells network stations in the area, an annual recharge of 44 M.cu.m has been estimated.

Considering the clayey nature of formation in the top aquifer, development of this resource is not considered promising on a large scale either in irrigation of water supply. Hydrological study reports reveal that Manipur valley is underlined by a thin veneer of alluvial deposits, which is largely clayey in nature, underlined by rocks of Tertiary age. Ground water occurs under un-confined and confined conditions. Since the upper formations are mainly silty and clayey, open wells have poor yield prospects. However the deeper zone, consisting of sand stones of Tertiary age, forms good aquifers which are under confined conditions, Auto flow conditions are observed in Imphal where the yield of the tube wells vary from 0.5 to 4 m³/hr.

WETLANDS OF MANIPUR

The National Wetland Atlas 2010, developed by Space Application Centre has identified 167 wetlands (≥ 2.25 Ha) and 541 wetlands (<2.25 Ha) covering 63,616 ha *i.e.*, 2.85% of total geographic area under different types of wetlands like lake/pond (61.5%), river/steam (26.2%), waterlogged (5.5%) and aquaculture pond. Analysis of wetland status in terms of open water and aquatic vegetation showed (in table 6.1) that around 71% of wetland area is under open water category during post monsoon and 62% during pre-monsoon respectively. Aquatic vegetation (floating/emergent) occupies around 26% of wetland area during post monsoon and 37% during pre-monsoon respectively.

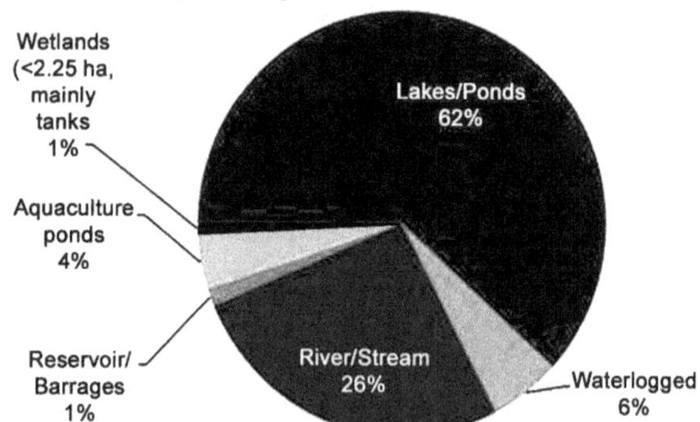

Percentage of wetland area in Manipur

Out of 9 (nine) districts in Manipur, three districts are rich in wetland viz. Bishnupur (30.7% of total district of total district geographic area under wetland), Thoubal (30.3% of total district geographical area) and Imphal West (2.6% of total geographical area under wetland). Chandel district has the lowest area under wetland *i.e.*, 0.44%. Senapati and Thoubal have observed with very high concentration of small wetlands (< 2.25 ha).

• • •

Climate

The climate of Manipur is mostly tropical with alpine climate. The rapid changes in topography results in climatic changes within short distance. The northeastern region has an amiable climate and is very cold in the winters. The temperature in the summer is 32 degrees C and in the winters it falls below zero. The rains last from May till mid-October. The average rainfall experienced is 1467.5 mm. Manipur is a state where you can see hills all around. The state is situated at 790 meters above the sea level. The climate varies according to the elevations of the land forms in the state. The weather in the plains is however, similar to that of the other states in the country. But the hilly regions are different and enjoy a pleasant climate with dry and low temperature. The weather in the state is highly influenced by the winds blowing from the Bay of Bengal and is conducive for heavy rainfall in the rainy season. The state experiences three main seasons like summer, winter and the rainy season.

A year in Manipur can be broadly divided into four seasons. The summer season being with early march and extends upto May, then the rainy season starts by mid-May upto September. October and November are the retreating monsoon months and the period from December to the end of February is the winter season. The winter and summer seasons are dry while rainy and retreating monsoon seasons are wet. The temperature during these months experiences an average of 28 degree Celsius. The weather is bright and sunny and the hills experience a dry and warm climate, while the plains are hot and dry like any other part of the country. Many tourists can also be seen during these months to experience the hilly climate of these regions. During the winter the average temperature is 8 degree Celsius and is mostly experienced in the plains, while the hilly regions are cold and freezing below zero degrees Celsius. Cold winds can be experienced that can snow the hilly regions to some extent.

As the Himalayan region is close by and the hills are actually an extension of the Himalayas, the climate here is similar to the Himalayan region, but not extreme. Winters begin from November and stay on till February. The coldest month is January, as cold winds freeze the atmosphere. The monsoon season begins in May and continues till the mid of October. The average rainfall received is 1467.5 mm annually. The rain fall distribution varies from region to region in Manipur. Imphal receives 933 mm of rain, while Tamenglong receives 2593 mm. The rains help in the agriculture of the state and enriches the soil and help in production of good grains.

The impact of terrain diversity, altitudinal variation and river regime has become eloquent in the seasonal variability of climate from one place to another. The Barak basin & lower foothills of Manipur Western hills have a warmer climate than the central valley and surrounding hills. Similarly, the western part of the state is more moist than the eastern because of its location on the windward slope of the hills. The climate of Manipur can be broadly classified into three as

(a) temperate prevailing in the higher altitude of hill where temperate fruits & vegetables can be grown throughout the year;

(b) Sub-tropical prevailing in the lower attitudes hills & central valley plain where winter lasts from November to February and rainy season from May to September. The transition period of March, April and October can be described as spring and autumn though short.

(c) Tropical prevailing in Jiri Plains and foothills - during March. In this plain and foothills all the tropical crops can be raised.

The mean rainfall in the state is around 1518.36 mm. that the monsoon confers upon Manipur a very handsome rainfall as

South-West monsoon (June-September)	–	5085.39 mm
Post monsoon period (October.-December)	–	329.77 mm
Winter monsoon (January-February)	–	47.80 mm
Pre monsoon (March-May)	–	610.50 mm
Annual Mean Total Rainfall	**–**	**1518.36 mm**

Although the State receives adequate rainfall for agricultural purpose, it suffers from temporal and location variations. There are great variations of rainfall in different districts. There is scarcity of water for economic activities in some districts.

● ● ●

Soils

The soil cover can be divided into two broad types, viz. the red ferrogenous soil in the hill area and the alluvium in the valley. The soil generally contains small rock fragments, sand and sandy clay and are of varieties. The top soils on the steep slopes are very thin. In the plain areas, especially flood plains and deltas, the soil is of considerable thickness. Soil on the steep hill slopes is subjected to high erosion resulting into formation of sheets and gullies and barren rock slopes. The normal pH value ranges from 5.4 to 6.8.

Manipur is endowed with wide range of climates, physiographic settings, geology and vegetative sequences. The interaction amongst these factors in the ecosystem with time and space leads to result in the formation of different kinds of soils with different properties, limitations and potentials.

It is revealed that the soils have been derived primarily from shales and sandstone. Climate and relief have played a dominant role in the development of these soils weathering is intense due to high precipitation under favourable condition of temperature and vegetation. The state comes under the warm perhumid agro-eco region.

DISTRIBUTION AND CLASSIFICATION OF SOILS

The soil of Manipur belong to 4 orders, 8 suborders, 13 greatgroups and 23 subgroups. It is observed that the Inceptisols are the dominant soils followed by Ultisols, Entisols and Alfisols and occupy 38.4%, 36.4%, 23.1% of the total geographical area of the State, respectively. Lake and marshy land occupy 1.9 per cent.

Distribution of Soil Order and Sub-orders

Sl. No.	Soil order	Suborder	Area ('000 ha)	Per cent of TGA
1.	Inceptisols		858.3	38.4
		Ocrepts	654.6	29.3
		Acrepts	203.7	9.1
2.	Ultisols		811.0	36.4
		Humults	374.0	16.8
		Udults	436.9	19.6
3.	Entisols	Orthents	515.6	23.1
4.	Alfisols	Udalfs	3.8	0.2
5.	Miscellaneous Marshy land		42.4	1.9
		Total	2231.0	100.0

Characterisation of Soils Under Different Agro-Ecological Subregions

The state comes under the hot and warm humid/per-humid agro-eco region. However, at microlevel, it can be divided into three distint-subregions(zone) with thermic and hyperthermic temperature regimes as follows:

1. Warm-humid agro-eco zone with thermic ecosystem and LGP 300-330 days.
2. Hot -humid agro-eco zone with hyperthermic ecosystem and LGP 270-300 days.
3. Warm Per-humid agro-eco zone with thermic ecosystem and LGP 330-365 days.

SOILS OF WARM HUMID AGRO-ECOZONE

The soils are derived from shale and sandstone and mostly occur on the hills of varying slopes. Soils occuring on the gently sloping foot hills are deep, well drained with greyish brown to yellowish brown in colour. Soils are classified as Type Haplohumults, Umbric Dystrochrepts and Ultic Hapludalfs.

Soils on steep to very steep hill slopes are deep under thick vegetative cover and otherwise they are shallow with exposed stratified grey coloured shale layers. The soils are classified as Typic Kanhapludults, Umbric Dystrochrepts. Typic Udorthents, Typic Haplohumults and Typic Hapludults.

The soils are acidic with high organic matter content. Available phosphate is very low in the soils of upper reaches while it is very low in the soils of upper reaches while it is medium in the soils of narrow valleys which may be due to the formation of Ferric (Fe^{3+}) phosphate or organometalic complexes not easily available to plant.

Valley and fllod plain soils derived from alluvium are deep to very deep, poorly to moderately well draiend. The soils are slightly acidic to neutral with high humus content. The ground waterable is generally high and the soils are classified as Typic and Mollic Haplaquepts, Fuvaquentic Humaquepts, Typic Haplaquent and Typic Fluvaquents.

Land Use

The upper reaches of the hills are under forest cover of decidous trees while mixed forest species comprising bamboos, wild bananas etc. occur in the lower steep hills. Jhum cultivation is practiced in places of convenient slope grades on medium hill ranges in normal cycles of 5-10 years. Maize, Sesamum, potato, Ginger, Tapioca and vegetables are grown under the shifting cultivation system. Horticultural crops like Orange, Pineapple, Lemon, etc. are also terraced on hill slopes and used for permanent cultivation. Scars of Jhum fields with secondary growth of vegetation are commonly occured. Valley lands are generally well bunded and used for intensive and permanent agriculture. The ' beel' areas are occupied by luxurient growth of submerged weeds of mixed species.

Soil Constraints and potentials

The salient problems and potentials of the soils are:

Constraints: Hill soils being acidic are not suitable for plant growth and traditional shifting cultivation alongwith indiscriminate cutting and burning of forests in every year in ters of timber, fire wood etc. have been affecting seriously the ecological balance of the area. Such practices leave the soil surface barren in addition to loss of fertile top soil surface through erosion. Water holding capacity is also reduced which again affect the availability of water in the lower reaches.

The valley soils are mostly restricted to rice, but these are low in available phosphorous content and susceptible to flood hazards. Due to high clay content in places farming operation becomes very difficult.

To sum up, the soil constraints are:
- Soil acidity
- Low cation exchange capacity

- Soil erosion due to shifting cultivation and deforestation
- Low base status leading to toxicity of Fe and Al.
- Low availability and high phosphate fixation
- High ground waterable and flloding in valley soils.

Potentials: The soils and agroclimate of this hilly region are ideal for the development of horticulture. It is, however, necessary to establish nurseries for varieties specific for the region. It is also possible to exploit these soils for cultivation of tea.

Beels and lakes can be utilised scientifically to expand and improve fish production in the area.

SOILS OF HOT HUMID AGRO-ECOZONE

The agro eco-zone encompasses parts of Imphal (Jiribam area) Tamenglong and Churachandpur districts bordering Assam and Mizoram and occupies about 12.8 per cent of TGA of the state. This zone experiences hot summers and cold winters with seasonal dry spells which even extend from November to April. The estimated length of growing period ranges from 270 to 300 days and moisture index ranges from 20-40 per cent. Mean annual precipitation of Jiribam station is 2088.7 mm and potential evapotranspiration of 1377.9 mm with an annual average temperature of 24.4°.

The soils of this region are heterogenous in nature and developed in gently sloping narrow valleys and strongly sloping hills with moderate to severe erosion hazards. These soils are in general, well to excessively drained, fine to loamy skeletal and classified as Umbric/Type Dystrochrepts; Typic Udorthents and Typic Haplohumults. These soils are moderately to strongly acidic, humus rich and have low base saturation. Soils developed in narrow valleys are deep, poorly drained, fine in texture and with slight erosion hazard.

Land Use

The area is primarily under forest cover, sesamum potato, maize, ginger, tapioca and vegetables are grown under the shifting cultivation system. Horticultural crops like Orange, Pineapple, Lemon, Pears etc. are grown in these areas. Narrow valleys are cultivated permanently for Paddy and Maize in general.

Soil Constraints and Potentials

The salient problems and potentials of these soils are :

Constraints: Hill soils of this region are strongly acidic and have low base status and comparatively less moisture holding capacity. These are low in available phosphate contents and highly susceptible to erosion due to heavy and swift runoff over the steeps slopes. Due to shifting cultivation landslides and mass movement are additional man made problems of the region.

To sum up, these soils suffers from:

- Soil acidity
- Low exchange capacity
- Soil erosion
- Low base status
- Limiting soil depth in steep hill slope, and
- Shifting cultivation and landslides

Potentials: The soils of the region being highly acidic and base unsaturated, crops tolerant to acidity will grow effectively under such agroclimate. Horticultural crops like Pineapple, Pears, Peach, Plum, Lemon, Orange and Banana may grow successfully with proper management.

SOILS OF WARM PERHUMID THERMIC AGRO-ECOZONE

This region comprising the south-western part of the state gradually merging to Mizoram has longest growing period. The land/surface configuration is mostly dissected hills with narrow valley. The region covers 14.4 per cent of the total geagraphical area of the state. The moisture is available through out the year barring some seasonal deficit during November, December and January. The estimated length of growing period varied from 330-365 days.

The main soil types of this area include Typic/Umbric Dystrochrepts, Typic Haplohumults/Typic Udorthents and Typic Palehumults. The organic carbon content of the soils are high and have low base saturation and low CEC. Soils are highly acidic.

Land Use

The area is under mostly forest, Sesamum, Potato, Maize, Tapioca and vegetables are grown under jhum cultivation. Some areas are used for fruit tree crops. Narrow valleys are generally used for Paddy cultivation.

Soil Constraints and Potential

Constraints: The soils of this agro eco sub-region suffers from

- Soil acidity
- Soil erosion
- Low base status
- Limiting soil depth in steep hill slopes
- Jhum cultivation and land slides

Potentials: Soils of this region being highly acidic and low in base saturation and cation exchange capacity is preferred for crops tolerance to acidity. This region is also suitable for horticultural crops like Pineapple, Pears, Peach, Plum and Banana if planted under little soil and water conservation measures. This region is also favourable for agroforestry and other silvipastural systems.

• • •

Forest & Wild Life

For a hilly State like Manipur, forest products are the most important natural resources for environmental protection and maintaining ecological balance. According to Forest Report, 2017 by Forest Survey of India (FSI), Dehradun, the forest cover of Manipur is 17,346 sq. kms. as against 16,994 sq. kms. in 2015. The distribution of forest cover according to the FSI is shown in the Table below.

District-wise Forest Cover of Manipur
(State of Forest Report 2017)

(Area in km²)

District	Geographical Area	Very Dense Forest	Mod. Dense Forest	Open Forest	Total	Percent of GA
Bishnupur	496	0	1	21	22	4.44
Chandel	3,313	11	970	1,926	2,907	87.75
Churachandpur	4,570	42	1,663	2,464	4,169	91.23
Imphal East	709	0	61	217	278	39.21
Imphal West	519	0	16	38	54	10.40
Senapati	3,271	272	751	1,161	2,184	66.77
Tamenglong	4,391	390	1,754	1,809	3,953	90.03
Thoubal	514	0	2	71	73	14.20
Ukhrul	4,544	193	1,292	2,221	3,706	81.56
Total	**22,327**	**908**	**6,510**	**9,928**	**17,346**	**77.69**

Forest plays threefold roles *i.e.*, protective, productive and aesthetic, each being equally important. Based on the legal status, the forest can be categorised as reserved, protected and unclassed forests. Reserved Forest is one which is permanently dedicated either to the production of timber or to other forest produces and in which right of grazing and cultivation is seldom allowed. In protected forests, these rights are allowed subject to a few mild restrictions. Unclassed Forest consists largely of inaccessible forest or unoccupied waste.

Area under Forest by Legal Status

Year	Reserved Forests	Protected Forests	Unclassed Forests	Other Forests	Total
2007-08	1,467	4,171	11,780	–	17,418
2008-09	1,467	4,171	11,780	–	17,418
2009-10	1,467	4,171	11,780	–	17,418
2010-11	1,467	4,171	11,780	–	17,418
2011-12	1,467	4,171	11,780	–	17,418
2012-13	1,467	4,171	11,780	–	17,418
2015-16	1,467	4,171	11,780	–	17,418
2016-17	1,467	4,171	11,780	–	17,418

CLASSIFICATION OF FORESTS

Area under forest includes all lands classed as forests under any legal enactment dealing with forests or administered as forests whether state owned or private and whether wooded or maintained as potential forest land. The area of crops raised in the forests and grazing lands or area open for grazing within the forests are generally included under the forests area.

Division of Forests

In spite of its smallness in size, the state's vegetation is rich and varied in character. This is because of the different climatic conditions found in the state and its peculiar physiography. The forest area of the state falls into four distinct zones viz. (i) Burma Border Forests (ii) Ukhrul Pine Forests (iii) Forest overlooking the valley and (iv) Barak Drainage Forests. The Burma Border Forests lie along the Indo-Burma Border. The Kabaw Valley marks the eastern boundary of these forests. The Ukhrul pine forests are scattered almost all over the hills surrounding the valley area. The Barak Drainage forests area situated in the hills of the west of valley area along the cost of the Barak River and its tributaries viz. Jiri, Tuivai, Leimatak and Makru.

The main timber species available in Manipur are Teak, Uningthou, Khasi-pine, Dipterecarpes species (Yangou and Khangra), Michelia Champa (Leihao), Terminalia species (Tolhao), Cedrela Toona (Tairen), Schima Walliechii (Usoi) etc. The quality of timber available in Manipur is very suitable for furniture and construction purposes.

FOREST PRODUCTS

With a view to maintaining ecological balance, the Government has restricted the felling of trees in the forest areas. As a result, the felling of trees is done on limited scale. The estimated production of timber in 2007-08 (about 8.3 thousand cubic metres which valued at ₹ 68.04 lakhs) is less than the production of 8.9 thousand cubic metres in 2006-07 valued at ₹ 82.59 lakhs. The estimated production of firewood in 2007-08 is 21.52 thousand tonnes (valued at 11.86 lakhs) as compared with 90.32 thousand tonnes produced in 2006-07 (valued at ₹ 13.52 lakhs). The value of forest products in 2007-08 is estimated at ₹ 135.31 lakhs as compared with ₹ 144.14 lakhs in 2006-07. Bamboo is accounted for ₹ 5.85 lakhs in the value of minor forest products in 2007-08.

ECONOMIC AND COMMERCIAL PLANTATION

One of the most important activities of forestry sector is raising of suitable plantation and their subsequent maintenance. In addition to the plantation by the Forest Department, the plantation schemes that are being implemented in the State are artificial plantation, a forestation creation of plantation crop, social forestry and recreation forests. Besides, plants that are naturally regenerated are also added over large areas every year to facilitate sustained growth. And also final plantation/restocking over 540 Ha. was taken up during the year 2007-08. A scheme for Rubber Plantation was also taken up to produce rubber as well as uplift the economy of the local people by providing employment to the backward families and to rehabilitate the wastelands. In spite of its vast forest resources, its share in the state income is very negligible and the expenditure is much greater than its revenue.

ORCHIDS

Blessed with an amazing variety of flora and fauna, 67% of the geographical area of Manipur is hill tract covered forests. Depending on the altitude of hill ranges, the climatic condition varies from tropical to sub-alpine. The wet forests and the pine forests occur between 900-2700 m above MSL and they together sustain a host of rare and endemic plant and animal life. Coveted the world over as some of the most beautiful and precious blooms, orchids have an aura of exotic, mysteries about them.

In Manipur, they are abound in their natural habitat growing in soil or on trees and shrubs speaking their beauty and colour, stunning the eye that is not used to seeing them in such profusion. There are 500 varieties of orchids which grow in Manipur of which 472 have been identified.

SOCIAL FORESTRY

Social Forestry scheme is constituted by three major components viz., (i) Farm Forestry Extension (Distribution of Seedlings), (ii) Fuelwood and Fodder Plantation and (iii) Roadside Plantation.

Under the Farm Forestry Extension scheme the people are encouraged to take up plantation activities in their own fields not only to meet their daily requirements of firewood but also to supplement their income by selling the firewood and fodder from these plantations.

In order to maintain ecological balance, the Fuel wood and Fodder Plantation scheme was taken up. Under the scheme the Forest Department taken up plantation on community and Panchayat land to develop woods and maintain it up to the third year of plantation. Thereafter, the plantation are hand over to the villagers. During 2008-09, plantations of over 600 ha. and advance work over 635 ha. were carried out. During 2009-10, final plantations over 635 ha. and advance work over 495 ha. were carried out.

Roadside plantation refers to the plantation of ornamental species in single or double rows along the National/State highways with the objectives of improving the aesthetic beauty of the surroundings and also provide protection to the roadside.

Wild Life

Manipur has a rich and wide variety of flora and fauna. Manipur has a special responsibility towards the rest of country and indeed the world at large. The mountains, foothills and plains house a zoogeographic diversity of flora and fauna. The species that are to be protected are, Sangai (dancing deer), Uchek Langmeidon (the great Indian hornbill), Nongyin etc.

Keibul Lamjao National Park: Spread in an area of 40 sq km, Keibul Lamjao National Park in Manipur was established in the year 1966 as a Sanctuary and in the year 1977 as a National Park. Keibul Lamjao National Park Manipur is probably the world's only 'floating sanctuary' that comprises 40 sq km of wetland overgrown with 1.5 metre deep floating vegetation (called phumdi). The park has several distinguishing features. Besides the vegetation and terrain, an important highlight of the park is the Loktak Lake (6,475 ha), the largest freshwater lake in India; a large portion of which falls within the park. It is about 53 km from Imphal. November to April is the best time to travel here.

Manipur Zoological Garden: About 6 km. from Imphal, towards the west, in Manipur Zoological Garden at Iroishemba lying on the Imphal Kangchup Road. Some rare to be found species can be seen in this zoological garden. A trip to the Manipur Zoological Garden, at the foot of the pine-growing hillocks in the westernmost corner of Lamphelpat is really enjoyable. November to April is considered as the best time to travel here under the temperate weather conditions

One can have an opportunity to see the graceful brow antlered deer (Sangai), one of the rarest species in the world, in sylvan surroundings of the Garden.

The Keilam Hill Range: This hill range in Churachandpur District has a variety of animals and birds. Uchek Langmeidon (the great Indian horn bill) and other kinds of hornbills are said to be found in this jungle area of hills. Indeed, this hill range is noted for its abundance in a variety of wild animals and birds. Some of them are Uchek, Langmeidon, tiger, elephant etc.

The Siroi-Kashong Range of Hills: This range of hills is rich in natural and valuable flora and fauna. Manipur's state bird "Nongyin" is found in the areas of Siroi-Kashong range of hills in Ukhrul District. This range stretches from north to south in Ukhrul District. The state's flower "Siroi Lily" is grown only on Siroi Hills of this range.

Angoching: It is yet another place which has been the habitat of various rare and indigenous flora and fauna of Manipur state. It is located at about 90 kms. east of Ukhrul. In this area grows a hill lily of the name 'Khayang Lily" which is closely related to Siroi Lily. Khayang Lily is also a beautiful hill lily of elegance.

Yaigangpokpi Lokchao Wild Life Sanctuary: Opened up in 1989 at Lokchao Yaingangpokpi, it has about 100 kinds of plants, 70 varieties of birds and 50 species of wild animals. It is spread in 184.8 sq km of area. Important fauna of this sanctuary includes tiger, leopard, elephant etc.

Zeliad Wildlife Sanctuary: This wildlife sanctuary in Tamenglong district is spread in an area of 21 square kilometre. Important fauna of this sanctuary includes tiger, hog deer, elephant, wild dog etc.

Area and Location of Wild Life Sanctuaries and National Parks in Manipur

Sl. No.	Particulars	Location (District)	Area in sq. km.
1.	Keibul Lamjao National Park	Bishnupur	40.00
2.	Yangoupokpi Lokchao Wildlife Sanctuary	Chandel	184.80
3.	Bunning Wildlife Sanctuary	Tamenglong	115.80
4.	Zeliad Wildlife Sanctuary	Tamenglong	21.00
5.	Kailam Wildlife Sanctuary	Churachandpur	187.50
6.	Jiri-Makru Wildlife Sanctuary	Tamenglong	198.00
7.	Shiroi Hill National Park	Ukhrul	41.00

8 | Agriculture

The economy of Manipur state being primarily dependent on agriculture, emphasis has been given on augmenting agricultural production of the state. Agriculture still occupies the most prominent position in the state's economy. Traditionally, people in the hills practice jhuming or shifting cultivation in general *i.e.*, they cultivate on high slopes, then abandon the plots after a few years and cultivate in another hill plot. Arable land is by and large marginal and hence agriculture had persistently been on subsistence level in Manipur.

Agriculture, being the main occupation of the people of Manipur, it has an important place in the economy of the state. Agriculture sector contributes a major share to the total State Domestic Product (SDP). 52.81% of the total workers in Manipur are cultivators and agricultural labourers according to 2011 Population Census. In fact, the SDP fluctuates depending on the performance of agricultural sector. Despite the crucial importance of this primary sector in the state's economy, the irregular and erratic behaviour of monsoon accompanied by inadequate irrigation facilities have resulted in severe fluctuations in agricultural production. Agriculture becomes a living proposition rather than a commercial proposition. Thus, from the view point of employment and income, agriculture plays a very crucial role in the state's economy.

SIZE OF HOLDING

The agricultural holding/land holding is the amount of land held by a farmer. In Manipur, arable land is limited and majority of the farming community have small and marginal land holdings which make them difficult to practice any subsistence farming. The area of operational holding is about 172 thousand hectares operated by 151 thousand farmers as per the agricultural census 2010-11. The area operated in small and marginal holdings accounted for 59.88 per cent in 2010-11.

Pattern of Land Utilisation

Land Utilisation statistics for the entire State of Manipur are not available because hill areas are not cadastrally surveyed. The plains of Manipur occupy about 2,238 sq. kms. which accounts for about 10 per cent of the total geographical area. A firm information regarding the land utilization of the entire State cannot be built up since land records are available only for the cadastrally surveyed area of the Manipur Valley and a very small pocket of the hills while no complete and regular land utilization survey have been undertaken by the authorities, such as Agriculture/Horticulture/ Settlement and Land Records/Revenue Departments. As per the land utilization statistics of 2000-2001, out of the total geographical area, the reporting area is about 1,90,446 hectares. An area of 26,900 hectares of land is not available for cultivation. Fallow land covers 200 hectares and other uncultivated land excluding the fallow land covers 8,055 hectares which account for about 4.23 per cent of the total reporting area.

Agricultural Production

Permanent cultivation is generally practiced in the valley districts, while terrace cultivation is practiced in some pockets of the hills where jhuming or shifting cultivation is widely adopted in most of the hill districts. Rice is the staple food of Manipur and is grown in both the hill and plain areas. Cultivation is almost entirely mono-crop with rice accounting about 98% of food-grains production.

During 2014-15, the food-grain production excluding pulses was 493.57 thousand tonnes thereby showing a increase of 1.02% from the previous year of 488.60 thousand tonnes in 2013.14. The estimated requirement of food grains for human consumption excluding livestock/poultry/seed/wastage etc. in the state would be of the order of 608.50 thousand tonnes in 2014-15.

The production of rice for Manipur for the year 2014-15 was estimated at 4.82 lakh tonnes as against 4.77 lakh tonnes in 2013-14. In case of maize, the estimated area, the average yield and production for the agricultural year 2014-15 was recorded as 5.30 thousand hectares, 2135.85 kgs. per hectare and 11.32 thousand tonnes respectively. Among the districts, Imphal East District had the highest production of rice with 91.40 thousand tones (18.95%) which was followed by Imphal West with 79.92 thousand tonnes (16.57%). The lowest was recorded in Tamenglong District having only 20.19 thousand tonnes (4.19%) during the year 2014-15.

Estimated Area and Production of Cereal Crops

Year	Rice		Maize	
	Area ('000 hectares)	Production ('000 tonnes)	Area ('000 hectares)	Production ('000 tonnes)
2010-11	168.78	377.37	5.01	11.91
2011-12	172.83	387.17	5.90	11.28
2012-13	175.04	426.50	5.27	11.10
2013-14	176.47	477.05	5.15	11.55
2014-15	178.20	482.25	5.30	11.32
2015-16	175.16	433.32	5.42	10.71

Source: *Directorate of Economics & Statistics, Govt. of Manipur*

High Yielding Varieties (HYV) Programme

The High Yielding Varieties Programmes which are introduced in India since the mid-sixties play a significant role in boosting agricultural production. However, the adoption of HYVs in the State has been found to be very slow particularly in the hill areas and also with regard to other crops except for paddy.

According to the results of Crop Estimation survey conducted by the Directorate of Economics & Statistics, the estimated area under HYVs and Improved varieties (IV) of paddy in 2014-15 is more than the previous year. The total area under HYVs and IVs of paddy constitutes about 37.98 per cent of the total area under paddy in 2014-15 as against 36.94 per cent in 2013-14.

The adoption of HYVs of paddy in the hill districts perhaps due to surface configuration of the hill areas continued to be negligible while that of IVs is quite encouraging. The proportion in the hill areas for the HYVs and IVs was 14.44 per cent in 2014-15 as against 18.60 per cent in 2013-14.

During 2010-11, it was found that HYVs of paddy were mainly used in the valley areas of the state. Of these total areas of 168.78 thousand hectares under paddy, the area under HYVs paddy was found to be 36.82 thousand hectares which was 20.55 per cent of the total area under paddy in the state. Out of 36.82 thousand hectares under HYVs, 33.47 thousand hectares was found in the valley and the remaining 3.34 thousand hectares was found in the hill areas. With the irrigation potentials created under major, medium and minor irrigation projects, double cropping has been adopted more successfully in a number of pockets of the valley districts of Manipur.

COMMERCIAL CROPS

The development of commercial crops like cotton, kabrangchak, oilseeds and sugarcane is very essential for enhancing the growth of agro-based industries in the State of Manipur. The estimated areas under some important commercial crops are given below.

Estimated Area Under Important Commercial Crops

(Area in '000 hectares)

Year	Cotton	Kabrangchak	Oilseeds	Sugarcane
2011-12	0.45	-	1.34	0.28
2012-13	-	-	1.50	0.27
2013-14	-	0.04	1.04	0.08
2014-15	-	0.10	0.94	0.26

Source: Directorate of Economics & Statistics, Govt. of Manipur

Rubber

Rubber Plantation under Forest Department, Manipur started in 1977-78 in Jiribam area covering about 938 hactares.

Potential Area

Jiribam area is, in fact, a non-traditional area for the Rubber Crop. However, due to prevalence of optimum climate, edaphic conditions required for successful growth of the crop, Jiribam has got good potential for undertaking plantation of rubber in a large commercial scale. Besides, there is a good transport facility to connect the area with good markets of Rubber Crop.

The outlying areas of Jiribam town are quite good potential areas for growing rubber trees. Plantations in a large scale can be taken up in areas on both the sides of Man Bahadur Road as far as Choudhurikhal. Special targets to utilise abandoned jhum areas in a productive manner by way of rubber plantation can be set and achieved. Higher the investment, higher would be the financial returns.

Application of Fertilizer

Chemical fertilizers play an important role in increasing the agricultural production particularly when used with the high yielding varieties which are responsive to recommended doses of fertilizers. The increase in agricultural production was possible as a result of adoption of quality seeds, appropriate doses of fertilizers and plant protection chemicals, coupled with assured irrigation. The improved and certified seeds have been the catalyst for making inputs cost effective.

HORTICULTURE

Manipur has plenty of scope and potential to grow various horticultural crops because of varied agro-climatic conditions. The major fruits grown in the state are pineapple, lemon, orange, banana, guava, peaches etc.

Growing of fruits and vegetables on small plots of land provides additional income to the farmers undertaking crop husbandry enterprises. Another advantage of growing fruits is that these can be grown on uneven and undulating lands. In this way, it gives additional benefits as forests cover for such lands which are liable to run off and erosion.

The cultivation of horticulture crops is by and large practised as non-commercial enterprise by farmers in their homestead and orchard, it hardly helps in development of proper market of horticultural crops. But in recent years, cultivation of horticultural crops like pineapple, potato and vegetables are being developed on commercial scale in many places of the state.

To promote healthy growth of horticulture in Manipur, it is essential to develop horticulture marketing and improve transport system as the present low level of horticulture production is due to perishable nature coupled with improper marketing facilities.

Tropical and Sub-tropical Fruits

Among fruits, Banana, Pineapple and Citrus take a major share in area and production. The other fruits which are grown in sizeable area are Guava, Papaya etc. Banana is native to this region (Tamenglong). Pineapple is mostly grown on hill slopes as rainfed crop. Giant Kew and Queen are the two leading varieties being grown.

Temperate fruits

Peach, pear and plum are being grown successfully on higher altitudes mostly low chilling varities, are performing well.

Pear : Leconte, Smith, Keifer, Coslin etc.
Peach : Flordasum, Shane-Punjab, Sharbati.
Plum : Santa Rosa, Doris, Mariposa.

Vegetables

The scenario in vegetable is much more promising in Manipur. Low productivity in most of the vegetable crops grown is directly connected to the use of genetically inferior varieties coupled with low input farming and incidence of insect pests and diseases. Several Improved and high yielding varieties and F1 hybrids are now available for large scale adoption. In Manipur the valley land, after the harvest of paddy, is being successfully utilized for large scale cultivation of vegetables. Now the farmers have started using F1 and high yielding varieties.

The state abounds in cucurbitaceous vegetables like Pumpkin, Bottle gourd, Ridge gourd, Cucumber and Dolichos, Vigna, Phosphocarpus and Phaseolous and Phaseolous vulgaris (French bean). Among solanaceous vegetables, brinjal, tomato, chillies and capsicum hold great promise. In cole crops, Cabbage and cauliflower are grown in limited area. Among exotic vegetables, brussels sprout and broccoli also hold good promise due to favourable climatic conditions but these are not popular among the farmers.

Mushroom

Mushroom, a nutritionary food item is common among the people of Manipur since ages. Cultivation of Mushroom is getting momentum mainly on Agaricus, Volvariella and Pleurotus. Introduction of Mushroom cultivation as an industry will be the pivotal role for employment and income generation.

Root & Tuber Crops

Indegeneous food-crops like Colocassia, Sweet potato, Tapioca etc. played main role in remote hill areas. Development of agro-technique in this regard will suffix the need.

Spices

Three commercial crops need mention in this respect, viz, ginger, turmeric and large cardamom. In ginger, varieties viz. Nadia, Poona, Suprabha were found promising. In case of turmeric G.L. Puram, RTC and Lakadong were found promising. Large cardamom is a potential crop for the state.

Aromatic & Medicinal Plants

The vast plant resource (medicinal) recorded until now are limited to about 1200 to 1300 species. Out of this partly a few hundred(400/500) are used by the local people for the treatment of ailments so far recorded and local uses of the rest could not be available. The villagers living in direct national plant-environment rather than the modern allopathy treatment should be emphasized as priority.

Moreover, aromatic plants also will play a main role in social, economic upliftment and environmental friendship.

ANIMAL HUSBANDRY

Amongst the allied sectors of Agriculture, Livestock/Poultry is another important sector. Development of animal husbandry is an essential feature as livestock plays a pivotal role particularly in the state's rural economy. A large number of small and marginal farmers, agricultural labourers and other economically weaker sections depend upon livestock for gainful employment.

The primary objective of animal husbandry development activities is to augment animal based products like milk, meat, egg, wool, hide and skins etc. In order to ensure a steady growth of these livestock and poultry products and also by-products, the department of Veterinary and Animal Husbandry Services has taken up development programmes such as

(i) animal health and disease control,

(ii) cattle development,

(iii) pig breeding,

(iv) poultry development,

(v) feed and fodder development and

(vi) dairy development and milk supply schemes.

Livestock Wealth

The main categories of livestock reared in Manipur are cattle, buffalo, sheep, goat, dog, pig, etc. Cattles and buffaloes provide motive power in wet cultivation. Rearing of pigs and poultry are found to be very important sources of income generating activities. The total livestock population according to livestock census, 2012 was recorded to be 6.93 lakhs as against 7.87 lakhs in the livestock census, 2007. Thus, there was a decrease of 11.94 per cent in the livestock population of the State. Cattle population constitutes 38.09 per cent of the total livestock population. In 2012, the total cattle population was about 2 lakhs as compared to 3 lakhs in 2007 census. In case of poultry, the total population in 2012 census was 24.80 lakhs as compared to 22.89 lakhs in 2007.

Livestock Products

According to the livestock census conducted in 2012, there were 6.93 lakhs livestock in Manipur. Of these 2.64 lakhs were cattle, 0.66 lakhs were buffaloes and 2.77 lakhs were pigs. The poultry population was recorded to be 24.80 lakhs. The main livestock productions in the state are milk, egg and meat. The total milk production in 2015-16 was 81.77 thousand tonnes which was less than the production of 82.17 thousand tonnes in 2014-15. The estimated production of eggs in 2015-16 was numbering at 924.37 lakhs showing a decrease over the production of 1,130.96 lakhs in 2014-15. The estimated meat production for the year 2015-16 was 11.32 thousand tonnes which was less than 45.83 % over the production of 26.57 thousand tonnes in 2014-15.

Animal Health and Disease Control

To keep livestock and poultry healthy and also to protect them from a number of deathly epidemic diseases, the Department has formed a network of veterinary services such as Hospitals, Dispensaries and Veterinary aid Centers throughout the State for treatment and control of diseases. By the end of March 2012, there were in all 55 veterinary hospitals, 143 (109 veterinary dispensaries and 34 Aid centers) dispensaries functioning in the State.

FISHERIES

Fish is the main food item of the majority of the people in the State, particularly the Meiteis who are mainly concentrated in the valley.

Fishery Resources

The State has no marine fisheries. It has vast potential of fisheries resources comprising ponds, tanks, natural lakes, marshy areas, swampy areas, rivers, reservoirs, submerged cropped land, low lying paddy fields etc. The largest source of fish is the Loktak Lake.

The total water area in Manipur State have shrunk from around 1,00,000 ha. in 1990 to around 56,461.5 ha. in 2009-10. About 18,000 ha of water areas have been brought under fish culture operation.

The swamps and marshy areas are lying barren without any effective utilisation. The lakes, reservoirs, beels, tanks, canals, etc. cover an area of about 13,221.45 ha. whereas rivers, streams etc. account for 13,888.27 ha.

These swamps can be profitably utilized for culture of various indigeneous natural fishes such as Ukabi (Anabas tesdudineus), Ngamu (Lata fish), Ngaton (Labeo bata), Ngakrijou (Lepidocephalichthys SPP), Sareng Khoibi (Botia SPP), Nganap (Pengia SPP), Ngatin (Labeo Pangusia), Ngakra (Barbus tor), Ngasang (Esomus denricus), Phabounga (Puntius SPP), Ngamhai (Chanda SPP), Pengba (Osteobrama belangeri) etc.

Fish Products

The production of fish in Manipur for the year 2015-16 was estimated to be 31.99 thousand tonnes as against 30.59 thousand tonnes in 2010-11. The per capita production of fish for 2014-15 was 8.08 kgs as compared to the estimated per capita requirements of 10.50 kgs., registering a shortfall of 2.42 kgs. per head per annum and the per capita production fish for 2010-11 was 8.01 kgs. as compared to the estimated per capita requirements at 10.50 kgs., with a short fall of 2.49 kgs. per head per annum.

The total requirement of fish far exceeds its indigenous production. Large quantities of fishes are being imported from outside the State every year to fill this gap. The estimated requirement of fish for the year 2004-2005 was 23.00 thousand tonnes whereas the actual fish production was 17.80 thousand tonnes. This huge gap is to be met by harnessing the vast fishery resources of State by adopting advanced scientific techniques of fish culture and consolidating the available infrastructures already laid and by introducing new schemes and projects. This will enable to meet not only the requirement of fish in the State but also for export to neighboring States like Assam, Nagaland, Mizoram and even to the neighboring country, Myanmar.

The Fishery Department, Manipur has taken up a Project 'Development of Reservoir Fisheries in Manipur' to enhance production of fish. During 2014-15, the other following schemes for development of Fisheries in the State.

(i) Mass Scale production of State Fish Pengba

(ii) Pen Culture in and around Loktak Lake and other Wet land areas

(iii) Development of Derelict/Swampy waterlogged areas.

Govt. Fish Farms In Manipur

Sl.No.	District	Name of Fish Farm
1.	Imphal West	D.L.F.S.F. Lamphel
2.	Imphal East	F.R.C. Khudrakpam
3.	Thoubal	D.L.F.S.F. Wangbal
4.	Thoubal	Waithou E.F.F.
5.	Bishnupur	D.F.F.S.F. Ningthoukhong.
6.	Bishnupur	Regional Pengba Seed Farm Haotak
7.	Bishnupur	Takmu E.F.F. Takmu
8.	Senapati	D.L.F.S.F. Keithelmanbi
9.	Senapati	Cold Water Fish Farm, Molhoi
10.	Ukhrul	Mirang Fish Seed Farm
11.	Chandel	Fish Seed Farm, Komlathabi
12.	Chandel	Fish Seed Farm, Khambathel
13.	Churachandpur	Fish Seed Farm, Phailian
14.	Churachandpur	Fish Seed Farm, Tuibong
15.	Tamenglong	Fish Seed Farm, Tamenglong
16.	Tamenglong	Fish Seed Farm, Khoupum
17.	Jirbam Sub Disn	Fish Seed Farm, Patchao
18.	Jiribam Sub Division	Compite Fish Farm, Kutikhong

MAJOR FISH FARMERS DEVELOPMENT AGENCIES

1. Fish Farmers Development Agency, Imphal
2. Fish Farmers Development Agency, Thoubal
3. Fish Farmers Development Agency, Bishnupur
4. Fish Farmers Development Agency, Ukhrul
5. Fish Farmers Development Agency, Senapati
6. Fish Farmers Development Agency, Tamenglong
7. Fish Farmers Development Agency, Churachandpur
8. Fish Farmers Development Agency, Chandel

SERICULTURE

Sericulture plays a vital role in the improvement of economic conditions of the artisans of the Manipur state. It is an important labour-intensive and agro-based industry generating employment opportunities for the rural people with lowest investment cost. Sericulture has a long tradition and has been practised by the farmers from time immemorial but on a limited scale. But the sericulture industry was confined only in a few villages. Mulberry silk worm rearing and reeling was confined to four villages viz Khurkhul, Leimaram, Pheiyeng and Thongjao etc. whereas Eri silk rearing was conducted for domestic consumption by the womenfolk. Silk weaving industry was confined to another four village's viz. Chingmeirong Kabo Leikai, Thangmeiband, Awang Kongpal and Maibam Leikai only. And the sericulture industry has been extended to other villages and also to the hill districts of the state during the plan period.

Manipur has 4 (four) varieties of Silk viz., Mulberry, Eri, Muga and Oak Tasar. To provide employment particularly to womenfolk, Manipur Sericulture Project (MSP) was initiated with the assistance of the Government of Japan through Government of India. Under MSP-II, 200 ha of land was brought under Silkwork Food Plantation and 20 Kissan Nurseries have been established in 4 valley districts of Manipur during 2014-15. Again, under the Rashtriya Krishi Vikas Yojana (RKVY), Industrial Oak Tasar Seed Production Centre-I at Thumkhonglok Bishnupur and Post Cocoon Tech. Working Units (2 each at Imphal West, Imphal East, Thoubal and Bishnupur and 1 each at Churachanpur and Ulkhrul are established during 2015-16. With the help of Central Silk Board, the Catalytic Development Programme (CDP) has been implemented which covered sericulture farmer excluded in the MSP.

Manipur Sericulture Project

During the Ninth Five Year Plan, the State Govt. had taken up a project entitled "Manipur Sericulture Project" with assistance from OECF (Overseas Economic Co-operation Fund) now renamed as JBIC, Japan in order to increase the annual production of silk yarn to the tune of 328 MT. Under this project, the advance technology and sophisticated machineries used in Japan could be transferred to India with a view to increase the production of raw silk in terms of both quality and quantity so as to meet the demand of international market. The project also envisage development of sericulture facilities covering (a) Construction of infrastructural facilities such as Seed Farm, Grainages, Research Station, District Storage and Cocoon marketing Centres, (b) Development of Plantation of Mulberry and Eri, (c) Construction of reeling and spinning facilities, twisting, etc. (d) Development of technical training centres for rendering technical assistance & training etc. The overall development plan on this project has been formulated including a total 2,720 hectares of Mulberry, 1,500 hectares of Eri and functioning all the necessary supporting facilities. The project has been implemented with an outlay of ₹ 490.59 crores since 20th July, 1998, in two phases.

Catalytic Development Programme (CDP)

With the help of the Central Silk Board (CSB), the State Government has implemented the CDP since 2003-04. The Central Silk Board has approved 23 microschemes for implementation in Manipur with an output of ₹ 228.04 lakhs during the Tenth Plan Period (2002-07).

Under this programme, Cluster Development Project, as special project, is introduced for the Eleventh Five Year Plan period (2007-2012), which will be aided by the CSB, MOT, and Government of India as catalyst.

Irrigation

The state, although small in geographical area is comparatively rich in water resources especially in surface water. There are number of lakes in the valley such as Loktak, Ikopat, Kharungpat, Lamjaopat and Pumlelpat. In addition to this, the state has two major river basins viz the Barak river basin and the Manipur river basin. The average annual yield of the two major basins of the state has been broadly estimated to be 1.8487 million hectare metre (14.98 million acre feet.)

MAJOR AND MEDIUM IRRIGATION PROJECTS

The state did not have any major and medium irrigation project up to 1972-73 and agriculture was solely dependent on capricious rainfall. Hence, assured water supply for irrigation is of utmost importance.

In fact, major, medium and multipurpose irrigation projects have been introduced very late in the state. Major and medium irrigation was started only from the 4th plan period onwards. The state has so far taken up 8 projects under the major, medium and multipurpose irrigation projects. Of these 8 projects, 3 projects namely Thoubal Project, Singda dam Project and Khuga dam Project are multipurpose. Loktak Lift Irrigation (LLI) is the major project and four are medium projects namely, Imphal Barage, Khoupum Dam, Sekmai Barrage and Dolaithabi projects. The Loktak Lift Irrigation Project is one of the biggest lift irrigation project in the North Eastern Region of India. Among these eight projects, three of them are on-going which are (i) Khuga Multipurpose Project, (ii) Thoubal Multipurpose Project & (iii) Dolaithabi Barrage Project. These 8 projects on completion will give an ultimate annual irrigation potential of 1,09,785 ha. with water supply and power components of 19 MGD and 10 MW respectively.

Khoupum Dam Project, LLI Project, Imphal Barrage and Sekmai Barrage Projects have already been completed and given irrigation benefits. The Singda Multipurpose Project was approved by the Planning Commission in the year 1974 and its construction was started from 1975. The irrigation and water supply components of the project was completed in 1995-96. Since then, irrigation potential of 4000 ha. has been created and 4 MGD of raw water is supplied to state PHE Deptt. Out of this 8 Major and Medium Irrigation and Multipurpose Projects Khoupum Dam, Imphal Barrage, Sekmai Barrage, Loktak Lift irrigation, Singda Multipurpose Project and the Barrage component at Keithelmanbi and a part of left Canal of Thoubal Multipurpose Project have been completed. The ongoing projects are (i) Khuga Multipurpose Project (ii) Head Work and remaining Part of Canal System of Thoubal Multipurpose Project and (iii) Dolaithabi Barrage project.

From the completed and partially completed projects Irrigation potential of 36,847 ha has been created up to 2008-09 with utilization of 27,000 ha. In addition 1,200 ha and 900 ha of low lying areas of Loushipat and Poiroupat respectively have been reclaimed by Thoubal Multipurpose Project.

Appreciable Progress of the ongoing Major and Medium irrigation and multipurpose projects could not be achieved onwards 2003-2004 up till date owing to financial constraint coupled with the prevailing law and order in the state.

Khuga Multipurpose Project

The Khuga Multipurpose Project was sanctioned for ₹ 15.00 crores in 1980 by the Planning Commission. The Project will create 1500 ha of annual irrigation Supply of 5 MGD of raw water for water supply and generate 1.50 MW of power. The Project works were taken up in 1982-83. Owing to rescission of the 1st contract and fixation of 2nd contract in 1986, law & order situations, financial constraints, ethnic clashes etc., completion of the Project has been delayed and rescheduled in 2010-11. The head work component has been completed and commissioned on 12th November, 2010 with a partial irrigation potential of 10000 ha. The progressive expenditure upto March, 2012 is ₹ 401.03 crores. The outlay for 2015-16 is ₹ 7.10 crores.

Thoubal Multipurpose Project

The Thoubal Multipurpose Project was approved by the Planning Commission in 1980 for ₹ 47.25 crores. The project when completed will create irrigation potential of 33,390 ha, 10 MGD of drinking water and generate 7.50 MW of hydro-power. The barrage component has been completed in 1991.

Since then, a partial irrigation potential of 21,260 ha had been created upto March, 2015. As part of the Thoubal Multipurpose Project, scheme for providing raw water from the Thoubal Dam upto the treatment plant near

Sanjenbam Village, Imphal East District is taken up to augment water supply of the Imphal City by 45 MLD (Million Litres per Day). The whole component of laying of pipes are targeted for completion by March, 2017.The Thoubal Hydro Power Component, which envisaged installation of 3 units of 2.50 MW, is targeted for completion during 2016-17.

Dolaithabi Multipurpose Project

The Dolaithabi Project was sanctioned for ₹ 18.86 crores by the Planning Commission and sanctioned by the state Government in 1992. The Project was originally planned for completion by 1996-97. However, owing to rescission of the original contract, financial constraint etc. the work is now targeted for completion during March 2017.

Land acquisition for barrage has been completed and 80% for canals was completed. Foundation excavation for main barrage has been completed and 38% of concrete work including super structures has been completed upto February, 2013.

Additional irrigation potential of 61,950 ha, 15.00 MGD of water supply and 10.75 MW of power will be accrued to the state on completion of the ongoing projects. Out of these 4MGD of raw water is also supplied from Khuga Multipurpose Project to the State PHED. Table shows the overall benefits to be accrued to state on completion of the said projects in the Twelfth Plan.

Irrigation Potential/Benefit to be accrued to the State during the12th Plan

Sl. No.	Projects	Ultimate Benefits			
		CCA (in Ha.)	Annual Irrigation (in Ha.)	Water Supply (in MGD)	Power Generation (in MW)
1.	Chakpi Multipurpose Project	9860.00	15260.00	3.00	7.50
2.	Regional Jiri Irrigation Project	5750.00	9770.00	1.20	-
3.	Iril Multipurpose Project	5500.00	8300.00	10.00	15.00
4.	Sekmai Multi-purpose Project	9000.00	13600.00	1.80	-
	Total	**30110.00**	**46930.00**	**16.00**	**22.50**

Source: Annual Administrative Report 2014-15, Irrigation and Flood Control Deptt.

The cumulative irrigation potential to be created under major, medium and multipurpose irrigation projects up to the end of Fifth, Sixth, Seventh, Eighth, Ninth and Tenth Plan were 800 ha., 40,000 ha., 59,000 ha., 63,100 ha., 28,500 ha. and 28,500 ha. respectively. The short-fall is due to restriction in the command area, encroachment, heavy siltation of the canal beds etc. By the middle of XIth Plan the irrigation potential from completed/partly completed projects was 36,847 ha. with utilisation of 27,000 ha.

It is proposed to complete all the ongoing projects within the Eleventh Five Year Plan period. Three new projects viz. Dam on Iril River at Yangoi, Dam on Chakpi River at Chakpikarong, Dam on Sekmai River at Kangoi Hiranpham and Transfer of Chakpi Water to Loktak Lake are proposed to be taken up during the Eleventh Plan (2007-12).

Irrigation Programme which was initially started with meagre plan investment of ₹ 1.41 crores during the Fourth Plan has been increased to the order of ₹ 20 crores, ₹ 40 crores, ₹ 74 crores, ₹ 125 crores and ₹ 222 crores during the 5th, 6th, 7th, 8th and 9th plan respectively. During the Tenth Plan the outlay for Major and Medium irrigation was ₹ 414.57 crores. The projected outlay for the Eleventh Plan is ₹ 386.14 crores and that the annual plan for 2009-10 is proposed to be ₹ 223.59 crores.

MINOR IRRIGATION

The scope of minor irrigation is very high due to the existence of numerous small valleys in the far flung hill districts and gentle slopes all over the state where permanent terraced fields are to be constructed for cultivation. Even though minor irrigation scheme is very small, their overall impact is quite substantial. The schemes are inexpensive, easy to build, maintain and operate within the short gestation period. Even for plain areas in the valley districts supplemented irrigation is to be provided during the dry spell of monsoon and drought by minor irrigation schemes, whereas in the permanent terraced field in the hill districts, irrigation is to be provided by Contour Canals throughout the monsoon as water from the elevated terraced plots reaches towards the lower plots (basin). Therefore, emphasis is to be laid on the Minor Irrigation Scheme.

Since the minor irrigation scheme plays a vital role in the state, maximum priorities are given to accelerate the minor irrigation activities. The scheme-wise programmes taken up during the Eleventh Plan are (*i*) River Lift Irrigation (RLI) (*ii*) Surface Flow Scheme and (*iii*) Construction of Tube Wells. (*iv*) Roof-top rain water harvesting.

River Lift Irrigation

River Lift Irrigation is very significant during the rabi and first crops of paddy. Under this scheme, 6 (six) numbers of pumping sets are targeted to be provided in the command area of 450 hectare in the hills whereas 20 (twenty) numbers of pumping sets will be provided in the command area of 4000 hectare in the valley. During the Eleventh Plan, the projected outlay is ₹ 940.12 lakhs with the target to create irrigation potential of 5,000 hectare and proposed outlay for annual plan 2009-10 is ₹ 350.00 lakhs.

Surface Flow Scheme

Surface Flow Scheme provides irrigation during kharif. The scheme is essential to grow H.Y.V. of rice to safeguard against reduction in yield and in proper water management and to respond to higher input of fertilizers to get proper yield. The scheme is supplemented with drainage and waste water disposal to eliminate water logging and salinity. During the Tenth Plan, a new scheme known as Tank Irrigation will be taken up as a pilot demonstration. During the Eleventh Plan the projected outlay for the scheme was ₹ 1745.20 lakhs with a target of creating 23,000 hectares of Irrigation potential. The annual plan outlay for the scheme for 2009-10 was ₹ 450.00 lakhs.

Construction of Tube wells

Under this scheme-wise, tapping of ground water through tube wells is taken up to provide irrigation water even during lean season and also to enhance double cropping and provide maximum irrigation potential. During the Eleventh Plan, ₹ 100.00 lakhs was proposed with to create irrigation potential of 500 hectares and the annual plan outlay was ₹ 100.00 lakhs.

FLOOD CONTROL

The state has two main river basins viz. (i) the Barak basin and (ii) the Manipur river basin. The Barak River which is the main river in the Barak basin, originates from the hill in the northern part of Manipur and ultimately flows into the Cachar district of Assam without traversing through the valley areas of the State. It, therefore, does not affect the valley much so far as flood is concerned.

The Manipur River which is the main drainage channel of Manipur valley then flows towards Burma through the southern hills. The major river in this basin are (i) Imphal/Manipur, (ii) Iril, (iii) Thoubal, (iv) Nambul, (v) Nambol, (vi) Wangjing,(vii) Sekmai, (viii) Khuga (ix) Merakhong and

(x) Kongba etc. The main river viz the Imphal River originates from the hills near Kangpokpi about 45 kms. from Imphal and is joined by the Iril river at Lilong, 10 kms. south of Imphal and by Thoubal river at the Irong Ichin near Mayang Imphal, the Sekmai river at Sekmaijin. After this, the Imphal River is known as Manipur River. The Khuga River joins the Manipur River near Ithai, upstream of Ithai Barrage. The Manipur River is connected with the Loktak Lake through a natural cut called Khordak. The Loktak Lake is the biggest water expanse in the State. The lake occupies prominent place in the hydrological system of the State. The average area of the lake is 216 sq. kms. All the rivers originating from western hill viz. the Nambul, the Merakhong, the Nambol, the Thongjaorok, the Ningthoukhong, the Potsangbam, the Khujairok and the Moirang rivers etc. drain into this lake along with a number of other smaller streams and streamlets. Other major lakes such as Ikokpat, Kharungpat, Lamjaopat, Pumlelpat which are on the left side of the Manipur river are also connected with this river through a number of natural drainages. All these major lakes act as flood reservoir of the rivers of the Manipur basin.

Ecological changes such as heavy deforestation and Jhum cultivation in upper catchments of the rivers, reclamation of low lying areas which earlier serves as flood reservoirs and inadequate carrying capacity of the rivers are some of the major factors contributing to the flood problems. The flood control works have been taken up in a systematic manner since the 3rd Five Year Plan after the devastating flood of 1966. Floods occurred in the state in 1966, 1967, 1974, 1976, 1980, 1982, 1984, 1985, 1986, 1987, 1989, 1997 and 2002 causes' heavy damages to properties, crops, and loss of human lives and miseries in the state. A separate flood control division had been set up in 1980 and a master plan was prepared.

Flood control measures in the state mostly consists of construction of new embankment, strengthening of existing bunds, improvement of drainage, construction of sluices, special protection and erosion control etc. The state has also started formulation of basin-wise/sub-basin-wise flood control project. Flood control projects for the rivers which have been causing maximum flood damages are being taken up on priority. Projects of other rivers are also formulated for taking up in a gradual manner.

Flood Management Programme (FMP)

Under the FMP, the Irrigation and Flood Control Department (IFCD), Manipur has taken up 22 schemes. In order to mitigate flood and also provide other allied benefits from the existing water bodies, Repair, Renovation and Restoration (RRR) of 4 (four) water bodies have been approved and are being implemented during 2015-16. The target for achievements for XIIth Plan (2012-17) is as given below.

 (i) Embankment - 267 Km.

 (ii) Drainage - 260 Km.

 (iii) Anti Erosion - 204 Km.

 (iv) Culverts - 99 Nos.

 (v) Water bodies - 4 Nos.

COMMAND AREA DEVELOPMENT PROGRAMME

Command Area Development (CAD) programme, 50 per cent centrally sponsored continuing scheme of the Ministry of Water Resources, Govt. of India was implemented in Manipur with the creation of Command Area Development Authority (CADA) since the Year 1982-1983 in the selected Command Area of Loktak Lift Irrigation Project.

The scope and objective of the CAD Programme is to integrate all the activities crucial for increasing agricultural productivity and production in the command area of irrigation projects leading to better utilisation of irrigation potentials created by Major & Medium and Minor Irrigation Projects. The main works are construction of field element, field drains, land leveling etc. and conducting adaptive trials, training of farmers in irrigation, water management, enforcement of Warabandi for suitable distribution of irrigation water to the farmer's field etc. Initially, CAD programme was implemented in the Loktak Lift Irrigation Project having a Cultivable Command Area (CCA) of 24.00 thousand ha in the year 1982-83. The next CAD programme was taken up in the Command Area of Sekmai Barrage Project in 1986-87. Similarly, the third programme for Imphal Barrage has also been started from 1993-94. The CAD programme for Thoubal Multipurpose Project (Barrage Component) are taken up under CADP in the commands of Minor Irrigation Scheme in the year 1995-96. Later, the Government of India has also included one medium Irrigation project and 8 clusters of Minor Irrigation projects in the year 2000-01 and implementation of Command Area Development and Water Management (CADWM) Programme have already been stated since 2003-04.

Command Area Development Projects

(in '000 ha.)

Sl. No.	Name of the Project	Culturable Command Area	Ultimate irrigation potential
1.	Loktak Lift Irrigation	24.000	40.000
2.	Sekmai Barrage Project	5.000	8.500
3.	Imphal Barrage Project	4.800	6.000
4.	Thoubal Multipurpose Project	17.350	30.000
5.	Singda Dam Project	2.400	4.100
6.	Khuga Dam project (KDP-I)	10.000	15.000
7.	Khoupum Dam project (KDP-2)	0.600	1.000
8.	Haipi and Lamlang MI project	0.945	1.607
9.	Aihang, Sitalok and Serou MI Project	1.464	2.599
10.	Ethei Maru MI Project	2.000	3.400
11.	Saikot, Masemlok and Wangoo MI Project	1.123	1.986
12.	MI project phase – II	22.685	38.566
	Total	**92.367**	**152.758**

Source: Draft Annual Plan, Planning Deptt., Manipur.

Out of above projects, Loktak Lift Irrigation, Sekmai Barrage, Thoubal Multipurpose (Barrage Component of 2400 Ha. CCA), Singda Dam Multipurpose, Imphal Barrage and 8 M.I. scheme/projects have been completed under CADWM programme. During the Annual Plan 2007-08 & 2014-15, 4 cluster of new MI Scheme and during 2010-11, two new major projects have been included in the CADWM programme.

● ● ●

Mineral Resources

Minerals provide a base for the rapid industrialization. It is imperative, therefore, that proper attention is paid to their development. The State Government has formulated a New Mineral Policy (NMP). It is to develop mineral-based industries by identifying lack of infrastructure, lack of investment and flow of credit from banks and exploration of local resources and manpower to achieve the industrial growth. With the objective of the strengthening organisational set up, streamlining of mineral administrative machineries, augmentation and intensification of mineral exploration, commencement of mining activities and participation in general water exploration and geo-physical investigations, it is proposed to provide sufficient fund during the Ninth Five Year Plan. To achieve the objectives phasing programme for exploration and investigation of minerals, collaborative efforts for strengthening of the Geology and Mining Division is initiated by creating Mining section. So far 58 per cent of the total area of Manipur has been covered by systematic geological mapping and 42 per cent still remains to be covered.

The Geological Survey of India (GSI) has undertaken systematic survey in the three districts of Manipur viz. Ukhrul, Churachandpur and Chandel and discovered considerable quantities of valuable mineral deposits like limestone, copper, lignite, nickel, chromite, asbestos, salt etc. Some of the important mineral resources are given below.

LIMESTONE

Limestone is an important material for manufacturing of cement. It is mainly available in different parts of Ukhrul District viz. Hundung, Mata, Khangoi, Sokpao, Lambui and Kasom. It is also available between 32/4 and 32/6 milestone on Imphal Moreh Road in Chandel District. Limestones are located at Lambui, Kasom, Paorei, Phungcham, Kazing Malung, Shokpau, Yongphu, Shingda, Marao, Singkap, Shangshak, Koshu, Nungou, Mawai, Songphel, Siraukhong, Cretland, Chingsou, Humine, Makan, of

Ukhrul District. Only in Ukhrul District, the total inferred deposit of limestone has been estimated to 6.35 million tonnes and 5.76 million tonnes at Phungyar and Meiring respectively.

ASBESTOS

The veins and veinlets of antigorite and chrysotile asbestos have been found in the massive serpentine bearing rocks near Moreh, Nepali Basti and Kwatha but none of these occurrences seem to be of economic importance. A small quantity of asbestos is also available in the eastern part of Ukhrul District.

CHROMITE

Deposits of chromite containing metallurgical grade have been located near the Shiroi hill of the Ukhrul District and hinted the possibility of large deposits in future. Besides, quantity of chromite is also available near the Nepali Basti of Chandel District covering an area of about 90 sq. km. and having maximum thickness of 0.3 metre.

More than 25 occurrences of chromite have so far been located in Manipur. These are located at Lunghar, Phangrai, Sirohi, Gamnom, Pushing, Khangkhui, Yentem, Nungbi, Hangkau, Apong, Chingai, Poi, Pinghang, Nampisha, Kangpat, and Chattrick Khunou of Ukhrul District and Kwatha, Sibong, Khudengthabi and Minou-Mangkang of Chandel District.

COPPER

The Geological Survey of India (GSI) has found copper in the Chandel District and Nickel containing copper sulphate, chalcopyrite, chalcocite and metals at Nungau and Kongal Thana. A small quantity of copper is also available at Ningthi & Kwatha of the Chandel District and Humie of the Ukhrul District.

NICKEL

Nickel associated with the serpentinite rock has been located at Nampesh and Kwatha areas of the Chandel District. The GSI in their geochemical and other methods has found metallic nickel dispersed in the soil in fairy high concentration of nickel varying upto 0.9 per cent. Soil samples in the Moreh area containing weathered serpentinite rock also show the availability of nickel varying from 0.24 to 0.9 per cent.

LIGNITE

The GSI has found deposits of lignite in Kangvai village of Turenloo valley of Churachandpur District. The total quantity of lignite has been estimated at 12,262 tonnes which can be used in manufacturing cement in the cement plant in Ukhrul district.

SALT

Salt is mainly available in Waikhong, Sikhong, Chandrakhong and Keithel Manbi. Most of the salt springs are being tapped by driving one metre diameter lined wells for manufacture of salt in a small-scale.

Minerals and their Producing Areas

Sl. No.	Mineral	Area
1.	Limestone	Hundung, Phungyar, Meiring mata, Khangoi, Shokvao, Lambui & Kasom in Ukhrul
2.	Asbestos	Nepali basti, Kwatha, Moreh in Chandel
3.	Chromites	Vicinity of Shiroi hill, Ukhrul, Napali Basti in Chandel
4.	Coppers	Nigthi and Kwatha in Chandel, Humie in Ukhrul
5.	Nickel	Nambashi and Kwatha of Chandel
6.	Lignite	Kanvai village of Turenloo valley in Churachanpur
7.	Salt	Waikhong, Sikhong, Chandrakhong and Keithel Manbi.

MAJOR PROJECTS

The Department pursued with the Ministry of Mines, Government of India for obtaining clearance of a project proposal on mineral exploration namely "Contribution to a sustainable socio-economic development of Manipur State: Supply of equipment along with related assistance to Department of Geology & Mining, Government of Manipur" to be implemented with the assistance of BRGM, France. The proposal is under consideration of Ministry of Mines for onward transmission to the Ministry of Economic Affairs, Government of India. The estimated cost of the project is about ₹ 10.00 crore.

Another project proposal named "DOVEMAP" (Development of Village Economy through Mineral Appraisal Programme) has also submitted to the Ministry of Rural Development, Government of India for funding. The aim of the project is amongst other, to locate low cost but large potential mineral resources in the villages and to study various factors and parameters affecting development aspects of rural economy encompassing minerals, water and terrain for planned exploitation.

The Geology & Mining Division is also presently engaged in the sponsored works on geotechnical investigations of the Loktak Downstream Project, NHPC.

● ● ●

Industry

Manipur is rich in natural resources but due to difficult terrain, inadequate infrastructural facilities and varying climatic conditions, the state could not develop much in the industrial sector of its economy. In the initial stage, Govt. policy in the state was one of revival and revitalization of the traditional handlooms and handicrafts of the local habitats. At present, there is no industries worth mentioning except traditional oriented ones such as khadi and village industries, handlooms and handicrafts. Manipur continue to remain an industrially backward state. The contribution of the manufacturing sector to the total gross state domestic product at current prices is found to be 2.7 per cent according to the advance estimates for the year 2015-16.

Keeping in mind the trend of industrial development and the present local conditions of the state and in consonance with industrial policy of the Government of India, the Govt. of Manipur in its policy announcement of 1990, has decided to focus attention to the small scale and agro-based industries without discouraging the medium and large-scale industries. It is expected to serve the objective of employment generation and dispersal of industries in rural and urban areas.

The New Industrial policy, 1996 of the state has laid emphasis on creating a strong industrial base and employment opportunities in the state through provision of various growth inducing factors based on locally available resources. It is based on locally available raw materials and minerals. In order to promote rapid industrialization, the State Government has over the years been offering attractive package of incentives and concessions to invigorate industries.

INDUSTRIALIZATION

Industrialization implies the creation and growth of factories, mills, power plants and so on. It refers to the development of manufacturing and other related activities. Without rapid industrialization, economic development is almost impossible. The state Government has made persistent efforts for rapid industrialization of the state thereby generating more employment opportunities, alleviation of poverty and removal of economic disparities.

Large & Medium Industries of Manipur

S. No.	Name	Year of Establishments	Product	Sector
1.	Manipur Spinning Mills Corporation, Loitam Khunou, Imphal	1973	Acrylic Yarn	State Govt.
2.	Kandsari Sugar Mill, Thoubal Dist.	1973	Sugar	State Govt.
3.	Manipur Cycles Corporation, Imphal	1985	Assembling Manufacturing Cycle	State Govt.
4.	Manipur Cement Limited, Hundung,	1992	Cement	State Govt.
5.	Manipur Pulp & Allied, Dist. Imphal, Jiribum	NA	Bamboo Chipping Product	State Govt.
6.	Manipur Vanaspati & Allied Industries Limited, Thangal Bazar, Imphal	1988	Edible Ghee	State Govt.
7.	Manipur State Drugs & Pharmaceutical Limited, Imphal	1987	Pharmaceutical Product	State Govt.
8.	MAGFRUIT Limited	NA	Fruit Processing	State Govt.
9.	Manipur Electronics Development Corporation, Imphal	1987	TV, Radio Assembling	State Govt.
10.	Meerless Steel Limited, Kanglatombi	NA	Rods	Private Sector
11.	Shree Manipur Flour Mills Limited, Mantripukhuri, Imphal,	1988	Wheat Flour	Private Sector
12.	K.B. Sons Private Limited, Lamsang, Imphal	NA	Brick Industries	Private Sector

Major Govt. and Other Industrial Units

- Silk Reeling and Spinning Factory Takyel, Imphal.
- Manipur Sugar Mills Ltd., Kabowakching.
- Khansari Sugar Factory, Khangabok.
- The Manipur State Drugs and Pharmaceutical Limited.
- Manipur Spinning Mills Corporation, Loitang Khunao.
- Manipur Electrics Development Corporation Ltd., Takyel, Imphal.
- Loktak Industries, Takyel.
- Lismart Industries, Lamphel Pat.
- Manipur Plastic Industries, Takyel.
- Bamboo Chipping Plant, Kadametala, Jiribam.
- Mini Cement Factory, Hundung, Ukhrul.
- Manipur Cycle Corporation, Takyel.
- Mechanised Dye House, Iroisemba.

Almost all the Public Sector undertaking like those shown below were facing financial problems and paucity of fund for maintenance inspite of providing package of incentives and concessions as laid out in its industrial policies and programmes.

1. Manipur Cycles Corporation Ltd. (MCCL)
2. Manipur Cement Ltd. (MCL)
3. Manipur Spinning Mills Corporation Ltd. (MSMCL)
4. Manipur Pulp & Allied Products Ltd. (MPAPL)
5. Manipur Food Industries Corporation Ltd. (MFIC)
6. Manipur Drugs and Pharmaceutical Ltd. (MSDPL)
7. Manipur Handloom & Handicrafts Development Corporation Ltd. (MHHDCL)
8. Manipur Electronic Development Corporation Ltd. (MANITRON)
9. Manipur Industrial Development Corporation Ltd. (MANIDCO)

As a result, the Government has decided to wind up five companies namely Manipur Cycles Corporation Ltd. (MCCL), Manipur Cement Ltd. (MCL), Manipur Spinning Mills Corporation Ltd. (MSMCL), Manipur Drugs and Pharmaceutical Ltd. (Joint Sector) and Manipur Pulp & Allied Products Ltd. (MPAPL), as they are all loss making industries. Proposals for privatization also failed as there were no buyer of the units. Regarding MDPL, the Government has been consulting the central Government for its viability. As for Manipur Vanaspati & Allied Industries Ltd., the Company was about to wind up but for the stay order issued by the Guwahati High Court. MHHDC, MANITRON and MANIDCO will be revitalized so as enable to stand themselves with one time assistance. Proposals for revival of these three corporations were submitted to the State Government for inclusion in the memorandum to the Twelfth Finance Commission. The staff of the Public Sector undertakings which are under process of winding up were already retrenched. Regarding the MFIC, the process has been reviewed and it shall continue as Implementing Agency of the Food Park Project set up at Nilakuthi.

A sum of ₹ 7.50 lakhs has been provided in 2006-07(B.E.) to be released as grants-in-aid to those corporation which are under the process of winding up for payment of salaries/wages of the staff retained to complete the updating of accounts of these companies. There is also a proposal voluntary retirement of 7 staff of MANIDCO during 2008-09 and ₹ 33.28 lakhs was allotted for this purpose during 2009-10 and no fund was allotted to public sector undertakings (PSUs) which are under process of winding up.

SMALL-SCALE INDUSTRIES

Small-Scale Industries (SSI) is an important segment of the economy, contributing substantially in the form of production, employment and exports. It has continued to play a vital role in the fulfillment of socio-economic objectives. The principal factor for defining small-scale Industries has always been based on the size of investment. Small-Scale Industries are those industries whose investment in fixed assets such as plants and machineries does not exceed ₹ 100.00 lakhs (₹ 1 crore). This has been brought down from earlier limit of ₹ 300.00 lakhs (₹ 3 crores) w.e.f. 24.12.99 in order to give a fillip to small units with low investments. The investment limit for tiny units continues to be ₹ 25.00 lakhs. Investment in plant and machinery in respect of industry related Small-Scale Service and Business Enterprises (SSSBE) was increased to ₹ 10.00 lakhs from ₹ 5.00 lakhs. According to these new definitions, all the industrial units except those of cottage and village industries in Manipur belong to the category of small-scale industries.

With the objective of providing employment to unemployed youth in the state and generate additional income, the 'Make in Manipur' was launched on 26th November, 2015 with a focus on
　(i) Cultivation & processing of aromatic and medicinal plants,
　(ii) Cultivation & processing of spices,
　(iii) Bee keeping & honey processing,
　(iv) Spawn production & mushroom processing,
　(v) Fish & pork processing,
　(vi) Bamboo processing and
　(vii) Rubber & Tea Plantation.

In order to develop manpower for carrying out the above activities, 36 personnel had been trained as Master Trainers at Fragrance and Flavour Development Centre (FFDC), Kanauj. In addition, 25 post graduate trainers have been selected from institution like Central Agricultural University, Manipur University and National Institute of Technology. Further, 9 Livelihood Business Incubators in each district alongwith Technical Business Incubators and Common Faculty Centres are being established. In order to ensure success of the programme, overall infrastructure support is being placed, to be provided through Industrial Estates in each districts, Food Parks, SEZs in Kuraopokpi, Tera Urok and Border Haats.

HANDLOOM

Handloom industry is the largest cottage industry in the state. It is a traditional cottage industry providing avenues of employment opportunities to the people of Manipur. Basically, it is a labour-intensive family occupation in which all the members of a family can participate. Majority of the handloom weavers in the state are self-employed artisans who are carrying on their profession in their own homes with the assistance of their family members in pre-loom and post loom process. Manipur ranks the fourth position in terms of the number of looms in the country. It has more than 2.8 lakhs looms comprising of fly shuttle, throw shuttle and loin-looms with a weaver population of more than 4.62 lakhs which is 2nd position among the states according to National Handloom Census, 1995-96.

In artistic weaving also there are many accountable designs which are still famous such as Ningthou Phee, Lamthang Khulak, Khamen-Chatpa, Shamilanmi, Moirangphee, Lashing Phee, Leiroom, Hijamayek, Tindongbi, Leirong, Akoibi designs etc. Each design has its own history as to how and by whom they were invented. In the art of design and printing, Manipur can be proud of possessing good knowledge of dyeing of fast colour on various kinds of hard printing of cloths since time immemorial by using indigenous plant leaves etc.

As Manipur has adequate potential for development of handloom industry various welfare as well as handloom development scheme for promotion and development of handloom industry including employment generating programme are taken up in the State. Most of the scheme supporting the weavers is Centrally Sponsored Schemes (CSS). For the provision of welfare measures and better working conditions to handloom weavers, a package of group insurance scheme, health package scheme, workshed cum-housing scheme, project package scheme, integrated handloom village development project etc. are being implemented in the handloom sector.

Project Package Scheme

The project package scheme, being implemented since 1992-93, is one of the major schemes to provide the requisite support to weavers in an integrated and co-ordinated manner. The scheme envisages formulation and implementation of specific need base projects for development by a particular handloom product or development of a particular area of weavers.

Integrated Handloom Village Development Project

Integrated Handloom Village Development project (IHVDP) aims at providing a comprehensive support in all areas covering all types of facilities in terms of skilled upgradation, productivity infrastructure and to give fillip to the motivation level. Construction of common facility centre, workshed, supply of looms, imparting training programme and providing of infrastructure are the main components of the scheme.

Deen Dayal Hathkargha Protsahan Yojana

Deen Dayal Hathkargha Protsahan (DDHP) Yojana was a scheme introduced for women belonging to the SC/ST/OBC as a promotional scheme of handloom sector. It is a centrally sponsored scheme which has come into force with effect from 01.04.2000. Product development, production support, institutional support, imparting training programme, providing of infrastructure, marketing support etc. both at macro & micro level in an integrated and co-ordinated manner for an overall development of the handloom sector are the main components of the scheme. The pattern of assistance between the central and the state is 90:10 unless specified for the component.

HANDICRAFTS

Handicrafts are another important industry in the state. It has its own unique identity amongst the various crafts of the country. Handicrafts industry of Manipur may be mentioned with special accounts for contributing to the economic structure and development of the state. The handicrafts of Manipur are treated in high class in themselves, drawing the main theme and subject matter from episode of Khamba Thoibi and latter Radha Krishna background of their religions belief and designs depiction of Pakhangba. With simple processes of indigenous nature, craftsman here produce handicrafts of excellence in the form of cloths embroidery, cane and bamboo, ivory, stone and wood carving, metal crafts, deer horn decoratives and supari, walking sticks, dolls and toys etc. Various kouna products, artistic weaving, wood carving etc. have a distinct place of its own.

The State Government has made full efforts for overall development of handloom and handicrafts industries in the state. Manipur Handloom & Handicrafts Development Corporation and Manipur Development Society are the two agencies of the state government taking utmost efforts for production and marketing of handloom and handicrafts products. Manipur State Handloom Weavers Co-operative Society is apex co-operative society taking pivotal role in the co-operative sector for development of handloom & handicrafts in the state. There is also departmental raw-materials bank to meet the requirement of various types and quality of yarn of weavers at reasonable price. The Mechanised Dye House now run under the Deptt. is also making full efforts to make available quality dyed yarn for the weavers of the State. Although there are various schemes for the growth and development of handloom and handicrafts in the state, only few could be implemented due to want of fund.

    (a) State Award to Master Craftsman,

(b) Modernisation of Handicrafts and

(c) Development of Kouna Product

Considering the significance of the role of handloom and handicrafts in India in terms of employment and income generation in addition to the aesthetic value of the products, the 6th Economic Census conducted all over India covered this sector for the first time. The district-wise handicrafts and handloom establishments, in terms of per centage, found in the rural and urban areas of Manipur as per the findings of the 6th EC is shown below.

Percentage Distribution of Handicraft and Handloom, 2013

Sl. No.	District/State	Percentage of handicrafts & handloom unit		
		Rural	Urban	Combined
1.	Senapati	2.82	0.09	1.92
2.	Tamenglong	0.81	0.25	0.63
3.	Churachandpur	11.63	0.14	7.83
4.	Chandel	2.90	0.21	2.01
5.	Ukhrul	2.87	0.57	2.11
6.	Imphal West	13.56	36.38	21.09
7.	Imphal East	25.62	22.74	24.67
8.	Bishnupur	14.06	14.17	14.10
9.	Thoubal	25.73	25.46	25.64
	Manipur	100.00	100.00	100.00

Source: Final Results of Sixth Economic Census, 2013

KHADI AND VILLAGE INDUSTRIES

The Khadi and Village Industries Commission (KVIC) was established by the Govt. of India in the year 1957. The Khadi and Village Industries is not only providing employment to people in rural and semi-urban areas at low investment per job, but also utilises local skill resources and provides part-time as well as full time work to rural artisans, women and minorities. It was only in the year 1966 that the State Board for the development of Khadi and Village Industries was constituted by the Government of Manipur. The traditional sector of industries fall within the purview of organisations such as Khadi and Village Industries Commission. The KVIC include artisans in tiny industrial units and defines it as any industry located in a village or town inhabited by population not exceeding 10,000 which produces goods and renders services with or without the use of power in which the fixed capital per head does not exceed ₹ 15,000. In the State, the KVIC has given special attention for economic upliftment of the Scheduled Castes/ Scheduled Tribes and women in general.

FOOD PROCESSING INDUSTRIES (FPI)

Food Processing Industries took a vital role in the development of industries and generation of large employment in the state. During the year 2014-15, a plan fund of ₹ 52.00 lakhs was provided for Food Processing Industries.

For the further development of FPI, the following promotional Schemes have been taken up.

(i) National Mission on Food Processing

(ii) Training on FPI

Food Park

The Foundation Stone for a Food Park was laid down on 10.11.2006 at Nilakuthi in an area of about 31 acres of land with a project cost of ₹ 1361.45 lakhs. During 2006-07, the State and Central Government have released a sum of ₹ 272 lakhs and ₹ 160 lakhs respectively. NABARD has agreed to extend a term loan of ₹ 620 lakhs for the project. The project cost was revised to ₹ 3172.40 lakhs and NABARD has also agreed to rise its term loan to ₹ 1574.16 lakhs. The approved provision of fund for the year 2009-10 was ₹ 1196.00 lakhs.

The implementing agency of the Food Park Project is the Manipur Food Industries Corporation Ltd. The State Government is planning to upgrade the proposed Food Park into Mega Food Park. There will be 40-50 Food Processing Units for which common facilities like Cold storage, warehousing, Quality Control Lab., Weight Bridge, Post Office, Bank, Water & Power supply will be made available in the Food Park. For the convenience of the food processing units, construction of a bridge connecting the Park at Nilakuthi and NH-39 over Imphal River has also started.

BAMBOO PROCESSING INDUSTRIES

Considering the fact that Manipur share about 25% of the total growing stock of bamboo of the North Eastern Region of India and 14% of the country, Manipur State stands to prominently benefit from the national programme for bamboo development. The bamboo growing area within and around Jiribam, covering the bamboo abundant area of Tamenglong district and Tipaimukh area of Churachandpur district is about 2969 sq. km., which is about 80% of the total bamboo growing area in Manipur.

Therefore, preparation have been made to set up a Bamboo Technology Park at Jiribam. The main object of setting up the park is to promote various bamboo based industries. The processing units will be set up on Public Private Partnership under Special Purpose Vehicle (SPV) model in association with the National Mission on Bamboo Application (NMBA), Government of India.

SCHEMES FOR INDUSTRIAL DEVELOPMENT

District Industries Centre

District industries Centre (DIC) came into limelight in pursuance of the Industrial Policy Resolutions of the Government of India adopted in 1977. The DICs were established in all the District Headquarters with 2 (two) sub centres at Jiribam and Kangpokpi subdivision of Manipur. Its emphasis is laid on dispersal of industries in the district headquarters, small towns and rural areas. The intention of the policy makers is to make the DICs to work as catalysts for promotion of cottage and small industries. It provides all the resources with its facilities required by the entrepreneurs including identification of suitable schemes, preparation of feasibility reports, arrangements for supply of machinery and equipments, provision of raw-materials and facilities for marketing and extension services. Various schemes like Seed/Margin Money, Self-Employment for Educated Unemployed Youths and Prime Minister's Rozgar Yojana were instrumental in the growth of industries in the state.

Prime Minister's Rozgar Yojana

A special scheme 'Prime Minister's Rozgar Yojana (PMRY) was drawn up to be operated through the District Industries Centre for providing self employment opportunities to educated unemployed youths. The Scheme covered all educated unemployed youths who passed or failed matric or ITI passed or having undergone Government sponsored technical course for a minimum duration of six months and within the age group of 18 to 35 years (relaxed upto 40 years for the North Eastern States and 45 years for SC/ST, Ex-Serviceman, physically handicapped persons & women). Beneficiaries of the PMRY scheme were selected from the relatively less affluent sections of the society, whose annual family income does not exceed ₹ 24,000 (relaxed upto ₹ 40,000 per annum for North Eastern States.) PMRY scheme provided loans, financial assistance to educated unemployed persons who are willing to employ in any one of the trades viz., industry, service and business. The scheme was launched on 2nd Oct., 1993.

Integrated Handloom Development Scheme (IHDS)

The IHDS, a Centrally Sponsored Scheme, was introduced to facilitate the sustainable development of handloom weavers located in and outside identified handloom clusters within a range of 300-500 looms in to a cohesive self-managing and competitive socio-economic unit.

Under this scheme, a sum of ₹ 800.00 lakhs was provided in 2009-10 which is meant to give benefit to 1395 nos. Primary Handloom Weavers Co-operative Societies for covering 44640 weavers under the component of Market Incentive and 33 nos. of Handloom Cluster Development projects set up covering 5115 weavers providing yarn, looms and its accessories, training, margin money for obtaining bank loan, computer aided textile design, deputing designers in each cluster, exhibition, buyer-seller meet, exposure visits to advanced clusters etc.

Prime Minister's Employment Generation Programme (PMEGP)

This scheme was implemented by the District Industries Centre (DIC) with Khadi & Village Industries Commission as Nodal Agency at the National level. In addition to the DIC other implementing agencies of the scheme are Khadi & Village Industries Commission State office and Manipur Khadi & Village Industries Board. The total target of beneficiaries under the scheme for Manipur during 2008-09 was 195 projects. The total numbers of employment created under the scheme for the year 2014-15 were 3258. During the year 2015-16, 184 numbers of projects were sanctioned.

INDUSTRIAL GROWTH CENTRES

Growth Centres are large villages or small towns which have the potential to become the nuclei for the socio-economic development of the surrounding area. The Growth Centres can be identified by the different orders with respect to the quality and quantity of services and facilities, service area and population. A growth centre of lowest order should have services such as agricultural input centre, primary and middle school, maternity and child care centres and daily market. At highest level, it must have manufacturing industries, hospitals, colleges etc.

The pace of development of backward areas is a cause for concern. With the doing away of the system of licensing of industries and coming into play of market forces, the industries tend to gravitate towards already developed areas which provide better infrastructure, easier availability of skilled work force and forward and backward linkages in terms of availability of raw-materials and markets for products. Thus, the regional imbalances in industrial development may tend to increase. So it is imperative to take special measures to promote development of industries in backward areas.

For tackling the problem of regional imbalances in industrial development, to some extent at least, the Growth Centres Schemes was initiated in the Eighth Plan.

Under the Growth Centres Schemes, the central Govt. has approved the Industrial Growth Centre Project at Lamlai-Napet at a project cost of ₹ 30.00 crores of which ₹ 15.00 crores will be the Govt. of India contribution, ₹ 5.00 crores as State Govt. contribution, ₹ 4.00 crores as loan and equity contribution from the financial institutions and ₹ 6.00 crores as loans and equity from other sources. A sum of ₹ 1.50 crores was sanctioned and released by the Government of India. A proposal for shifting the site of the Centre is under examination.

INDO-MYANMAR BORDER TRADE PROMOTION

The opening of the Border Trade between India and Myanmar was an important achievement during the Eighth plan period. The Indo-Myanmar Border Trade was inaugurated in 12th April, 1995 by the then Union Minister of State for Commerce as a follow-up measure of the Trade Agreement signed between India and Myanmar on the 21st Jan., 1994 at New Delhi. Subsequently exchange of 22 items have been allowed by the residents across the border. The development has to boost up the export potential of India/Manipur by creating adequate infrastructure for promotion of export oriented industrial units. To facilitate the trade, trade centers are being constructed at Moreh and another at Imphal. The importance of setting up of trade centers for providing facilities to the trades and entrepreneurs of Manipur with the new avenue of opening up of regulated border trade between Myanmar and India was considered by Planning Commission, Government of India.

Accordingly, the Centre is to provide infrastructural facilities such as telecommunication, export-import information cell, show room-cum-sales counters, conference hall, boarding and lodging facilities, guest-room and restaurants, bank and other relevant Govt. extension counters to facilitate the trades/businessmen/ entrepreneurs in creating a business like congenial atmosphere. However, the Director General of Foreign Trade has permitted the bilateral/border trade along with the Indo-Myanmar border as per the prevailing customary practices for the commodities namely, mustard/rape seed, pulses and beans, fresh vegetables, fruits, garlics, onion, chillies, spices (excluding nutmeg, maee, cloves, cassia & cinnamon), bamboo, minor forest products (excluding teak), betel nuts and leaves, food items for local consumption, tobacco, tomato, reed broom, sesame, resin, corriander seeds, soyabeans, roasted sunflower seeds, katha, ginger etc. The main items of exports were wheat flour, bleaching powder, fenugreek seeds, Ani seeds, Cumin seeds, Soyabari, dry chillies, agarbati, suman rose powder, Pea, Garlic, Dry Buffallo Offal etc. while the import items were Betel nuts, Turmeric, Red Kidney bean (Rajma), Kuth roots, gram. Resin, reed-brooms, dry ginger etc.

Sources of Energy

Power or electricity is the most convenient and versatile form of energy. It plays a key role in the industrial, agricultural and commercial sectors of the economy and is also the most crucial source of supplying domestic energy requirements. The demand has, therefore, been growing at a rate faster than other forms of energy.

The power supply position in Manipur showed a marked improvement with the commissioning of the Loktak Hydro Electric Project in August, 1984. The demand of power was met mainly from Grid Power and a little from diesel and hydro generation. More emphasis was given to utilize Loktak Hydro Power to the maximum extent possible and to curtail the uneconomical generation of power from diesel generating sets.

The erstwhile Electricity Department, Manipur was unbundled and corporatized into the following two State Owned functionally independent successor entities w.e.f. 1st February, 2014, in pursuance of Electricity Act, 2003:

(I) Manipur State Power Company Limited (MSPCL)

(II) Manipur State Power Distribution Company Limited (MSPDCL)

POWER GENERATION

The installed capacity of power in the state has remained the same as 11,845 KW during 1999-00 to 2001-02. However, during 2002-03 the installed capacity increased to 47,252 in 2002-03 KW. During the year 2003-04 the installed capacity reduced to 47,052 KW. Then there was an increase from the years 2004-05 to the tune of 47,252 KW. The installed capacity were 45,020 KW, and 36,600 KW in 2011-12 and 2013-14 respectively.

Hydro Power generation depends on supply of water. The installed capacity and generation of power in the state during 2014-15 are presented in Table.

District-wise Installed Capacity and Generation of Electricity, 2014-15

Year	Installed Capacity (KW)	Electricity generated (in lakh kw)
Senapati	-	-
Tamenglong	-	-
Churachandpur	-	-
Chandel	-	-
Ukhrul	-	-
Imphal East	4,000	4.00
Imphal West	25,490	2.52
Bishnupur	-	-
Thoubal	-	-
Manipur	**29,490**	**6.52**

Source: MSPDCL, Manipur.

REQUIREMENT OF POWER

The requirement of power for all categories of consumers viz., domestic, commercial, industrial, water works and public lighting has been gradually increasing year after another. This has been due to the fact that all the development activities like education, health care, telecommunication, electronic media and computerisation etc. have been depending by and large on electricity.

Demand and Supply of Power in Manipur

Year	Power (MW)		
	Demand	Part of the Demand Met	Shortfall
2010-11	184	110	74
2011-12	171	115	56
2012-13	201	119	82
2013-14	229	130	99
2014-15	262	232	30
2015-16	301	167.19	133.81

Source: Manipur State Power Distribution Company Limited, (MSPDCL).

It can be seen from the table that the demand of power has always surpassed the supply.

Requirement of Power & Energy

Year	Peak load (MW)	Energy requirement (MU)
2010-11	184	838
2011-12	171	615
2012-13	201	722
2013-14	229	824
2014-15	262	956
2015-16	301	1080

It is expected to have an increasing trend in the demand of power due to increase in population, enterprises and modernisation/mechanisation of various economic activities.

AVAILABILITY OF POWER

The power supply in Manipur depends entirely on the share of power allocated from the Central sector plants namely, Loktak Hydro Electric Plant, Kopili-Khangdong Hydro Electric Plant, Assam Gas Based Power Plant at Kathalguri and Agartala Gas Turbine power plant at Ramchandranagar, Eastern Regional Electricity Board, Meghalaya State Electricity Board, Ranganadi Hydro Electric Plant and Doyang Hydro Electric Plant in the North Eastern region. The availability, however, decreases in the lean season when the generation is reduced following the recession of water levels in the rain fed reservoirs of the Central sector Hydel plants. Sometimes, the availability of the power from these plants was so poor that even the demand of vital installations like hospital, radio station, doordarshan kendra and other telecommunication stations could not be met. When the water levels in the Hydel plants went down below minimum draw down level, the generation is likely to be stopped anytime if rain does not come.

Therefore, the shortage of power is the major cause for the slow development in the state. The state continues to be deficit in electric energy. Purchases of power from outside the state have been rising at a higher rate. As per 18th Electric Power Supply (EPS) of Central Electricity Authority, the estimated requirement of power for 2015-16 was 10,800 Lakh kWH

The generation of all the central sector Power Project of North Eastern Region are shared among the states of the region as per the allocation made by the Govt. of India leaving 20% as unallocated share. During the year 2014-15, the allocated share of power for Manipur from the Central Sector Generating Stations of the North-Eastern Region is as given in Table.

Share of Power for Manipur from Central Sector, 2015-16

Sl. No.	Name of the Project	Installed Capacity MW	Share of Manipur	
			Per cent	MW
1.	Loktak Hydro Electric Project (NHPC)	105	36.57	38.4*
2.	Khongdong HPS	50	5.33	3
3.	Kopilli + Kopilli HPS	200	6.17	12
4.	Kopilli HEP Stage-II	25	6.0	2
5.	Kathalguri GPS	291	6.9	23
6.	Agartala GPS	84	7.0	6
7.	Agartala GPS Extra Unit-I	23	6.85	1.6
8.	Doyang HPS	75	6.7	5
9.	Ranganadi HPS	405	7.16	29
10.	Pallatana GPP	726	5.79	42
	Total	1,984	94.47	162.00

Inclusive of allocation of surrendered share 8 MW by Meghalaya to Manipur
Source: Annual Administrative Report, 2015-16, Manipur State Power Company Limited

RURAL ELECTRIFICATION

Manipur is a small state with an area of 22,327 sq. kms. and population about 23 lakhs people. Over 75 per cent of the population lives in rural areas comprising 2,524 inhabited villages as on 21st January, 2009. By the end of 2009-10, 2002 villages were electrified. Accordingly, the state has made a good progress in rural electrification achieving 79.32 per cent of the total villages up to the end of 31st March, 2010.

District-wise Rural Electrification in Manipur, 2015-16 (as on 31st December)

District	Number of Villages Electrified
(1)	(2)
Senapati	5
Tamenglong	5
Churachandpur	36
Chandel	22
Ukhrul	8

Source: Electricity Department, Government of Manipur

Integrated Rural Energy Programme (IREP)

The implementation of Integrated Rural Energy Programme (IREP) covered 5 blocks, 7 blocks and 12 blocks during 1992-93, 1993-94 and 1995-96 respectively and 7 blocks in 1997-98. The programme covered 19 IREP Blocks upto 1998-99. Various energy devices like bio-gas, Improved chulha, solar lantern tube-light with electronic choke and solar cooker and pressure cooker, improved crematorium, compact fluorescent lamp etc., were made available to the beneficiaries for efficient use of energy.

During the year 2009-10, the IREP Scheme funds are proposed to be provided to the Zilla Parishads of Valley Districts as part of the devolution of powers to the Institutions of Zilla Parishads and to the Deputy Commissioners for the Hill Districts. The items taken up during the year are LED Reading Light system totaling 10000 units in 4 valley districts of Manipur which will help public, particularly students.

PATTERN OF POWER CONSUMPTION

The overall consumption of electricity increased from 1972.06 lakh kWh in 2008-09 to 2200.30 lakh kWh in 2009-10. The pattern of consumption of power in the state shows that the domestic consumption was highest compared to others. In 2009-10, it rose to 1274.85 lakh kWh. In 2009-10, domestic consumption accounted for 57.94 per cent of the total followed by 28.54 per cent and 7.28 per cent consumption by public water work and bulk water supply work and commercial & small power sector respectively.

ENERGY CONSUMPTION

The household sector is the largest consumer of energy in Manipur, accounting 40 to 50 per cent of total energy consumption. The bulk of energy consumed by households consists of traditional fuels such as firewood, animal dung and agricultural residues.

In urban areas, a growing demand for modern household fuels such as LPG, electricity and Kerosene is creating additional concern.

Percentage of Households using Different Fuels for Cooking, 2011

Item	Manipur	All India
Cowdung	0.00	4.57
Electricity	0.05	0.10
Coal/Coke/ Charcoal	1.25	1.51
L.P.G.	50.05	36.81
Fire wood and chips	48.10	50.73
Gobar Gas	0.05	0.10
Kerosene	0.50	4.26
Others	-	1.92

POWER DEVELOPMENT

Manipur has no sufficient generation of its own but it needs more power to meet the growing demand. Electricity has become an essential commodity and therefore it requires attention of all sections of the society viz. non-government organizations, social workers and general public besides the Government.

Hydro Power Development

Hydro-electric power plays a major role in the field of power development in the state. But the performance of the hydro-power stations has been seasonably variable. The mini/micro hydel projects are suitable for remote areas where the sub-transmission system is hard to reach. The state government started taking up various Micro Hydel, Medium/Small Hydro Electric Projects and Mini/Micro Hydro Electric projects. A comparative picture of the mini/micro hydel projects upto 25 MW capacity ending 2009-10 for the North Eastern States (NES) of India is indicated below.

Small Hydro Power projects upto 25 MW Capacity in the NES of India

North Eastern State/ All India	Project set-up		Project under Implementation	
	Number	Capacity (MW)	Number	Capacity (MW)
1. Arunachal Pradesh	68	45.24	56	41.82
2. Assam	3	2.11	4	15.00
3. Manipur	8	5.45	3	2.75
4. Meghalaya	4	31.03	3	1.70
5. Mizoram	16	17.47	3	15.50
6. Nagaland	10	28.67	4	4.20
7. Sikkim	14	39.11	4	13.20
8. Tripura	3	16.01	-	-
All India	**611**	**2045.61**	**225**	**668.86**

Source: Compendium of Environment Statistics, India 2010, New Delhi

Manipur has substantial hydro power potential of about 2000 MW, which is sufficient not only to meet the local requirement for domestic and industrial uses but leave surplus for marketing outside. The State Power Department has so far identified about a dozen of hydro power potential sites in the State and they are at different stages of implementation.

Name of Project	Capacity(MW)
Loktak Down Stream HE-Project	2 × 33
Tipaimukh HE-Project	6 × 250
Pabram HE-Project	2 × 95
Irang HE-Project	4 × 15
Tuivai HE-Project	3 × 17
Nungleiband HE-Project	2 × 35
Khongnem Chakha HE-Project	2 × 33.5
Maklang–Tuyungbi HE-Project	3 × 15

- **Loktak Down Stream HE-Project:** The project is located near Tousang Khunou village of Tamenglong district on Leimatak river.

- **Tipaimukh HE-Project:** The project is located near Manipur-Mizoram border in Churachandpur district.

- **Pabram HE-Project:** The project is located near Tamenglong Khunjao in Tamenglong District.

- **Irang HE-Project:** The project is located near Taobam village on NH-53 in Tamenglong District.

- **Tuivai HE-Project:** The project site is located near Dailkhai village in Thanlon Sub-Division of Churachandpur District.

- **Nungleiband HE-Project:** The project is located near Nungleiband village in Tamenglong District.

- **Khongnem Chakha HE-Project:** The project is located near Maram Centre in Senapati District.

- **Makang-Tuyungbi HE-Project:** The project is located at the confluence of river Maklang and Tuyungbi near Khonglo village in Ukhrul District.

Diesel/Heavy Fuel Generation

As hydel projects take a long time to construct it became imperative that the department take up Diesel/Heavy Fuel based power project as a short term measure to meet the power demands of the state.

The State has many Diesel Generating Stations of various capacities and make located at strategic locations throughout the state. These power house are run only when there is a Grid failure and during the lean season when Hydel generation in the NE Region are drastically reduced due to shortage of water in the reservoirs.

Besides and above the small Diesel Generating Set, the state also has a Heavy Fuel Based Power Plant (6 × 6 MW) at Leimakhong.

Water-Power Development

Water-power is derived from the running rivers and lakes in the form of electricity. Dams and anicuts are constructed and the river water is made to run huge water turbines. Electricity so produced from water-power is known as hydro electric power. About 64 per cent of electricity generated in the state is from hydel sources. The other important use of water is in irrigation.

Renewable Energy

For implementation of renewable energy programme in the State, the Ministry of Non-Conventional Energy Sources, (MNES), renamed as National Solar Mission (NSM), Government of India have directed all the states to form State Nodal Agency (SNA). Accordingly, Manipur Renewable Energy Development Agency (MANIREDA) was established as the SNA for planning, development and implementation of various renewable energy programme in Manipur. The agency is placed under the control of the Power Department during 2014-15 for better integration and coordination of renewable energy with conventional energy. The cumulative achievements of the Agency are given below.

Solar Renewable Energy(RE) Projects and Biomass Gasifier Power Project :

	Name of the Renewable Energy(RE) Projects	Number of System/ Projects installed	Total installed capacity (in KW)
A.	Solar {Demonstration & Remote Village Electrification (RVE) }		
1.	Solar Home Lighting System	17,505	921
2.	Solar Street Lighting System	8,946	745
3.	Solar Lantern	8,139	77
4.	Solar Power Pack	305	37
5.	Solar Photo Voltaic(SPV) Power Plant	20	377.5
6.	1 KWP (each) Stand Alone type SPV Power Plant	399	399
7.	Solar Water Pump	30	27
8.	Implementation of energy awareness cum educational parks	10	20
9.	Implementation of 1 KWp	46	46
10.	Implementation of 5KWp	67	335
B.	Biomass Gasifier Power Project	3	600

● ● ●

Population and Health

Population of a country is its most important asset and resource for all kinds of development. In terms of size of population, Manipur is the fourth largest State in the North Eastern Region of India. Population of Manipur constitutes 6.24 per cent of the total population of 8 (eight) north eastern states including Sikkim where it comprises nearly 0.24 per cent of the total population of India. Population pressure is found to be increasing day by day reducing the man-land ratio from about 1: 7.85 hectares in 1901 to 1: 0.78 hectares in 2011. With such a size of population to support on so small area, the State of Manipur finds itself in great difficulty in making any significant dent on its poverty and economic backwardness.

POPULATION

Manipur is a small State with an area of 22,327 sq. kms. which constitutes 0.7 per cent of the Indian Union according to 2011 Census. It is situated in the far flung north-eastern border of India. In terms of area, Manipur ranks twentieth among the states of India and fourth in the north-eastern states of India.

The total geographical area of the State was recorded as 22,356 sq. kms. in 1971 Census. It was recorded as 22,327 sq. kms. in 1981. The area of the State has remained the same as 22,327 sq. kms. according to 1991, 2001 and 2011 Censuses.

Geo-climatically, the state may be clubbed into 2 (two) regions such as the hill and the valley. The valley region is very small with an area of 2,238 sq. kms. which is 10 per cent of the total State area, but this is one of the most thickly populated region of the state. The hill constitutes 20,089 sq. kms. *i.e.*, 90 per cent of the total State area and therefore, it is approximately 9 times the size of the valley area. The density of population per sq. km. in the hill is 61 as against 730 in the valley.

97

Population of Manipur by Districts 2011

District/Region/ State	Population		Population Density (per sq. km.)
	'000 Nos.	% to total	
Senapati	479	16.8	146
Tamenglong	141	4.9	32
Churachandpur	274	9.6	60
Chandel	144	5.0	44
Ukhrul	184	6.5	40
A. Hill	**1222**	**42.8**	**61**
Imphal East	456	16.0	643
Imphal West	518	18.1	998
Bishnupur	237	8.3	479
Thoubal	422	14.8	821
B. Valley	**1633**	**57.2**	**730**
Manipur	**2,856**	**100.0**	**128**

Source: Manipur Economic Survey 2015-16

The population of Manipur as per the 2011 Census was 28.6 lakhs consisting of 14.4 lakhs males and 14.2 lakhs females. In absolute term, the population of Manipur has increased by 5.62 lakhs during the decade 2001-2011. The decadal growth rate in 2011 over 2001 was found to be 24.50 per cent.

Population of Manipur

Year	Person	Male	Female
1961	7,80,037	3,87,058	3,92,979
1971	10,72,753	5,41,675	5,31,078
1981	14,20,953	7,21,006	6,99,947
1991	18,37,149	9,38,359	8,98,790
2001	22,93,896	11,61,952	11,31,944
2011	28,55,794	14,38,586	14,17,208

Source: Manipur Economic Survey 2015-16

GROWTH OF POPULATION

In 1961, the population of Manipur was 7.80 lakhs which rose to 28.56 lakhs in 2011. Following Table presents the decennial growth rates of Manipur as compared to those of all India.

Population Growth of Manipur vis-à-vis India

Census Year	Total Population (in lakhs)		Decennial growth (per cent)	
	Manipur	All-India	Manipur	All-India
1961	7.80	4,392.34	-	-
1971	10.73	5,481.60	(+) 37.53	(+) 24.80
1981	14.21	6,833.29	(+) 32.46	(+) 24.66
1991	18.37	8,463.03	(+) 29.29	(+) 23.85
2001	22.94	10,287.37	(+) 24.86	(+) 21.56
2011	28.56	12,108.55	(+) 24.50	(+) 17.70

The decade 1961-1971 registered highest growth rate which was recorded to 37.53%. Thereafter, the decadal growth rate decreased to 32.46% in 1971-1981, and it further declined 24.50% in 2001-2011. The district wise absolute growth in the total population in 2011 over 2001 is shown in following Table.

District wise Absolute Growth (2001-2011)

District/State	Population						Absolute Population Growth
	2001 Census			2011 Census			
	Male	Female	Total	Male	Female	Total	
Senapati	146548	137073	283621	247323	231825	479148	195527
Tamenglong	58014	53485	111499	72371	68280	140651	29152
Churachandpur	117232	110673	227905	138820	135323	274143	46238
Chandel	59741	58586	118327	74579	69603	144182	25855
Ukhrul	73465	67313	140778	94718	89280	183998	43220
Imphal East	198371	196505	394876	226094	230019	456113	61237
Imphal West	221781	222601	444382	255054	262938	517992	73610
Bishnupur	104550	103818	208368	118782	118617	237399	29031
Thoubal	182250	181890	364140	210845	211323	422168	58028
Manipur	**1161952**	**1131944**	**2293896**	**1438586**	**1417208**	**2855794**	**561898**

Considering the literacy rates, low sex ratios, higher mean age at marriage, changes in consumption patterns, various health interventions, people's awareness of small family norms, lesser immigrations etc., it was naturally expected to have a lesser growth rate in the decade 2001-2011. The decade 2001-2011 registered a growth rate of 24.50% as against 17.70% of All-India.

Decennial Population Growth Rates

Region/District/ State	Population ('00 nos.)		Decennial Growth (%)
	2001	2011	2001-2011
A. Hill	**8,821**	**12,221**	**38.54**
Senapati	2,836	4,791	68.94
Tamenglong	1,115	1,407	26.19
Churachandpur	2,279	2,741	20.27
Chandel	1,183	1,442	21.89
Ukhrul	1,408	1,840	30.68
B. Valley	**14,118**	**16,337**	**15.72**
Imphal East	3,949	4,561	15.50
Imphal West	4,444	5,180	16.56
Bishnupur	2,084	2,374	13.92
Thoubal	3,641	4,222	15.96
Manipur	**22,939**	**28,558**	**24.50**

DENSITY OF POPULATION

Density of population refers to the number of persons living per sq. km. of geographical area, which indicates whether a region or country is thickly populated or thinly populated. In 1961, the density of population of Manipur was recorded at 35 and in 1971, it was only 48 persons per sq. k.m. which rose to 64 in 1981 and further to 82 in 1991. According to 2011 Census, density of population of Manipur was 128 persons per sq. km. as against 103 persons per sq. km. in 2001 Census. Among the districts, Imphal West District had the highest density which is followed by Thoubal. The lowest was recorded in Tamenglong District with only 32 persons per sq. km. in 2011.

Population Density

District	Population (in lakhs)	Density (per sq. km.)
Senapati	4.79	146
Tamenglong	1.41	32
Churachandpur	2.74	60
Chandel	1.44	44
Ukhrul	1.84	40
Imphal East	4.56	643
Imphal West	5.18	998
Bishnupur	2.37	479
Thoubal	4.22	821

SEX RATIO

The sex ratio is the number of females per thousand males. In 1961, the number of females per thousand males in the Rural and Urban areas of Manipur stood at 1,018 and 985 respectively. In the following period, the sex ratio decreased to 951 in 1991 and 969 in 2011 in the case of rural areas while for the urban areas, the ratio decreased to 969 in 1981 but rose to 1026 in 2011. The combined sex ratio of the State was 1,015 which declined 958 in 1991 but in 2011, it was 985 which was found to be slightly higher than the all India Sex-Ratio which stood at 943. Among the districts of Manipur, the highest Sex Ratio is recorded at Imphal West District (1,031) and the least in Chandel District (933).

Sex Ratio of Population

District	Sex ratio		
	Rural	**Urban**	**Combined**
Senapati	936	1,010	937
Tamenglong	940	968	943
Churachandpur	973	1,004	975
Chandel	932	943	933
Ukhrul	941	954	943
Imphal East	995	1,051	1,017
Imphal West	1013	1,042	1,031
Bishnupur	994	994	999
Thoubal	999	1,008	1,002
Manipur	**969**	**1,026**	**985**

RURAL AND URBAN POPULATION

According to 2011, 70.79% of the total population are found in rural areas while 29.21% are settled in the urban areas. Similar pattern are observed at the regional level also. However, the concentration of population in the rural areas is much higher in the hill region (92.70%) as compared to the valley region (54.40%). The per centage of urban population to the District population is found to be highest in Imphal West Districts (62.33%) among the Valley Districts and in Ukhrul District (14.78%) among the Hill Districts. And the least concentration of urban population is found in Senapati District with only 1.56% and the second least in Churachandpur District with 6.70%.

Rural-Urban Population of Manipur

District	Population			% of total population	
	Rural	Urban	Total	Rural	Urban
Senapati	4,71,672	7,476	4,79,148	98.44	1.56
Tamenglong	1,21,288	19,363	1,40,651	86.23	13.77
Churachandpur	2,55,786	18,357	2,74,143	93.30	6.70
Chandel	1,27,335	16,847	1,44,182	88.32	11.68
Ukhrul	1,56,811	27,187	1,83,998	85.22	14.78
A. HILL	11,32,892	89,230	12,22,122	92.70	7.30
Imphal East	2,72,906	1,83,207	4,56,113	59.83	40.17
Imphal West	1,95,113	3,22,879	5,17,992	37.67	62.33
Bishnupur	1,49,894	87,505	2,37,399	63.14	36.86
Thoubal	2,70,835	1,51,333	4,22,168	64.15	36.02
B. VALLEY	8,88,748	7,44,924	1,633,672	54.40	45.60
Manipur	**20,21,640**	**8,34,154**	**28,55,794**	**70.79**	**29.21**

LITERACY RATE

The extent of literacy reflects the qualitative aspect of the population. Higher literacy emancipates economic and social backwardness. The literacy rate had shown an increase from 59.9 per cent in 1991 to 76.94 per cent in 2011.

Male-Female Literacy Rate of Manipur

District	Literacy rate		
	Male	Female	Person
Senapati	69.21	57.67	63.60
Tamenglong	76.09	63.69	70.05
Churachandpur	86.97	78.50	82.78
Chandel	77.78	63.96	71.11
Ukhrul	85.25	76.95	81.35
Imphal East	88.77	75.32	81.95
Imphal West	92.24	80.17	86.08
Bishnupur	85.11	66.68	75.85
Thoubal	85.00	64.09	74.47
Manipur	**83.58**	**70.26**	**76.94**

Source: *Manipur Economic Survey 2015-16*

URBANISATION

Urbanisation stands for growth of towns and non-agricultural activities. It is generally associated with the growth of industrialization, trade and commerce. According to 2011 census, urban population of state is 8,34,154.

Urbanisation in Manipur

Year	No. of Towns	Urban population	Percentage to total Population	
			Urban	Rural
1961	1	67,717	8.68	91.32
1971	8	1,41,492	13.19	86.81
1981	32	3,75,460	26.42	73.58
1991	31	5,05,645	27.52	72.48
2001	33	5,75,968	25.11	74.89
2011	51	8,34,154	29.21	70.79

Population were found in the urban area constituting 51 towns (28 statutory and 23 census towns) in the state as against 1 (one) town in 1961. It appears that the process of urbanization has been very slow in the state which perhaps indicates a slower occupational shift.

SC AND ST POPULATION

According to 2011 Census, the ST population was 11.67 lakhs as against 7.41 lakhs in 2001 Census. The total SC population was 97 thousand in 2011 census as against 60 thousands in 2001 Census. The Scheduled Tribes in Manipur are Aimol, Anal, Angami, Chiru, Chothe, Gangte, Hmar, Kabui (substituted as Kabui, Inpui, Rongmei), Kacha Naga (substituted as Kacha Naga, Liangmai, Zeme), Koirao (substituted as Koirao, Thangal), Koireng, Kom, Lamgang, Mizo, Lushai, Maram, Maring, Mao, Monsang, Moyon, Paite, Purum, Ralte, Sema, Simte, Sahte, Tangkhul, Thadou, Vaiphei, Zou, Poumei Naga, Tarao, Kharam, any kuki tribes and Mate. And the Scheduled Castes communities in Manipur are Loi, Yaithibi, Dhobi, Muchi or Rabidas, Namsudra, Patni and Sutradhar.

Number of SC and ST of Manipur by Sex

Year	Scheduled Castes	Scheduled Tribes	% to total state population	
			S.C.	S.T.
1961	13,376	2,49,049	1.71	31.93
1971	16,376	3,34,466	1.53	31.18
1981	17,753	3,87,977	1.25	27.30
1991	37,105	6,32,173	2.02	34.41
2001	60,037	7,41,141	2.77	34.20
2011	97,328	11,67,422	3.41	40.88

According to the 2011 Census, about 95 per cent of the scheduled tribe population are found in the hill districts of Manipur while the remaining 5 per cent are in the valley districts. In the case of the scheduled caste population, about 98 per cent are concentrated in the valley districts as against 2 per cent in the hill districts.

POPULATION BY RELIGION

Attempts are made to provide a picture of the religious pursuits of the people of Manipur. The Hindus who constitute about 46 (forty-six) per cent of the total population are mostly settling in the valley districts. The Muslims who constitute about 9 per cent of the total population are also settling in the valley areas. Most of the tribes are Christians and they are mostly settling in the hills. Other small communities like Sikhs, Buddhists, Jains and others etc. constitute 10 per cent of the State's population.

Distribution of Population by Religion (1961-2001)

Religious Communities	Population					Percentage increase
	1961	1971	1981	1991	2001*	1991-2001
1. Hindu	4,81,112	6,32,597	8,53,180	10,59,470	9,96,894	(-) 5.91
2. Muslim	48,588	70,969	99,327	1,33,535	1,90,939	4.30
3. Christian	1,52,043	2,79,243	4,21,702	6,26,669	7,37,578	17.70
4. Sikh	523	1,028	992	1,301	1,653	27.06
5. Buddhist	325	495	473	711	1,926	170.89
6. Jain	778	1,408	975	1,337	1,461	9.27
7. Others	-	83,167	35,490	14,066	2,35,280	1572.69
8. Religions not stated	96,668	3,846	8,814	60	1,057	1661.67
Total	7,80,037	10,72,753	14,20,953	18,37,149	21,66,788	17.94

Excluding Mao Maram, Paomata and Purul Sub-division of Senapati District
Source: *Manipur Economic Survey 2015-16*

BIRTH, DEATH AND MORTALITY RATES

With the implementation of various socio-economic upliftment programmes, birth and death rates have been continuously decreasing since independence. In the rural areas of Manipur, the birth rate of population per annum is 14.6 in 2007 and the death rate is 4.4 in the same period. The urban birth rate registered a decline from 15.7 in 2008 to 15.1 in 2013 where the urban death rate falls from 5.4 to 4.2 in the same period. During the period between 2007 to 2013, the highest infant mortality rate of 18 in the rural areas and 12 in the urban areas was recorded in 2009 and 2011 respectively. In 2013, the IMR for the rural, urban and combined was the same *i.e.*, 10.

Estimated Birth, Death and Infant Mortality Rates

Item	Year						
	2007	2008	2009	2010	2011	2012	2013
1. Birth rate:							
Rural	14.4	15.9	15.4	14.8	14.2	14.4	14.5
Urban	15.2	15.7	15.5	15.3	15.0	15.2	15.1
Combined	14.6	15.8	15.4	14.9	14.4	14.6	14.7
2. Death rate:							
Rural	4.2	4.8	4.6	4.3	4.1	4.0	4.0
Urban	4.9	5.4	5.0	4.0	4.2	4.2	4.2
Combined	4.4	5.0	4.7	4.2	4.1	4.0	4.0
3. Natural Growth rate:							
Rural	10.2	11.1	10.8	10.5	10.2	10.4	10.5
Urban	10.3	10.3	10.5	11.3	10.2	11.0	10.9
Combined	10.2	10.9	10.7	10.7	10.3	10.6	10.6
4. Infant Mortality rate:							
Rural	13	16	18	15	11	10.0	10.0
Urban	9	8	11	9	12	11.0	10.0
Combined	12	14	16	14	11	10.0	10.0

Source: Manipur Economic Survey 2015-16

HEALTH

Over the years there has been an overall improvement in the health situation of the state. The substantial improvement is the result of many factors including improvement in public health, coupled with infectious disease prevention and control as also application of modern practices in diagnosis and treatment of various ailments.

Despite overall improvement in socio-economic status and increasing life expectancy, the prevalence of infectious diseases continues to be an area of major concern in Health Sector. To tackle the problem of communicable and non-communicable diseases, the State Health Department is implementing many new schemes.

Medical Facilities

The State Health Department of Manipur fully is committed in the total health cafe of its people in the spirit of Health for All. The priority is to provide the optimum health needs of the people in general and particularly to those living in Rural and Tribal areas of the State.

The Health system of the State is based upon the Primary Health Care approach as envisaged in the National Health Policy of 1983 with the objective of attainment of "Health for All" and "All for Health".

The three tier administrative set up of the Health Services in the State is as follows :

The highest level of the organisation is the Administrative level. A cabinet Minister heads it and major decisions concerning policies, programmes and proposals are taken at this level. The minister is supported by a Commissioner/Secretary, Joint Secretary, Deputy Secretary and Under Secretary of Manipur Secretariat.

At directorate level, the department is headed by the Director as the Technical and health Administrator of the state. The Director is assisted by Additional Directors, Joint Directors and Deputy Directors to give direction and undertake planning, supervision, evaluation and monitoring of various health programmes taken up in the state of Manipur.

The District level Health Administration is organised through the Chief Medical Officer (CMO) as the head who is assisted by District Level Programme Officers. The District Health Organization is responsible for implementation of various health programmes under primary health care through a network of various health care centres and hospitals in the district.

Health Infrastructure

The state has altogether more than 500 Primary Health Care Institutions, 13 hospitals including one state level hospital (J.N Hospital) as referral centre and 7 District Hospitals. Other Drug de-addiction centres, TB Centers, Leprosy Control Unit and STD Clinics are functioning in the State.

Major Hospitals of Manipur
  (i) Jawaharlal Nehru Hospital
  (ii) Churachandpur District Hospital
  (iii) Other District Hospitals
  (iv) Private Hospitals & Clinics
  (v) Regional Institute of Medical Sciences (RIMS)

Regional Institute of Medical Sciences (RIMS)

Regional Institute of Medical Sciences (RIMS) was established on 14th September 1972 in a picturesque Lamphelpat at the heart of Imphal, the capital city of Manipur.

This Institute is a joint venture of the north eastern states viz. Manipur, Meghalaya, Mizoram, Nagaland, Tripura and Arunachal Pradesh. It is fully funded by the Government of India through the North Eastern Council (NEC) and the six beneficiary states.

Medical facilities in the state were mainly provided by the State Government. It is the basic social input for healthy and efficient human resources. The Health and Family Welfare Department is providing services such as public health, control of communicable diseases, health education, family welfare, maternal and child health care through a network of 14 Civil Hospitals, 80 Primary Health Centres, 420 Primary Health Sub-Centres, 16 Community/Urban Health Centres, 20 Dispensaries as on 3l-3-2010. Special attention was also given from time to time to eradicate diseases like malaria, leprosy, T.B., Iodine Deficiency and Aids.

Number of Hospitals/Dispensaries and Beds

(in nos.)

Year	Hospital (including PHC/UHC/ CHC)	Dispensaries (including PHSC's)	Total	Bed	Population	
					Hospital/ Dispensaries	Bed
2011-12	106	440	546	1,066	5,414	2,773
2012-13	112	441	553	1,066	5,463	2,834
2013-14	112	441	553	1,542	5,583	2,002
2014-15	112	441	553	1,936	5,705	1,629
2015-16	112	441	553	1,480	5,829	2,178

Source: *Directorate of Health Services, Govt. of Manipur.*

During the year 2015-16, medical health care facilities were available to the people of Manipur through a network of 553 hospitals/dispensaries.

National Malaria Eradication Programme (NMEP)

This programme was implemented in the state as a Centrally Sponsored Scheme from December, 1994.

The programme could tackle malaria problems more effectively. Youth and voluntary organisations have been actively involved in malaria control activities. Since March, 2004, the nomenclature of the programme, NAMP has been changed to National Vector Borne Disease Control Programme (NVBDCP).

National Leprosy Control Programme (NLCP)

This programme was started during 1955 as a control programme under 'Mono-Drug Therapy' giving more stress on survey, Education and Treatment. The objective of the programme is to reduce the number of active leprosy cases by fifty per cent. National Leprosy Eradication programme was introduced on 1984 with an objective of eradicating leprosy by 2000. The main trategies were active case detection and promt treatment with Multi-Drug Therapy to reduce case load and transmission. Manipur has achieved the National Goal of prevalence rate of less than 1 per 10,000 population at the end of 2000-01. As on today Prevalence Rate of Manipur is 0.08 per 10,000 population which is one of the lowest in India.

National T.B. Control Programme (NTCP)

Under this programme, 100 bedded T.B. Hospital at Chingmeirong, 2 T.B. Clinics, one each at Churachandpur and Ukhrul and 4 District T.B. control centres one each at Imphal, Senapati, Tamenglong and Chandel are functioning since 1984-85.

The B.C.G. vaccination programme which is one of the most important Component of the T.B. Control Programme continued to provide B.C.G. vaccination to all eligible Children. R.N.T.C.P. project funded by the World Bank has been complemented in all the districts of Manipur State. Under the project, at present, there are more than 800 DOTS (Directly Observed Treatment Short Course) Centres, 13 TUs (Tuberculosis Units) and 56 DMCs (Designated Microscopy Centres).

National Programme for Control of Blindness (NPCB)

The objective of this programme is to reduce the incidence of blindness from the estimated level of 1.35% to 0.7%. During 2007-08, 2008-09 and 2009-10 the number of patients treated with Cataract Operation under NPCB was 210, 268 and 934 respectively.

Maternal Child Health-Cum-Expanded Programme on Immunisation

In order to curb the infant mortality rate and to provide safeguard against serious diseases, an intensive 'Child Immunisation Programme' is being implemented in the State. The objective of the programme is to cover 100 per cent of pregnant women with 2 or a boosters dose of T.T. and at least 85 per cent of the infants with 3 doses of D.P.T. and Polio and one dose of B.C.G and measles vaccine.

National Aids Control Programme

AIDS (Acquired Immuno Deficiency Syndrome) has become a major public health problem in the state since 1990. It is affecting a number of youths in Manipur. According to the National AIDS Control Organisation (NACO), Manipur ranks third highest as regarding the total number of HIV positive cases next to Maharashtra and Tamil Nadu states. The State Government with the help of NACO took up various activities in order to advert this looming catastrophic. The following measures were taken up,

(i) 100 per cent blood safety in all the blood banks in Manipur.

(ii) Introduction of AIDS education in school for class VI, VII, VIII and X.

(iii) Impart training to more than 81 per cent of doctors and 80 per cent of nurses/paramedicals in AIDS and related problems.

(iv) Implementation of the Manipur state AIDS policy.

(v) Increase in the number of NGOs financially supported by the National AIDS Control Programme.

(vi) Broaden partnership with NGOs.

National Iodine Deficiency Disorder Control Programme (NIDDCP)

Iodine deficiency is also one of the major public health problem in Manipur. The objective of this programme is to reduce the prevalence rate to below 5% as against 13% in 1996 and to achieve 100% household consumption of iodized salt.

National Rural Health Mission (NRHM)

Inorder to provide accessible, affordable and accountable quality health services even to the poorest households in the remotest rural region, the NRHM was launched in 12th April, 2005. In the North Eastern Region of India, the North Eastern Regional Resource Centre is playing a critical role in developing need-based programmes in the region. In Manipur, Health Societies were formed at State and district level. Rogi Kalyan Samiti were established at J.N. Hospital. District Hospitals of Churachandpur and Bishnupur were started upgrating to Indian Public Health Standard (IPHS) level. Sufficient manpower including AYUSH doctors and ASHAs has been deployed for implementing this programme.

SANITATION

Sanitation covers arrangements for drainage of rain water and effluents, collection and disposal of garbage and removal of human excreta. Proper sanitation is necessary condition for improvement in general health standards, productivity of labour force and quality of life. Sanitation has two aspects to it viz. (i) Rural Sanitation and (ii) Urban Sanitation.

Rural Sanitation

Rural Sanitation has been one of the most neglected sectors. In this regard, Rural in Manipur has remained as primitive as ever. The Government of India has now restructured Rural Sanitation Programme under the name of Total Sanitation Campaign with an objective of to provide sanitary latrines to every household of the state. So far 17 nos. of Rural Sanitation Mark/Production centre has been established and 32,764 nos. of Individual household latrines, 142 nos. of Sanitary Complex and 787 nos. of Sanitary Latrines for schools have been constructed. In addition total sanitary has been achieved in Maklang village (Imphal West district) and Utlou (Bishnupur district).

Under Swachh Bharat Mission (Gramin), which is a Flagship Programme of the Government of India, 2,41,581 numbers of individual household latrine, 320 numbers of sanitary complex, 3,019 numbers of school toilets, 20 numbers of RSM/PC and 1,201 numbers of Anganwadi toilets have been constructed as on November, 2015.

Urban Sanitation

For the upliftment of Urban Sanitation and drainage of the urban areas, a technical clearance of ₹ 36.69 crores has been given by the Ministry of

Urban Development, Government of India, New Delhi, for the construction of 5 (five) basines viz. Nambul, Waishel, Kongba, Imphal and Chandranadi basins of Greater Imphal area. Construction of 47,226 RM. of pucca drain and resectioning of 51,661 RM. were completed by the end of March 2007. The length of the pucca drain constructed during the year 2007-2008 was 5000 RMs.

Due to the absence of a proper sewerage system for Imphal City, the effluent from the numerous septic tanks, pits etc., discharges directly into the open drains, then to the rivers and ultimately reach the Loktak Lake. Further, open fields and low lying marshes become dumping ground on account of want of a scientific and hygienic method of disposal of night soil and garbage. This practice causes air, water and soil pollution and effects overall environmental degradation which is hazardous to health.

In order to minimize the adverse effects of open discharges of effluents from the individual household septic tanks pits and likely health hazards from the absence of proper sewerage system, a project formulated for conveyance and treatment of sewage for Imphal City with a revised cost of ₹ 323.78 crores is under construction. Imphal Sewerage System for Imphal Municipal Ward No. 1,2,3,4,5,6,14,15,24,25 and 26 under EAP/ France has been taken up since 2004. Presently, construction of treatment plant (27 MLD), five pumping station, primary sewer line (25.291 km.) and 62% of secondary sewer line has been completed.

● ● ●

Education

Education is a life long process by which an individual acquires and accumulates knowledge, skills, attitudes and insights. It starts from the cradle and ends at the grave for an individual. And life experiences are given to child through the informal agencies like family, social groups (clubs, associations, political parties, literary circle, debating societies, library, mass media radio, television, cinema, museum, tour etc.) and also through the agencies of formal education such as schools, colleges, universities etc.

However, education is one of the principal factors influencing the quality of the state's labour force. It has an important role in the socio-economic development of the State. Its contribution to economic growth and its impact on population controls life expectancy, infant mortality, improving nutritional status and strengthening civil institutions is well recognised. As per National Policy on Education, priority has been accorded to the universalisation of primary education for children in the age group of 6 to 14 years.

PROGRESS OF EDUCATION

There has been a great deal of accomplishment in the field of education since 1950-51. The number of educational institutions has increased from 538 in 1950-51 to over 3676 by the end of 2015-16.

Since 1950-51, the number of institutions imparting occupational and technical education has shown a phenomenal increase. Among these, different types of institutions like those connected with agriculture, arts and commerce, engineering, medicine, physical education, teachers training etc. are emphatically included. The University level education is imparted in subjects such as arts, sciences, vocational courses and specialised subjects etc. Universities also offer good higher research facilities. It has been observed that significant progress had been made in the spheres of education in the state.

The literacy rate in Manipur has gone up from 11 per cent in 1951 to 76.94 per cent in 2011. In the state, the rate of male literacy was as high as 83.58 per cent while rate of the female literacy stood at 70.26 per cent in 2011. Despite the rise in literacy rate, the absolute number of illiterates has increased due to fast growing population.

Districtwise Number of Literates Persons

Sl. No.	State/District	No. of Literate		
		Person	Male	Female
1.	Senapati	264477	148012	116465
2.	Tamenglong	85006	47403	37603
3.	Churachandpur	195935	104013	91922
4.	Chandel	90302	51053	39249
5.	Ukhrul	129829	70148	59631
6.	Imphal East	324664	173314	151350
7.	Imphal West	392626	205985	186641
8.	Bishnupur	156333	87313	69020
9.	Thoubal	259304	152617	116687
	Manipur	**1908476**	**1039858**	**868618**

Districtwise Literacy Rates

Sl. No.	State/District	Literacy rate		
		Person	Male	Female
1.	Senapati	63.60	69.21	57.67
2.	Tamenglong	70.05	76.09	63.69
3.	Churachandpur	82.78	86.97	78.50
4.	Chandel	71.11	77.78	63.96
5.	Ukhrul	81.35	85.52	76.95
6.	Imphal East	81.95	88.77	75.32
7.	Imphal West	86.08	92.24	80.17
8.	Bishnupur	75.85	85.11	66.68
9.	Thoubal	74.47	85.00	64.09
	Manipur	**76.94**	**83.58**	**70.26**

Source: Directorate of Census Operations, Manipur.

SCHOOL EDUCATION

As per the National Policy on Education 1986, a target had been set for the universalisation of primary education for children in the age group of 6 to 14 years. Under this policy, three aspects of elementary education viz. (i) universal access and enrolment (ii) universal retention of children upto 14 years of age and (iii) substantial improvement in the quality of education are to be achieved.

Several programmes like National Programme of Nutrition support to primary education (mid-day meal scheme) and promotion of girls' education were also undertaken in the state. Under mid-day meal scheme, the state is providing 3 kgs. of rice per student per month to the students of class I to V reading in 2997 Govt. and aided schools having primary classes. Under the scheme (Expanded Operation Black Board) of the Govt. of India, minimum teaching learning materials, like teachers equipment, teaching learning materials, games materials, play materials, books for library, furniture etc. were procured for 398 upper primary schools of the state during 2002-03. The total enrolment at the primary stage (Class I to V) decreased from 3,66,372 in 2011-12 to 3,24,231 in 2012-13. However, in the following year the numbers rose to 4,71,629 which recorded an increase of an absolute 1,47,398 over the previous year. But, the number of enrolment decrease to 3,55,297 in 2014-16 and further to 3,35,479 in 2015-16.

The school level education is primarily looked after by the State Government. The high school stage of education comprising of classes from class IX to X are under the academic control of the Board of Secondary Education, Manipur. And Higher Secondary Schools Education comprising of class XI to XII comes under the control of Council of Higher Secondary Education, Manipur.

The total number of high and higher secondary schools in the state were 872 by the end of 2010-11 which rose to 1,131 in 2015-16. The enrolment of students for high and higher secondary classes has increased from 2,34,211 in 2010-11 to 4,50,399 in 2015-16.

Sarva Shiksha Abhiyan (SSA)

The objective of the Sarva Shiksha Abhiyan (SSA) Project is to ensure universal education for children in the age group of 6-14 years through proactive participation of community in a mission mode as envisaged under the Right to Education (RTE) Act. According to the Unified District Information System for Education (U-DISE), there are 4,865 elementary schools during 2015-16 which includes 2,951 Primary Schools (I-V) and 1,914 Upper Primary Schools (VI-VIII).

Although, the enrolment of boys is higher than the girls, the net enrolment ratio (NER) of girls is greater than the boys which stood at 99.66% (Primary) and 81.33 % (Upper Primary). At both level, the NER of girls is more than the boys. NER is calculated by taking number of enrolment of students (6-10 in case of Primary and 11-14 for Upper Primary) divided by population of children belonging to the corresponding ages related to the level of education.

HIGHER EDUCATION

Higher education plays a crucial role in the national development process. The matters relating to higher education are looked after by Directorate of Higher Education (U). The total number of colleges for General Education in the state at the end of 2005 was 62 (all types including private colleges). All these colleges had teaching facilities for higher degree courses.

Manipur University

Manipur University was established on 5th June, 1980 under the Manipur University Act. 1980 (Manipur Act 8 of 1980), as a teaching cum-affiliating university at Imphal with territorial jurisdiction over the whole of the state of Manipur and it was converted into a central university on 13 October, 2005. The University has six schools of Studies including the School of Medical Science and currently there are 31 departments and 7 Centres of Studies.

Central Agricultural University, Imphal

The Central Agricultural University (CAU) was established under Department of Agricultural Research and Education (DARE) on 26th January, 1993 by an Act of Parliament the Central Agricultural University Act, 1992 with its headquarters at Imphal, Manipur.

The university has unique features of having jurisdiction over six States of North-Eastern Hilly Region (NEH) of India namely, Arunachal Pradesh, Manipur, Meghalaya, Mizoram, Sikkim and Tripura. Like other Agricultural Universities of India, the CAU also has integrated programmes of teaching, research and extension education.

The mission of the University is to be a centre of excellence in teaching, research and extension education in the field of agriculture and allied sectors.

The University aims to develop sustainable farming systems for improving productivity and profitability in agriculture and allied sectors and also train the farmers and extension functionaries for the effective dissemination of advanced agricultural technologies in North-East India.

Regional Institute of Medical Sciences, Imphal

Regional Institute of Medical Sciences, Imphal is situated at Lamphelpat, Imphal, Manipur. It is an autonomous institution under the Ministry of Health & Family Welfare, Government of India.

It is an institution of regional importance catering to the needs of the North Eastern Region in the field of medical education by providing undergraduate and post graduate courses, bringing together in one place the educational facilities for the training of personnel in all important branches of medical specialities.

National Institute of Technology, Manipur

National Institute of Technology (NIT), Manipur, a centrally funded institution, is set up to impart quality technical education to various levels of higher learning.

It has been established to cater to the needs of the thousands of students from the North East and outside in the field of Technical Education with National Institute of Technology Agartala, as its mentor institute and tremendous support from the State Govt. of Manipur. NIT Manipur started its first session on 1st August, 2010.

TECHNICAL EDUCATION

Technical education is basically meant to produce trained manpower in adequate numbers for speedy economic development of the state. Training have been diversified and programmes modified to take care of the needs of the modern development in technology. At the end of the Sixth Plan, the state had only a polytechnic having diploma courses in Civil, Electrical and Mechanical Engineering etc. But the existing arrangements for educating at degree level is by reserving specified number of seats in different Engineering Colleges of the country through the Ministry of Human Resource Development. One Engineering College (Govt. College of Technology) was started during the annual plan 1998-99 in 3 courses viz., Civil, Computer Science, Electronic & Communication Engineering with per intake capacity of 30 each further the produce of technically trained manpower for the upliftment of economic development of the state. Still, inspite of all these, progress of technical education is at a slow pace and the state is lagging behind and is quite below the level of the other states in the development of technical education.

Industrial Training Institute

There are 11 Industrial Training Institutes in the state which are imparting various engineering and non-engineering training courses based on locally suitable selfemployment activities under two schemes viz., Craftsman training and Apprenticeship training. Under the aegis of the Government of India (DGET), training are also imparted in the new diversified fields so as to meet the technological advancement.

ITIs in Manipur

Sl.	District	Name of ITI
1.	Bishnupur	Govt. ITI, Ningthoukhong
2.	Chandel	Govt. ITI, Chandel (Komlathabi)
3.	Churachandpur	Govt. ITI, Saikot
4.	Imphal East	● Govt. ITI, Jiribam (Jiribam Sub-Division) ● Govt. ITI, Phaknung
5.	Imphal West	● Govt. ITI, Takyel ● Govt. Women ITI, Takyel
6.	Senapati	Govt. ITI, Senapati
7.	Tamenglong	Govt. ITI, Tamenglong
8.	Thoubal	Govt. ITI, Kakching
9.	Ukhrul	Govt. ITI, Ukhrul

Source: Directorate of Craftsmen Training, Manipur

NON-FORMAL EDUCATION

To achieve the goal of universalisation of elementary education and fulfillment of the constitutional objectives, Non-Formal Education (NFE) for the elementary age group children is being developed as an alternative supportive system of formal schooling. The State Council of Educational Research and Training (SCERT), has been working for the upliftment of the quality of education in the elementary stage of education as well as the goal of the universalisation of elementary education by adopting proper strategies non-formal educational schemes for drop-out and non-starters in the age group of 0-14. The SCERT has also been entrusted with the implementation of the schemes of vocationalisation of education at plus two stage for self-employment as one of the main objectives. This scheme is equally shared by Central and State Governments. It is basically aimed at providing the institutional infrastructure necessary both for coverage of non-enrolled and non-attending children and strengthening the academic inputs of the action programme of non-formal education. During the Ninth Plan period, 3122 non-formal education centres have been functioning through 55 NFE projects with the total enrolment of 90,000 learners all over the state.

ADULT EDUCATION

The 'National Literacy Mission' (NLM) was established in 1988 by the Government of India with the aim of successful implementation of strategies of eradicating illiteracy in the age group of 15 to 35 years. Following prescribed detailed guidelines for the implementation of total literacy campaign, the state Government has taken a policy decision to implement Total Literacy Campaign (TLC) in a phase manner. A State Literacy Mission Authority (SLMA), Manipur was constituted as per the directive given by the NLM Authority, Government of India. In Manipur, the Department of Adult Education is implementing various Adult Education Programmes with the objective of eradicating illiteracy, retention of literacy among the adult learners and impart skill development schemes for neo-literates in the age group of 15-35 years and above.

Saakshar Bharat (SB) Mission in Manipur

The Government of India launched the Saakshar Bharat (Literate India) Programme on 8th September, 2009 with the aim of strengthening adult education. In Manipur, the programme is implemented in 4 Districts viz., Senapati, Tamenglong, Chandel and Thoubal, since January, 2010. There are 321 Adult Education Centres (AEC) in the 4 districts. A nationwide assessment/ test for the basic learner under SB Programme was conducted by the NLM in collaboration with the National Institute of Open Schooling (NIOS).

Rashtriya Madhyamik Shiksha Abhiyan (RMSA)

Rashtriya Madhyamik Shiksha Abhiyan (RMSA), a centrally sponsored scheme, was launched by the Government of India on 2nd March, 2009 with the objective of enrolling students into classes IX to XII to achieve universalisation of secondary education by 2017 and full retention by 2020. In Manipur, the scheme took off formally on 20th April, 2010. Under the scheme, the gross enrolment ratio and net enrolment ratio stood at 72.98% and 64.88% respectively in 2013-14 which increased to 76.9% and 66.87% in 2014-15.

Kasturba Gandhi Balika Vidyalaya (KGBV)

The SSA, SMA manages the KGBVs. There are altogether 11 KGBV (3 Chandel, 1 each in the remaining 8 Districts) in Manipur. Presently 1,118 girls are enrolled against the targeted nos. of 1,100. Out of the total enrolment, 31 girls are children with special needs.

POST LITERACY PROGRAMME (PLP)

The PLP was launched in Manipur during 2006-07 with the following objectives:

   (i) Remedy the deficiency of learning in the literacy phases or, in other woods, build up literacy skills satisfactory standards;

  (ii) Retention, re-enforcement, stabilization and upgrading of literacy skills and improvement of functional skills;

 (iii) Application in living and working situations but this need to be encouraged by positive measure. Through application of literacy, people begin to participate in the development process.

The programme is funded by the Central and State Government in the ratio of 2:1 and 4:1 in the Valley and Hill districts respectively. The target groups of the programme are :-

   (i) Drop outs of TLC,

  (ii) Uncovered (gap between figures of TLC survey and enrolment),

 (iii) Neo-literates and

 (iv) New entrants/school drop out who are in the age group of 15 years and above.

SCIENCE AND TECHNOLOGY

Science and Technology plays a vital role in the process of development and transformation of a traditional agrarian economy into a modern Industrial economy. Development in the fields of Science and Technology in Manipur is carried out under the auspices of the State Government. The Government has been consistently laying emphasis on the development of Science and Technology as a major instrument for achieving national goals of self-reliance and Socio-economic development.

Set up in January, 1985, the Science and Technology Department has been a Nodal Agency in the State for planning, co-ordinating and promoting science and technology for achieving the socio-economic objectives through meaningful applications in numerous developmental programmes.

Not only being an implementing agency, the department of Science & Technology also encourages the use of non-conventional sources of energy to minimise the excessive use of forest products. The Department also provides a feasible alternative for supplying energy to locations which cannot be provided with conventional sources of energy. Altogether, 16 schemes were implemented by the department under 3 (three) major schemes viz. (i) Scientific Research, (ii) Development of non-conventional sources of energy and (iii) Integrate Rural Energy planning.

Scientific Research

Under scientific research centre, the Department had undertaken several scheme viz. (i) Science Centres and Science popularisation, (ii) S & T. Entrepreneurship Development Programmes, (iii) Human Resource Development, (iv) Research and Development, (v) State Remote Sensing Centre and (vi) State Computer centre etc., to give a main thrust of all-round activities in the popularisation of science for welfare of various communities. To develop scientific temper among the students and people of the state, the Department had already set up 8 District Science Centres, 30 District level science Model laboratories. Besides, the programmes like science symposia, science quiz/essay/seminars/workshops, national children's science congress, science excursion etc. were very effective in raising the level of science popularisation among the younger generation.

One Tissue Culture Laboratory at Manipur University and one Food Testing Laboratory at D.M. College of science were set up under the Research and Development scheme. Another project on 'Micro-Propagation of certain orchids of Manipur using tissue culture techniques' was also completed by making the products available to the progressive growers. And it was found effective with remarkable progress in production of orchids during 1997-98.

The State Remote Sensing Centre had taken up a project on "Natural Resources" and completed the projects on 'Application of Remote Sensing Techniques in Geological Studies in Manipur' and 'Integrated Mission for sustainable development of Imphal District'. The Remote Sensing Centre has Installed ARC/INFO, GIS software to supplement the existing image processing computer facility. The State Computer Centre plays the role of introducing innovative and appropriate computer application for Government departments with the objective of improving efficiency and productivity. Training on Computer operations and use of software were provided in various departments. Facility of AUTOCAD drafting was successfully introduced in departments like PWD. An Online INTRANET based Govt./ Public information system has been set up. The Department is also providing computers and Modems under the scheme of computer for homes and computers were offered to schools at low cost for use under school Computers Education. During 2009-10, the Manipur Remote Sensing Application Centre (MARSAC) has taken up schemes like Land Use/Land Cover of Manipur, Wasteland Mapping of Manipur, Land Degradation Mapping of Manipur, Urban Information system for Imphal and Kakching municipalities etc.

Important Educational and Training Institutes in Manipur

College of Technology	Government College of Technoloqy (Takyelat, Imphal).
Jawaharlal Nehru Manipur Dance Academy	Imphal.
Shree Shree Govindajee Nartanalaya (Government Dance College)	Palace Compound, Imphal.
Manipur Science Centre	Imphal.
Arts College	D.M. College of Arts (Imphal). Imphal Arts College (Imphal).
Commerce College	D.M. College of Commerce (Imphal).
Law College	L.M.S. Law College (Imphal). L.M.G.M. Law College (Churachandpur). Royal Academy of Law (Bishnupur).
Theological College	Manipur Theological College (Imphal).
Agricultural College	College of Agriculture (Imphal).
Sainik School	Imphal.
Science College	Regional Institute of Medical Sciences (Imphal). Pamyala Arts and Science College (Churachandpur).
Rajyaka Sanskrit Toll (College)	D.M. College Compound
Teacher Training College	Hindi Teacher Training College (Imphal).
University	Manipur University (Canchipur). Central Agricultural University (Iroisemba, Imphal).
Polytechnic	Government Polytechnic (Imphal).

Centre for Electronics and Design Technology	Akampat (Imphal).
Regional Institute of Medical Sciences (Manipur)	Imphal
Farmer's Training Centre	Iroisemba
Central Institute of Plastic Engineering and Technology	Takyelpat
Government Ideal Blind School	Takyelpat
The Deaf and Mute School	Takyelpat
Manipur Sanskrit Mahavidyalaya	Brahmpur Nahabam
Vishwanath Sanskrit Vidyalaya	Kakching

● ● ●

15   Art and Culture

Manipur has immensely contributed to the composite culture of India. She is open to external influences of the east and the west inspite of her geographical isolation from the rest of India. Its culture under the able kings has retained its distinctiveness amidst the give and take with countries of the world. For administrative purpose Manipur was under the Governor of Assam during the British regime, religiously it belongs to Bengal but linguistically and culturally it is independent.

The culture of Manipur is the product of various forces-natives, Aryanism from the west and the Mongoloid from the eastern countries. Aryan culture penetrated by also degrees into the Meetei community, the hybrid race formed by the integration of such streams along with the people of the east and the west settling in the valley while the Nagas and Kukies of the hill areas remained comparatively unaffected.

Manipur is distinguished from other parts of India by such features as the marketing by women, women police organization (at a time when probably it did not exist in any other part of India), observance of the distinction between formal and informal dress, use of phanek (lower garment of women), wonderful practice of music and dance, abundance of tantric and love of freedom. Polo, of which Manipur is the mother, represents a special aspect of Manipuri culture.

Manipur is synonomous with dances to the world outside. The colourful and rhythemic expressions, both traditional and classical dance form need no introduction. Influenced by the Vaishnav culture, the dancers of the Meitei population supplemented by the folk dances of the hill tribes makes Manipur a unique stage for performing arts. The world is yet to see what Manipur can offer in performing arts.

FOLK DANCES

Some Famous folk dances of Manipur are as follows:

- **Maibi Laiching Jagoi :** One of the most popular festivals in the valley of Manipur mirrors the unique heritage of the ancient Pre-Vaisnavite Tradition of Manipur. It is celebrated during the month of March and April every year. The Lai-Haraoba Dance led by the Maibi and the Maibi's symbolised the creation of life and growth of civilization in a highly rhythmic and absorbing style and performed before the sylvan deity to bring peace and prosperity to the land.

- **Thougal Jagoi:** Thougal Jagoi is a part of the famous Manipuri Traditional Lai-Haraoba depicting the performance before the sylvan god and goddess to bring peace and prosperity to the land.

- **Paosa Jagoi:** Paosa Jagoi means conversation. This dance is a part of Manipuri Traditional "Kanglei Haraoba". Nongpok Panthoibi came out in search of Nongpok Ningthou. In the course of her journey she reached Nongmai-ching hillock and came across Nongpok Ningthou. As soon as she met him, they recalled the happenings in their past generation. They started merry making with a happy singing and dancing.

- **Tribal Dance: Kit Lam:** Kit Lam Dance is an example of the creative skills of Kubuis inhabiting the western hill ranges of Manipur. The Kubui's are well known for their exquisite tribal folk danes and heart throbbing musical renderings. The Kit Lam Dance is particularly known for vigorous and rhythmic covenant in highly sophisticate geometrical shape and design amidst background music and defening sound of the drum.

- **Thang-Ta:** Thang - Ta popularly known worldwide as Martial Art of Manipur is an art for self defence and also for offence having a deep spiritual foundation and long historical tradition right from the Prehistoric times which reminds one of Spartan life-style of the Greek. The agility and strikin movement of the sword men with exciting and artistic gesture makes the art a thriller for the audience.

- **Dhon Dholok Cholom:** Dhon Dholok Cholom is an indispensable part of the great Holi festival and belong to the post Vaishnative Culture of Manipur. Dhon Dholok is popularly known for agility and artistic precision in the part of the percussionists with thudering sound of the drums.

- **Pung Cholom:** Pung Cholom as a part of the Sankirtana music, by the drummers in spotlesswhite costume is known world wide for vigorous and acrobatic style of movement executed with great artistry and presision. The tales numbering more than forty are highly complicated and classical in rhythmic structure.

- **Basanta Ras:** Basanat Ras is one of the five traditional Manipur Ras Leela, based on the Bhagavata tradition of the Sringara Rasa of the Lord Krishna and his Gopies led by Shrimati Radhika as concieved by the great Gurus of Manipur. The Gopies led by Radhika responding to flute of the lord came to the appointed grove and danced together and concluded with the milan of the Lord Krisna and Radhika.

- **Lai Haraoba:** Lai Haraoba means the Festival of Gods. The traditional Lai Haraoba Dance, which enacts the 'Creation of the Universe', was initially a part of the Lai Haraoba festival. The dance is traditionally presented before the shrines of Umanglai, the ancestral God of the Meiteis, at the village temples.

  The principal performers are the maibas (priests) and maibis (priestesses), who are considered to be embodiments of purity. They invoke the deity through their repetitive and rhythmic movements, which are highly symbolic.

- **Kabui Dance:** During the Gang-Ngai festival, the Kabuis, inhabiting the Western hill ranges of Manipur, perform a series of dances in different stylized forms, accompanied by the sound of heavy drums and high pitched songs. The Shim Lam Dance and the Kit Lam Dance are some of dances of the Kabui Nagas. The Shim Lam dance is also known as the Fly Dance. According to Kabui legend, a prophet named Mhung was the creator of laws relating to all living creatures on the earth. Mhung performed a sacrifice called 'Jourumei', to which all the creatures were invited.

  The Kit Lam is a colourful dance performed by the Kabuis to celebrate their harvest. This annual festival mainly involves merrymaking. The rhythmic dance imitates the movement of the crickets.

- **Katabenlu Laam Kabui:** The Katabenlu Laam, which means Bangle Dance, is known for its intricate footwork and rhythmic movements.

- **Takin Taremlaam Kabul:** This dance is also performed at the Gang-Ngai Festival of the Kabuis in January. The Kabuis, through their dances, pay homage to their ancestors and worship the spirits of the home and hearth.

- **Mao Naga Dance:** The Mao Naga Dance is a popular dance of the Mao Naga community of Manipur, who reside in the northern mountains of Manipur.

  Young girls and boys perform the dance during the annual harvesting and seed-sowing festivals (Chikhuni). It involves intricate footwork along with graceful body movements.

- **Luivat Pheizak Dance:** The Luivat Pheizak Dance is one of the most popular dances of the Thangkhul Naga community of Manipur. This dance, which depicts the different stages of cultivation and the simple lifestyle of the Tangkhul Naga community, is performed during all traditional festivals.

- **Thang-Chungoi Yannaba:** This is a duel fight, where both the warriors carry a sword and a shield. The swordsmen use the Chungoi (shield) to protect themselves against possible attacks. The sword and the shield are wielded with agility and precision to thwart all attempts of attack.
- **Ta-Kousaba:** This dance mainly involves the use of the spear and is performed in an open area. There are nien kinds of Khusaral (steps with a spear), evolved by experts over the ages, which have been handed down through generations. In this performance, the artistes select one of the Khausarals and present it in the form of a dance.

  The warrior dancers hold a spear in one hand and a chung (a long shield) in the other. This dance forms part of the Kwak Jatia and Lai-Haraoba festivals.

- **Thang-Ta-Chaieraba:** This dance comprises a duel between the sword and the spear. While one dancer carries a sword and a shield, the other wields a spear but no shield.

  The man carrying the spear performs steps called Khousaba under the overarching principle called Khausaral. The steps used by the swordsman are known as Thanghairol. In this dance, both men try to defend each other's attack.

- **Thang Leitend Haiba:** Also known as decorated sword play, this dance is only performed by highly skilled swordmen. The choreography combines martial steps with complete mastery of the weapon.
- **Chei Khaipa:** This dance forms part of the Thang-Ta repertoire and is performed using one long stick and two shorter ones. It is a form of Cheitek Kotpi, an indigenous Manipuri game.
- **Lhou Sha:** The Lhou Sha is a war dance performed at every confrontation between two villages. The dance from has been preserved as part of the tradition of the Maring community of Manipur and marks the conclusion of significant festivals.

  The dance, which was initially performed by men only, has evolved into a folk art, including the tribe's womenfolk in its ambit.

- **Dhol Cholam:** The Dhol is a large drum used during Manipuri dances, especially on religious occasions. The Dhol Cholom is a form of singing and dancing to the accompaniment of the dhol and is part of the Manipuri Sankirtan tradition.

  Dhol Cholom, which involves the intricate interplay of drums and fire play, is performed during the Yaoshang festival.

- **Pena Cholom:** The Pena is a traditional string instrument of Manipur that is played during Sankirtan and on other religious occasions. In

Pena Cholom, the dancers execute graceful body movements while playing the Pena.

- **Khubak Ishei:** This is a festival dance performed during Rathayatra. The song of Dashavatar is performed while the artistes clap their hands as accompaniment to the dance. Khubak Ishei depicts the Tandava aspect of Manipuri dance.

MARTIAL ARTS

While Manipur is famous for her dances and other performing arts, little is known about the martial arts that are a part of Manipuri life. The grace, rhythem and the speed of the performers are by no means inferior to the dancers. The movements have the affinity to the Mongoloid styles. All such arts were performed at the *Lai-Haraoba* festival.

Some of the forms of Martial Arts and Sports are:

- **Chongba:** Thengou is a systematic pattern of movements sacred and ritualistic, in which the performer with sword or spear executes on the symbolic head of thousand petalled lotus or the *Ananta Nag* called *Pakhangba* in Manipuri, Thengou normally admits nine kinds of movements and it is believed that any mistake on the part of the performer would lead to serious misfortunes in the state. Hence Thengou is a closely guarded art form performed by only a handful that too under strict supervision of the masters.

- **Taa Khousarol (The Spear dance):** Similar to Thengou, Taa Khoursal also has nine kinds. This dance is more secular than Thengou. Every Khoursal has fixed sequences, which are handed down from generation to generations. It demands great skills and agility on the part of the performers. There are solo as well as duet performances as part of rituals and prayers for prosperity. Unlike Thengou, Khousarol is still in active form and is practised by priests and gurus.

- **Thanghairol (Art of Sword fight):** The art of sword fight, apart from the sequences and steps has non Manipuri terms like *Yalak, Kalak, Shut* etc. associated with it because of which it is believed that the art has been influenced and enriched by similar art of fencing in northern India. Although the art was banned by the British as policy of subjugating a warrior race, the old art is being revived again.

- **Mukna (Wrestling-Manipuri Style):** Free from any rituals, Mukna is primarily a sporting event or art participated with competitive spirit. The rules are rigid and there are only a few thrusts and leap associated with the art. Mukna is very popular at the Lai-Haraoba festivals.

Besides the above major martial art forms in Manipur, there are hosts of other popular forms practised by the youth.

FOLK MUSIC

- **Khullang Esei:** One of the most precious folk music of the Meiteis is the Khullang Esei, which is usually delivered in duet. It signifies exchange of romantic emotions between a lad and a lady through highly literary verses in the form of natural tunes without any musical accompaniment. It may also be considered as a tuned dialogue of poetic verses between a male and a female, mostly on romantic themes.

- **Khullong Ishei:** It is a folk song commonly sung by the Meiteis in villages when they go to work in the fields or go for fishing.

- **Pena Ishel:** This song is accompanied with the music produced through Pena. A Pena is a musical instrument, in which a slender bamboo rod is attached to the round dry shell of gourd of coconut.

- **Khubak Esei:** This kind of song is performed by two sides of participants standing at opposite sides and facing at each other. The rhythmic clapping of palms is its accompying music.

- **Ougri:** This is a very ancient type of songs and sung usually in praise of Sun, Moon, Kings etc. It is mostly sung in Lal Haraoba festivals.

- **Thoubal Chongba** is a tuneful song sung during the Thoubal chongba dance. The theme of the song is reglious.

- **Nat** is a classical music which is used during the ceremonies such as marriage, Upanayanams etc.

- **Gaur Padas** are songs in praise of Chaitanya Mahaprabhu.

- **Dhob** is sung with a large cymbal known as Jhal. The song is accompanied with the Manipuri style of beating of the drum.

- **Manohar Sai** are the songs named after Manohar Sai who came to Manipur in 19th century. The songs are accompanied with small cymbals called Ramkaratal and drum called Khol. the songs are devotional.

- **Napi Pala** is a song sung by women. It is a devotional song. The small cymbal called Mandira is used during this song.

- **Khubaishei** is a clapping music. No cymbals are used and the songs are sung accompanied with the clapping of hands. If the Khubaishei is sung by women only, then it is called Nupi khubaishei. It is sung in a standing position.

- **Raslila** songs are a class by themselves due to their special thematic approach. The songs carry deep religious essence. The tribal songs and music have variety and quality.

FAIR AND FESTIVAL

Manipur is a land of festivals. The Festivals run through the entire calender year. The entire cycle is filled with celebrations and festivities so much so that there is some observance or festivity in every month of the year. Fairs and festivals of Manipur not only rejuvenate but act also add sheen to the monotony of people's lives. Hardly a month passes without a festivals which, to the Manipur, is a symbol of his social and religious aspirations. The monotony of life is broken by providing physical diversions, mental recreation and emotional outlets which help one to lead a more relaxed and fuller life. Fairs and festivals of Manipur as a follows:

Yaoshang (Holi)

Celebrated for five days commencing from the full moon day of Phalguna (February/March), Yaoshang is the premier festival of Manipur. The *Thabal Chongba* - a kind of Manipuri folk dance, where boys and girls hold hands together and sings and dance in a circle, is particularly associated with this festival. Yaoshang to Manipur is what Durga Puja is to Bengal, Diwali in north India and Bihu to Assam. Another distinctive feature of the festival is community celebrations. For the purpose of holding community celebrations individuals both young and old rally around the community collecting money for the same.

Kut

It is an autumn festival of the different tribes of Kuki-Chin-Mizo groups of Manipur. The festival has been variously described at different places amongst different tribes as Chavang Kut or Khodou etc. It is a happy occasion for the villagers whose food stock is bountiful after a year of hard labour. It is observed on the 1st November every year.

It is a day of thanks-giving wherein the villagers thank the almighty for the bounty which they have laboured for in the last few years. Song and dance add colour to the festivities.

Gang-Ngai

Celebrated for five days in the month of December/January, Gang-Ngai is an important festival of the Kabui Nagas. The festival opens with the omen taking ceremony on the first day and the rest of the days are associated with common feast, dances of old men women and of boys and girls, presentation of farewell gifts etc. Since 1996 the date of the festivities has been fixed for the 21st January.

Cheiraoba—The Manipur New Year

During the festival special festive dishes are prepared which are first offered to various deities. Celebrated during the month of April, a part of the ritual entails villagers climbing the nearest hill tops in belief that it will enable them to rise to greater heights in their worldly life.

Kang - The Rath Yatra

One of the greatest festivals of the Hindus of Manipur, this festival is celebrated for ten days in the month of July. Lord Jagannath leaves his temple in a car known as 'Kang' in Manipur pulled by devotees who vie with one another for this honour.

Heikru Hitongba

This festival is celebrated in the month of September. Long narrow boats are used to accommodate a large number of rowers. Idol of Lord Vishnu is installed before the commencement of the race.

Ningol Chak-Kouba–A Social Festival

It is a remarkable social festival of the Meiteis. Married daughters of the family come to their parental house along with their children and enjoy sumptuous feast. It is a form of family reunion. It is celebrated on the second day of the new moon in the month of *Hiyangei* (November) as per Manipur Calender system.

Lui-Ngai-Ni

It is a collective festival of the Nagas observed on the 15th day of February every year. This is a seed-sowing festival after which tribes belonging to the Naga group begin their cultivation. Social-gathering, songs, dances and rejoicing highlight the festivity. The annual festival also plays a great role in boosting the moral and strengthening the bond of Naga solidarity.

Chumpha-Festival of Tangkhul Nagas

Celebrated for seven days in the month of December, the *Chumpha* festivals is a great festival of the Tangkhul Nagas. The festival is held after harvest. The last three days are devoted to social gatherings and rejoicing. Unlike other festivals, here women play a special role in the festival.

Christmas-Festival of Christians

Christmas is the greatest festival of all the Christians, observed for two days on December 24 and 25 with merriment, joy and gaiety.

Ramjan Id

Ramjan Id is the most popular festival of the Manipuri Muslims. It is observed in the usual spirit of joy and festivity as done in other muslim worlds. Ramjan is the ninth month of Hijri year.

Lai-Haraoba

Lai Haraoba means the Festival of Gods. The traditional Lai Haraoba Dance, which enacts the 'Creation of the Universe', was initially a part of the Lai Haraoba festival. The dance is traditionally presented before the shrines of Umanglai, the ancestral God of the Meiteis, at the village temples.

The principal performers are the maibas (priests) and maibis (priestesses), who are considered to be embodiments of purity. They invoke the deity through their repetitive and rhythmic movements, which are highly symbolic.

Rasa Lila

In Manipur, there are six Rasa Lilas, These Rasa Lilas are classical dances based on the various episodes in the life of Lord Krishna.

    (a) Kunja Rasa   : On the night of the full moon of Mera/Aswin/October.

    (b) Maharasa   : On the night of the full moon of Hiyangei (Kartik/November)

    (c) Basanta Rasa   : On the night of the full moon of Sajibu (Beisakhi/April)

    (d) Nitya Rasa   : This Rasa is about Radha and Gopies who play with Krishna. It is a stream of happiness, without separation, fear and anger in its theme. It has no specific time for performance.

    (e) Gostha Rasa   : The Gostha Rasa or Gopa Rasa in Manipur takes place on the 8th day of Kartak (Hiyangei/November).

    (f) Udukhol Rasa   : This festival commemorates the early life of LORD KRISHNA. This entertaining Rasa is performed in Manipur in the month of Mera (October-November).

CUSTOMS AND TRADITIONS

Manipur is mosaic of ancient traditions and customs. They are organized in such a manner that in temple institutions those reveal the real festivity and reflect the curious character of socio-religious life of the valley. It involves the ethics and aesthetics of Manipuris. Mass propagation of Hindu customs and traditions in Manipuri society is the indicator of their reverence towards the Hindu deities and temples.

Birth

In Meiteis the rites and rituals are now on the Hindu pattern but certain traditional rituals are also combined. During pregnancy the mother is not restricted on any kind of food. Savasti Puja is conducted on the birth of the child. A day is fixed by the Brahmin.

On the fixed day relatives from the child's mother side visit the house. They come in a procession. This procession is a unique one. The women wear saffron, fanek and white chader and woolen endi or white silk shawl. They carry presents in round baskets in which Muri Laddos, leaves, nuts, kalasa, fish and clothes for the child and the mother are placed.

The procession is arranged in a single file, the women followed by the men. When they reach the house, they keep the gifts around the newly born child. Kirtans are arranged. Kirtan party and the mother and the child sit round the Tulsi plant.

Eepan Thaba

The first ceremony after birth of a human life. On the 6 day of the birth of the child this ceremony is "a must" observed by the people of Manipur both in plain and the hills.

The hill people do not observe nowadays after embracing Christianity yet the people mostly the Meiteis are still observing this important ceremony along with Hindu Vaishnavism rituals.

At the Evening Function

Inside the house on the right side of the entrance door an altar (phambat) has to be made on which things needed for the child like clothes, comb, mirror, neck-chain, book and money will be displayed. Depending on whether the child is boy or girl some variation will be there.

Chaomba (Feeding Ceremony)

Cha-Omba has two words *i.e.* Cha-cooked food and Omba to feed, feeding the normal food. It is a feeding ceremony performed when the child is three month or five or seven months of a boy and six or eight in case of a girl, the child grows it needs foods other than the mother milk to nourish himself. For this reason Cha-Omba feeding ceremony of the child is necessary.

On this day the food of the child has to be arranged on separate dishes that were brought for the child on day of Shashthi Puja. After preparation of food and offering to god the father of the child will put chandan on the forehead of the child and the mother will feed the child keeping on her lap with appropriate words of prayer for at least five times.

COSTUMES

The traditional costumes of north eastern India are known for their colourful and vibrant attire. And Manipuri costumes hold no exception in standing out for their dynamic trends of clothing.

The traditional dresses of Manipuri females differ from occasion to occasion but the major traditional dresses comprise Innaphi, Phanek, Mayek-Naibi, Kanap-Phanek, Lai-Phi, and Chin-Phi.

- Innaphi is a shawl that is worn on the upper body. It's almost transparent in texture, which is a result of the way it's woven.
- Phanek is a hand woven dress like a sarongand is most commonly worn by Manipuri women. It's a wraparound skirt like dress. The traditional Phanek would be mostly either block colors or striped.
- A special type of Phanek is called Mayek-Naibi. The speciality and beauty of this Phanek is the horizontal stripes, which sure does beautifies the wearer of this dress.
- Kanap-Phanek, is a traditional cloth which is stitched by Meitai females.
- Lai-Phi is a yellow bordered beautiful white cloth.
- Chin-Phi, a Phanek full of embroidery, are the major traditional costumes of Manipuri women amongst several other costumes worn during several ceremonies.

Meitai women, usually, team up Phanek and Innaphi with a saree blouse. Along with the Manipuri females, men also have very distinctive traditional clothing. The traditional clothing for men comprises turban (which is called as "Pagdhi"), a jacket and a dhoti.

There is a special type of dhoti called KhamenChatpa; it's worn by superior members of the society during rituals and ceremonies. In ancient times, KhamenChatpa was given as reward to brave people by the king as the token of appreciation.

Different occasions call for different kinds of dressing in Manipur. They have different traditional attires that are worn during specific festivals. For example, during Rasa Leela Kumins and Potlois is worn.

And there are many other dresses which are worn during different dance festivals. Tribals in Manipur wear Phiranji, Lmaphie, Ningthoupee, and Saijounba.

As the state's economy developed and westernisation influence increased, it affected the fashion sense of the people in Manipur accordingly. Youngsters can be seen wearing shirts, tees, jackets, skirts, and jeans.

This change or modernisation is also due to the influence of Christianity. But as much as the modern or fashionable dresses have found its place in Manipur, the people are still inclined towards wearing their traditional costumes.

Modernisation has got the traditional attire modified to some extent and old designs of cloths have got a new modern-day look. The best example would be the women of Manipur wearing Innaphi with modern skirts.

Innaphi, are now made up of cotton and silk but in ancient times it was made up of bark of creepers named Uriphi. Now modern sarongs are used as skirts, shawls and also as beach wear.

FOOD AND FLAVOUR

The traditional Manipuri fine dining was a literally 'sit-down' affair with banana-leaf plates. Their love for rice can be seen in every household. Some take rice with meat, and some others prefer a fish delicacy along with the main dish. In fact Kabok, a traditional speciality, is mostly fried rice with a world of vegetables added in. The Iromba, an eclectic combination of fish, vegetables and bamboo shoots is served fermented. Along with all these, Manipuri menu of food and flavour contains many other delicious items. Some of them are given below:

- Heithongba is a pungent dish of lemon, sugar, salt, amla (Indian gooseberry) or tamarind.

- Moroi Morok Thongba, meaning different types of vegetables or 'little plants', is another speciality. Morok stands for green chillies so this dish may be a bit hot to taste.

- Madhur Jhan is a sweet made of milk, sugar and gram flour.

- Manipuri cuisine is a unique experience in itself. Their vegetarian thali is famous. Traditionally served at the Govindji temple on plantain leaves, it is very elaborate and has at least 20-25 items. The rice is served in the middle and little bowls made of plantain leaves surrounds it. They are used for serving chutney, lentils, vegetables and other preparations.

- A black lentil called Uti is compulsory at all feasts. Vegetables consist of cauliflower called Sak, pumpkin made into a hot and spicy curry, spinach, banana flower and a wonderful salad called Singju made of very finely shredded vegetables and raw papaya tossed in herbs.

- A dessert made of rice called Chak Sao is deep violet in colour and is combined with milk, sugar, coconut and dry fruits.
- Suktani is a combination of neem leaves, basak leaves and sugar.
- Sweet Kabok, made up of molasses and rice, is a famous name among the Manipuris.

  This and more make up the ceremonial thali. A normal thali has three to four items. Eromba chutney, a special fish delicacy of this state, is an essential part of every meal. It is made of fermented fish and bamboo shoot with chillies, boiled vegetables and potato.

- Fish is also an important part of Manipuri cuisine and is cooked in numerous ways.
- The drink called shekmai, made in a village with the same name, is a famous country wine of the state.
- **Chicken Chatni :** Simple boiled chicken mixed with chilli, ginger, native onion and spices.
- **Hancham :** Known in Mietei dialect as champhut, it is simple boiled vegetables without any spices.
- **Khamui :** Baked bread with special sticky rice. There are two methods of preparation; one is fried and the other is baked into cakes then wrap with panama or cardamom leaves and boiled.
- **Vaitei :** Ordinarily known as Khor, it is prepared with floured rice (sticky rice) made to ferment in a jar-filled water with floured sprouted-paddy grains.
- **Chakhan :** For those who don't relish the above drinks, simple fully boiled sticky rice with some soluble sweetening items are used.
- **Chathur :** Preparation, same as Vaitei as also the materials, but let to cool and ferment. This is used as cold drink.

FINE ART EDUCATION

Under Fine Art Education, grant-in-aid to Manipur State Kala Academy and Imphal Art College was extended for organising festivals/seminar/symposium etc. During the year 2001-02, Shri Shri Bal Mukunda Dev Music College and Govt. Dance College were established. The construction of cultural complex has been taken up during the said year.

The Imphal Art College, the only College of its kind in Manipur has been functioning as a standard college comparable to other Arts Colleges of other states. The College has been affiliated to Manipur University. The total number of students during the year 2014-15 was 67.

The Government Dance College has been functioning with the objectives of propagation and spread of knowledge of Manipur Dance, its pristine, purity among the people of' Manipur and other states of India. Altogether 77 student were undergoing various courses in the fields of classical Manipur Dance and Folk dances of Manipuri Laiharouba, Kabui dance and Mao dance etc. During the year 2014-15, 239 students were enrolled in Govt. Music College (now renamed as Shri Shri Bal Mukunda Dev Music College).

PROMOTION OF ARTS & CULTURE

The Manipur State Kala Academy: It is a composite Centre of Sahitya, Fine Arts and Dance & Music are regularly implementing various programmes in order to promote the unique cultural heritage of the state. 64 cultural personalities have got National Awards in different fields of culture w.e.f. 1956 till date. The Academy is conducting Sumang Leela Festival in regular basis. Under promotion of Art and Culture, the grant-in-aids are extended to voluntary organisation working in the, field of theatre, dance and music, public libraries and also to Manipur Film Development Corporation.

The Manipur Film Development Corporation Limited: It came into existence in 1987. It was established with the objective of upliftment of film industry in the state. Till date Manipur could produce 56 feature films and 50 documentary films. These have earned prestigious awards both at the national (10 nos.) and international (9 nos.) levels. This is definitely no mean achievement as the film lovers of the state toil under impossible circumstances.

ARCHIVES

The state Archives collects a number of valuable old records from the government departments/semi government offices/custodian and from individuals for preservation. The reprographic unit and micro film units have also been maintained to take necessary measures for the preservation and rehabilitation of the valuable records.

The state Archives is preserving the noncurrent records including books, papers, maps, photographs etc. which are more than 25 years old and other record which are less than 25 years old. A proposal for construction of a permanent 'Stack Area' was submitted under the 12th Finance Commission as first phase.

LIBRARY

There are 10 Government public libraries in Manipur. This includes 1 central library at Imphal, 8 hill district libraries, and one branch library of the State Central Library, Impha1 at Ningthoukhong of Bishnupur district. Moreover, there are 130 beneficiary, libraries run by clubs/voluntary organisations/ libraries which are reorganised by the State Government and treated as public libraries. After the State Central Library was burnt on 13.4.05, the library started running in the new building at the State Central Library and Manipur State Archives at Keishampat. Now, there are 47,234 books and 51 Nos. of regular News paper/journals.

ARCHAEOLOGY

The State Archaeology office has been conducting numerous systematic exploration and scientific excavation at different parts of the state.The important Pre-historic sites of (i) Khangkhui Cave, Ukhrul district (ii) Napachik Wangoo, Bishnupur district (iii) Nongpok Keithelmanbi, Thoubal district (iv) Tharon Cave and Rock Shifters Tamenglong district etc. were the results of these systematic excavation and exploration. Besides these, Proto-historic and historical sites of (1) Sekta Kei Mound, Sekta, Imphal East district (2) Khamrou, Imphal West district (3) Sangai Yumpham. Langthabal and (4) Koutruk, Imphal West district etc. have also been discovered and excavated. Till date 37 historical monuments have been declared as protected monuments and 861 Antiquites and Art objects have been registered.

Under the State Plan Assistance, the State Archaeology will develop the Maharaja Gambhir Singh Memorial Samadhi, Langthabal within 2007-08.

MUSEUM

Having been established on 23rd September, 1969, Manipur State Museum has now become a full-fledge Museum. At present, it has 7 Gallaries viz. (i) Ethnological Gallary (2) Archaeological Gallary (3) Natural History Gallary (4) Children's Gallery (5) Art Gallery and (6) Jallan's Gallery (7) Hiyang Hiren open Art Gallary. There is also one Museum at the INA Memorial Complex, Moirang where the museum objects of the 2nd world war particularly for the Indian National Army (INA) has been exhibiting. The latest collection by the State Museum are (a) Personal belongings of Potsangbam Mani Singh, Nongthombam/Pukhramba (b) Tribal ornaments (c) A very rare fossil (tooth) of Elephant presented by Sadokpam Rajeshwor

Singh, Phaknung Awang Leikai (d) 50 nos. of stamps presented by O. Tomba Singh (e) Shami Lanmi Phee presented by Meisnam Lalini Devi, Wangkhei and (f) Personal property of Ph. Madhumangol Sharma, who served as Hanjaba during Maharaj Budhachandra.

Manipur State Museum

This museum, located near the Imphal Pologround has a fairly good display of the state's heritage and a collection of portraits of Manipur's former rulers. Items of special interests are costumes, arms and weapons, relics and historical documents.

The Manipur State Museum was inaugurated by the late Prime Minister of India, Smt. Indira Gandhi on 23rd September, 1969. During 39 years, this Museum has become a fullfledged multipurpose Museum comprising of various Galleries like—Ethnology, Archaeology, Natural History, Painting, Jallan, Children's Gallery and an open air gallery for housing the 78ft long boat called Hiyang Hiren (Royal boat).

Apart from the normal functions of Museum, it took up various activities like Museum awareness programmes, Conservation of Biological specimens, Cultural appreciation course, Science fairs, Thematic exhibition, Mobile exhibition etc.

Manipur State Museum has also taken up numerous sponsor programmes through National and International Museums.

Sekta Archaeological Living Museum

Sekta Mound locally known as "Sekta Kei" is a protected archaeological site. The historical hotspot is located at Sekta village, about 16kms from Imphal on the Imphal-Ukhrul Road. It is a place where evidence of the practice of secondary burial was discovered. The site was jointly excavated by the Archaeological Survey of India and the State Archaeologists.

Some of the other state's well-known museums include Muttua Museum in Imphal, INA Martyrs Memorial Museum in Moirang, Tribal Museum and Research Centre in Sagotband and Kakching's People Museum.

Important Places of Worship

All the communities and religions celebrate their respective religious festivals or days with devotion and unflinching commitment.

Kangla Temple	—	4th Assam Rifles Ground
Sanamahee Temple	—	1st Batalion, M.R.
Jain Digamber Temple	—	Paona Road
Govindajee Temple	—	Palace Ground
Iskon Temple	—	Airport Road
Hanuman Thakur Temple	—	Near Palace Ground
Gurdwar Temple	—	Thangal Bazar
Jame Masjid	—	Masjid Road
Hiyangthang Lairembi Temple	—	Hiyangthan
M.B.C. Central Church	—	Deulahland
Moirang Thangjing Temple	—	Moirang

● ● ●

Transport and Communication

Transport and Communication is the basic infrastructure needed for generation of economic activity and for bringing about prosperity and well being in the state. A well developed transport and communication system plays a vital role in ensuring sustained economic growth. Development activities of this sector generated large employment opportunities. Manipur is served by two means of transport viz., roads and airways. The existing facilities of transport and communication are not adequate which continued to be a major constraint in the development process of the state.

ROAD TRANSPORT

Roads are the lifeline of the people of the state as the only means of transport for the state is the surfaced communication and road link in the accessible terrains. As such road has a special importance as vital infrastructure for economic development of the state. High priority is given in the plans and programme for construction of roads to develop the economy.

National Highway

National Highway is a highway which is declared as such under the National Highway Act, 1956. The National Highway system is the primary road grid of the state.

Highways and roads are regarded as arteries and veins of a state which are essential for its growth. The main artery of communication is the National High-way No. 39 connecting Imphal with Dimapur in the neighboring state of Nagaland. It runs through Mao in the extreme north of Manipur to the International border town of Moreh in the south-east. Dimapur is the railhead for road traffic to the state and in fact, this road is for so long her life line. The road passes through the hilly area of Senapati District and part of Nagaland Hill touching Kohima in between. The transport cost on this road is very high in view of frequent landslides on the hill tracts, restriction of transport services during night time due to unexpected events and one way trade movement because of little exports from Manipur.

Another road of' considerable economic importance is the 225 kms. long National Highway No. 53 viz. New Cachar Road, connecting Imphal with Jirighat in Manipur Assam border. It passes through dense forests and difficult terrains of Tamenglong District which remained, by far, the most inaccessible district in the state. The opening of this road brings the District closer to other parts, helps in exploring untapped resources of the district and give incentives for more production and general development besides being a second life-line for the state. For this, State of Manipur, the road needs further development in order to be the main life-line of the state.

State Highways and Major District Roads

The state Highways and major district roads form the secondary road system and take care of collection and distributary functions. The total length of State Highways was 1623 kms. at the end of March, 1998 and it has decreased to 675 kms. by the end of March, 1999 showing a decrease of 58.41 per cent over the previous year. The total length of State Highways in the state has remained unchanged till the end of 31st March, 2002. The length of surfaced road of National Highway was 1,745 Kms in 2017. On the other hand, the other roads like State Highways, PWD Roads, Rural Road, Urban Road and Project Road have changed over the years. The length of road according to category is presented in Table below.

Length of Road in Manipur

(In kms.)

Classification of Road	2012		2013	
	Total	Surfaced	Total	Surfaced
National Highways	1317	1317	1317	1317
State Highways	1137	1137	715	620
PWD Roads	8305	3475	9404	3407
Rural Road	6680	2964	7635	3919
Urban Road	212	156	166	111
Project Road	1600	1408	1601	1601

Source: Statistical Year Book, All India (MoSPI, GoI)

Manipur State Road Transport Corporation

In view of the geographical feature of Manipur, Road Transport is the only cheap and quick means of transport for the state. Consequently, there is need for greater thrust towards providing safe, comfortable, cheap and adequate facilities for transportation of passengers and essential commodities. With this in view, the existence of a State Road Transport Corporation Ltd. and its improvement is essential in the public interest.

The Manipur State Road Transport Corporation (MSRTC) plays an important social role in covering areas/routes which are not considered attractive and profitable for the private sector road transport enterprises.

Greater mobility of people has a crucial role in the economic and social growth of the country. Public sector role in passenger transport has been increasing since enactment of the Road Transport Corporation Act, 1950 which provided efficient, economic, adequate and co-ordinating public transport on business principles. MSRTC has played a very important role in bringing national integrity and communal harmony by operating its services in the remote areas.

AIR TRANSPORTATION

Manipur has an airport located at the capital city, Imphal. The airport at Imphal is the second largest airport in the Northeast region. There are regular flights from the Imphal airport to all the major cities like Kolkara, New Delhi, Pune, Aizwal, Silchar and Guwahati.

Indigo, Indian Airlines and Jetlite offers frequent flights 4 to 6 days a week. To further improve the air connectivity night landing facility is ready and airfield is being expanded to increase parking space for eight aircraft at a time.

Imphal Airport

The Imphal airport is the main airport in Manipur. The Imphal Airport is the second International airport in the northeast region, after Guwahati. The airport connects all the important towns and cities of India.

RAILWAY CONNECTIVITY

The state has neither railways nor navigable waterways and the transport system is synonymous with road communication. The only major functional railhead linking Manipur with the rest of India is at Dimapur town of Nagaland state which is 215 kms. away from Imphal. A railhead has been extended from Silchar to Jiribam. It covers only 1.5 kms. of railway line over the state of Manipur. The second railway line will be between Karong in Senapati district and Diphu in Assam through Dhansiri. The foundation stone was laid on November 17, 1998.

COMMUNICATION

Allied to the transport system is the communication system. The communication system comprises of postal services, telegraph services, telephone services etc. There has been a steady growth in the postal and telecommunication facilities in the state. There were 1394 post offices and 1 telegraph office in the year 2012-13.

Postal Facilities in Manipur

(in nos.)

Year	Post Office	Population served Per Post Office	Telegraph Office
2000-01	692	3342	2
2001-02	691	3457	2
2002-03	694	3442	2
2003-04	697	3501	3
2004-05	697	3572	3
2005-06	697	3644	3
2006-07	697	NA	2
2007-08	697	NA	1
2008-09	697	NA	1
2009-10	697	NA	1
2010-11*	1394	NA	1
2011-12	1394	NA	1
2012-13	1394	NA	1
2013-14	1394	NA	NA

*NA: Not Available * upto 31-12-2011*

Source: 1. Directorate of Postal Services, Manipur.

There were 48245 telephone connection in the state as on 31st March 2006 showing an increase of 3.94 per cent over the previous year, 2004-2005. However, from 2006-07 onward the number of telephone connection shows a decline. There were 47631 connection in the year 2006-07 and again in the year 2007-08 there were 34507 connection which depicts a decrease of 27.55% over the previous year 2006-07. However, in the year 2009-10 there were 32613 connection against 31241 connection in the previous year 2008-09 with an increase of 4.39 per cent. There were 28,458 telephone connection in the state during 2010-11 as on 31st March. But, in the year 2011-12, there were 28,150 connections.

District wise Telecommunication Facilities in Manipur, 2015-16

(in nos.)

Sl. No.	District/State	Telegraph Office	Telephone Exchange	Telephone Working (DEL)	P.C.Os. (Local/STD/ Trunk)
1.	Senapati	—	9	1,089	70
2.	Tamenglong	—	2	463	7
3.	Churachandpur	—	4	1,219	29
4.	Chandel	—	4	985	55
5.	Ukhrul	—	1	563	35
6.	Imphal East	—	5	2,180	208
7.	Imphal West	—	13	12,203	403
8.	Bishnupur	—	5	427	5
9.	Thoubal	—	6	2,319	120
	Manipur State	—	49	21,448	961

- Nil Source: Office of the Telecom, District Manager, Imphal.

AIR & DOORDARSHAN

First Manipuri Programme was broadcast through AIR Gauhati for a period of 45 minutes only daily. It was somewhere around 1957-58. But, for Manipuri programmes, it was not too far away from their own station when All India Radio, Imphal commenced its public service broadcasting with a modest setup on 15th August 1963 under the station directorship of R.K. Acharya. Initially, it was consisting of a pilot studio and a 200 watt Medium wave (MW) transmitter. Within a couple of years, it was augmented to a one killowatt (kw) transmitter. This transmitter enabled AIR to cover Imphal town and surrounding villages only. The pilot studio was housed in the present Raj Bhavan complex and the transmitter in the DM college campus. To cover the entire state of Manipur, a 50 KW MW high power transmitter was commissioned near the Mayang Imphal village in a site measuring 34.5 acres in October 1972. This improved the coverage of the station substantially to an extent of 75% of the area of Manipur state. Studio center was shifted to present location at Palace compound during 1980.

Captive generators have been provided at the studio complex for operating the studios and FM transmitter. Studio setup consists of a drama, music and talk studio along with dubbing room and control room. Consider in still there are number of uncovered packets in the hill terrain, a SW transmitter of 50 kw was installed and commissioned on 1992 at Mayang Imphal center. Presently, AIR is successfully disseminating the state's culture and values through its wide reach.

From January 29, 2004, a Manipur Programme called 'LEIKOL' is being broadcast in AIR Delhi under the Bhasha Bharati Programme.

On the other hand first Doordarshan (TV) Kendra of Manipur was started on 30th April 1992 from Porompat, while the more entertaining version of Doordarshan, Metro Channel, was started on 23rd December, 1995.

NEWSPAPER & JOURNALS

Having situated in the easternmost corner of India, the wave of journalism could be felt only in the early part of 1920s. It is believed that, newspapers published from Calcutta have a great influence on the masses thereby signalling the idea of journalism in the state of Manipur. It may be pointed out that, geographical isolation, communication bottleneck, backwardness of the people may be some of the reasons for the lackadaisical development of the forth estate in Manipur.

History has it that, 'Meitei Chanu' was the first print journal in Manipur. It was edited by Hijam Irabot Singh during 1925-26. However, the journal could not survived long and it vanished away from the news stand after 5/6 issues were brought out. In 1933, another paper 'Dainik Manipur' was published under the editorship of Gokulchandra at the Churachand Printing Press. The paper was believed to be widely read not only in Manipur but also in Assam and neighbouring states. The publication discussed about religions, custom and traditions and political structure of the time. The newspaper, with a daily circulation of about 1,000 copies was known for its critical views against the then British Government in Manipur. The result was that, the newspaper had to be closed after five years of publication under the diktat of the Government.

In 1937, yet another newspaper 'Manipur Matam' was published from Tarun Press. The paper, edited by Rajkumar Shitaljit Singh hardly survived for about three years. It has a circulation of around 300 copies a day and was also believed to be circulated in Assam. By the early parts of 1939, a bi-weekly paper 'Manipur Paojel' was launched in Manipur. In those days, cases against journalists were not uncommon. Because of the Press in Manipur were a part of the Freedom Movement, the Government of the day came down heavily on them. K. Kunjabihari, an independent journalist was summoned by the Manipur Darbar and Sadar Panchayat. He became the first ever journalist in the State to have been put under bar. Due to a strong stand taken by the then British Government against the press, publication of newspaper/magazines were virtually impossible in those days. However, a concerted effort were made to bring out newspaper/magazine against all odds. In 1948, one year after India won her Freedom, a weekly magazine 'Praja' was published under the editorship of Loitam Yaima. A new chapter of journalism was witnessed after India won Independence from the British rule.

Statehood and the Press

The State of Manipur witnessed a sudden increase of newspapers and magazines after the attainment of full-fledged state in 1972. There was a big wave of journalism brewing in all parts of the State. The people of Manipur, particularly the 'hoi polloi' started to understand the importance of media in development process. Awareness among the public was visibly increasing. A new gear of media spirit was added to the journalists' community following the attainment of statehood. It is, therefore, no surprising to see the number of newspapers and magazines increasing by leaps and bounds. In the process, a new trend of journalism took its shape with political parties taking keen interest in media.

First in Newspapers and Magazines

Newspapers/Magazines	Name of the Publication (Year)	First Editor
❖ First Manipuri magazine	Meitei Leima (1917-18)	A. Thambou Singh
❖ First daily newspaper	Dainik Manipur Patrika (1932)	Gokulchandra Singh
❖ First journal	Meitei Chanu (1922)	Hijam Irabot
❖ First English journal	Meitei Leirang (1969)	—
❖ First weekly magazine	Praja (1948)	Loitman Yaima
❖ First bi-weekly newspaper	Manipur Paojel (1939)	K. Kunjabihari
❖ First Health journal	Meitei Maiba	Sagolsem Indramani

FILM & DRAMA

Manipur's first produced film, 'Meipak, Son of Manipur', was a documentry. It was released in 1972. However, the first attempted Manipuri film of Manipur was 'Mainu Pemcha'. A part of it was made in 1948-49 but unfortunately remaining parts of this movie could not be completed. On the other hand the beginning of staging Drama in Manipuri Language (Meeteilon) may be said to have first started from the year 1914 when students of Johnstone High School, Imphal staged a Drama called Arjungi Maithiba (Partha Parajay) in one of the earliest Manipuri Dramas that won First position in All India Drama Competition in 1954 was M.D.U's "Haorang Leishang Saphabee".

Some interesting facts about Manipur's film industry are:

- Manipur's first Feature Film was K.T. Films' "Matamgi Manipur". It was a 35 mm. Black and White film. It was released in April, 1972.

- 'Imagee Ningthem' of Manipur is a film which got International Award of the first time in the history of film world of Manipur.

- Manipur started producing colour feature films from the year 1985 onwards. The first colour feature film of Manipur is "Langlen Thadoi".

- "Brojendrogi Luhongba" was Manipur's second Feature Film. Late S.N.Chand produced and acted in the film.

- Movie "Matamgee Manipur" won a President Award in 1972. While N.S. Films' "Saphabee" in 1976 and "Olangthagi Wangmadasoo" in the year 1980.

- Leikhendro Singh in the film 'Imagee Ningthem' won a National Award for child actor.

- "Imagee Ningthem" won both National and International Award including Grand Pix at Nantes International Film Festival in 1982.

- The documentary film "Sangai" directed by the well-known director A. Shyam Sharma won five merit awards in the 12th International Film Festival of wild life in USA in the year 1989.

- "Sangai" was also declared as the outstanding film of the year at the London Film Festival in 1989.

- Another short and documentary film 'Pebet' directed by H. Kanhailal also won both National and International Award.

- "Eshanou" won awards at International level.

- "Sana Keithel" won a National Award.

- "Sanabi" and "Chatle-do Edi" also got National Awards.
- First Manipuri Women Film Producer is Smt. Khaidem Sakhi Devi (in "Langlen Thadoi") 1984.
- Manipuri Film's First Manipuri Play-back Singers were— *Male*–Bhudhachandra; *Females*—(i) Kamala & (ii) Jamuna.
- First Music Director of Manipuri Films is Aribam Shyam Sharma (in the film "Matamgi Manipur").
- First Manipuri Film Hero was Robindro Sharma.
- First Manipuri Film Heroine was Rashi Devi.
- "Manipur Film Development Council" was established in 1980 and it become a Corporation in 1987.
- "Film Society, Manipuri" was established in 1966.
- Imphal Cine Club was established in 1979 to promote good quality film in Manipur.
- Shree Shree Govindajee Film Company, established in 1946-47, was Manipur's Pioneer film making Organization.

First in Manipuri Film and Drama

❖ First Manipuri Feature Film	: Matamgi Manipur (9th April 1972) Directed by : Debkumar Bose
❖ First Manipuri Coloured Movie	: Langlen Thadoi (1984) Directed by : Kh. Pramodini
❖ First Manipuri Documentary Film	: Maipak–the Son of Manipur (November 9, 1971) Directed: Debkumar Bose
❖ First Manipuri-Full length Feature Film	: Langlen Thadoi (1984) Directed by : Kh. Pramodini
❖ First Manipuri Film Producer	: Karam Manmohan Singh (K.T. Films).
❖ First Manipuri Film Director	: S.N. Chand
❖ First Manipuri Film Actor	: Robindro Sharma
❖ First Manipuri Film Actress	: Rashi Devi
❖ First Manipuri Film to receive the best Feature Film Award in the Manipur State Film Festival	: Imagee Ningthem (1981) Directed by : Aribam Shyam Sharma

❖ First Manipuri Feature Film in direct 35 mm colour format	: Madhabee (1993) Directed by : L. Banka Sharma
❖ First Manipur Child to get the Best Child Actor Award	: Leikhendra Singh (At 8 years of age)
❖ First Manipuri Film to receive the best documentary film in the non-feature category in the first Manipur State Film Festival	: Sanaleibak Manipur (1980) Directed by : Aribam Shyam Sharma
❖ First Manipuri Documentary Film to be ever screened publicly	: Meipak the son of Manipur (1997) Directed by : Debkumar Bose
❖ First Manipuri Film, which is also the first Indian film to receive the prestigious "Grand Prix" at the Nante International Film Festival.	: Imagee Ningthem (1982). Directed by : Aribam Shyam Sharma
❖ First Manipuri film to be screened in Indian Panorama	: Matamgi Manipur
❖ First Manipuri Film to receive the President's Medal in the 20th National Film Festival	: Matamgi Manipur (1972).
❖ First Attempted Manipuri Feature Film	: Mainu Pemcha (Around the year 1948-49)
❖ Pioneer Film Making Organisation of Manipur	: Shree Shree Govindajee Film Company (Estd. 1946-47).
❖ Pioneer Film Society of Manipur	: Manipuri Film Society (Estd. 1966)
❖ First Manipuri play	: Narasingha (1925)
❖ Manipur's first permanent theatre house	: Manipur Friends Dramatic Union (1930)

Manipur Film Development Corporation

It is an autonomous body set for the promotion and development of film industry in the state of Manipur. It regularly organizes National Film Festivals etc. and perform many activities for the promotion of film industry in Manipur. It is located at Palace Compound, Imphal.

Manipur State Film Development Society (MSFDS)

The Manipur Film Development Corporation Limited (MFDC) is the successor to the erstwhile Manipur Film Development Council. The MFDC is a Public Undertaking and was registered as a Corporation in 1987 under the Companies Act (Act 1 of 1956) at the office of the Registrar of Companies, North East States of India, Shillong (Meghalaya).

Objectives & Functions

With an authorized share capital of ₹ 1.5 Crore, MSFDS was launched to promote and propagate film industry in the State. Its main objectives are to promote, develop, aid and assist to the cinematography trade and industry, and all of its allied and kindred trades and businesses, particularly the business of construction and running of studios, laboratories and theatres for the production of films, both celluloid and digital videos; television programs, organization of national and international film festivals, establishment of Film Archives, Library and Museum for the development of film industry on modern lines.

Tourism

Manipur, a little Shangrila located in North-East India, is a Jewel of India. This little corner is a paradise on Earth where Mother Nature has been extra generous in her bounty. Least touched and least discovered Manipur promises to be the great tourist discovery of the 21st century.

An oval shaped valley surrounded by blue green hills, rich in art and tradition has inspired description such as the "Switzerland of the East" with its cascading rapids, tripling rivers, varieties of flowers, exotic blooms and lakes. The people of Manipur include Meitei, Nagas, Kuki-Chin-Mizo and Gorkhas groups and Muslims and other colourful communities which have lived in complete harmony for centuries.

These are the people whose folklore, myths and legends, dances, indigenous games and martial arts, exotic handlooms and handicrafts are invested with the mystique of nature and an indefatigable "Joie de vivre".

The Department of Tourism, Government of Manipur came in to existence in August, 1972 as a publicity wing of the IPR Department. Over the years it has evolved into an independent department, considering the natural beauty and potential of the State, every effort should be taken to make it an efficient and vital department of Tourism in the State.

The State of Manipur, though tiny in size has immense scope for promotion of tourism with an area of only 22,327 sq. kms. It is situated in the eastern-most fringe of the country. It has a salubrious climate, exotic greenery and rich flora besides the rich culture. The State can broadly be divided into two parts, the valley and the hill. The location of the valley is such that it is being surrounded by a rows of rolling hills forming preventive barrier isolating the state from the rest of the country.

There are many places in Manipur which can be developed as tourist centres. Keibul Lamjao National Park on the bank of the Loktak Lake, the only habitat of Brow Antlered Deer locally known as 'Sangai'. INA (Indian National Army) Memorial at Moirang where INA hoisted tricolour flag for the first time on Indian soil, Siroy National Park at Ukhrul, Loktak lake, the biggest fresh water lake in the North-Eastern Region and Khongjom War Memorial, where the last war of Manipur Independence was fought, are the major tourist spot of the state. Besides there are other places which are worth seeing and which possessed immence potential for developing into a good tourist spot.

PILGRIMAGE TOURISM

Temples in Manipur are remarkable pilgrimage sites which makes the trip to this state more captivating. Almost all the temples of Manipur are created on Brahmanical rules of **Vastu Shastra** and have the Mandapas. The architectural style of the temples in Manipur resembles the Bengal temple architecture. The Vishnu temple of Bishanpur town in Manipur is the oldest temple of the state. This temple is a significant religious structure of Manipur and is an important pilgrimage site. The temple is a eminent pilgrimage sight of the Hindus. Shri Govindaji temple in Manipur is one of the most visited religious centers of the state. It is a popular Hindu temple and the deities worshipped here are the Hindu gods, Radha and Krishna Govinda. Located in an easily accessible place in the capital of the state, Imphal, the temple is visited by large numbers of pilgrims every year. The tourists also have a high regard for the temple structure. Built of red bricks, the temple features a rectangular medieval style of architecture.

NATURE TOURISM

The Keibul Lamjao National Park is one of its major tourist attractions. Located near the capital city of Imphal, this is a must visit tourist spot of Manipur. The sight of rare animals and birds is a delight for the nature lovers. Spread over forty square kilometers of wetland, the Keibul Lamjao National Park is debatably the world's only floating sanctuary. Apart from the foliage and topography the park consists of the Loktak Lake, which is the biggest freshwater lake in India. The star appeal, of the park is the browantlered deer. This is a breed of the Thamin deer. Because of its fragile way of walking it is also affectionately called Manipur's dancing deer. Other species of deer seen here comprise the hog deer, sambar and muntjac. Various birds such as the Waterfowl, the Hooded Crane, the Black Eagle and the Shaheen Falcon are found here. The major fresh water lake of Manipur is the Loktak Lake which is also well known by the name of 'Floating Lake' as it one of the exceptional lakes in the world which have the Phundies or floating islands on it. Tourists visiting the lake can also go for the nearby attraction which is the ancient temple of the pre-Hindu deity, Lord Thangjing, located in the Moirang. The Zoological gardens in Manipur is a prime attraction of the place. Flocks of vacationers stopover in the Zoological Gardens to see the diverse species of animals and birds that are kept there. The Zoological Gardens in Manipur is a well-maintained garden that is located at a distance of about six kilometers from Imphal in Manipur in India. A trip to the Zoological Gardens is actually a pleasant expedition for family and friends. The Khonghampat Orchidarium in Manipur is a nature lover's delight. The comforting fragrance of the flowers and wide-ranging colours refreshes the mind and spirit of the tourists. More than hundred and ten varieties of orchids, including quite a few rare species, are grown here.

LEISURE TOURISM

The Shahid minar in Manipur is a must see tourist location. The monument is an emblem of the bravery of the valiant soldiers who laid down their lives for their nation. The war cemetery in Manipur is also a popular destination. This place is toured by large numbers of visitors every year. The Manipur War Cemetery is an emblematic memorial raised as a reference for the supreme human sacrifices made by the officers and men of the associated forces during the Second World War. Ukhrul is the highest hill station of the state of Manipur. Siroi hills and Khang Khui lime caves are striking excursion destinations in this place. The Khayang peak is the highest peak of the region and the tourists from here can have exquisite views around the place. The Khangkhui Cave is an outstanding natural lime stone cave in Ukhrul and is a popular visiting site for the tourists. Langthabal in Manipur is a small hill situated about eight kilometers from Imphal. The place houses an old significant palace and efficiently planned temples. The different structures found here are marvelously placed between pine and jackfruit trees. Langthabal offers an impressive sight of the well-known Manipur University. This picturesque place is a must see location of Manipur. The Manipur State Museum focuses on tribal costumes, jewellery and weapons along with geological, archeological and natural history displays.

IMPORTANT ATTRACTIONS

Loktak Lake and Sendra Island: One of the most enchanting and biggest fresh-water lakes in the north-east is the Manipur's Loktak Lake. The Sendra Island Tourist Bungalow offers dazzling views of the lake, its rich plant and avian life and the intriguing floating weed, shallow bowl-like islands (Phumdi) and the fishermen who live on them harvesting water chestnuts.

Situated in the middle of the lake, the tourist home has a cafe and makes an ideal look-out. Boating has been introduced along the lake's labyrinthine waterways.

Also on the southern part of the lake is the world's only floating national park, the Keibul Lamjao National Park, a unique habitat of the rare Sangai, the brow antlered deer or the 'dancing deer'. The entire lake complex is a wildlife enthusiast's dream.

Sadu Chiru Waterfall: Sadu Chiru waterfall is more popular known as Keimaram fall because of its closeness to Leimaram in the Bishnupur District of Manipur. It is around 29 km from Imphal and fall under the Senapati District.

The waterfall is 15 m high and came cascading down from thich tropical forest. There are two more falls hidden beneath this green forest, but they are not open to public, because of the precarious and sheep landscape.

Kaina: Occupying an important place in the hearts of Hindus, Kaina is a famous religious centre of Manipur. It is a hillock elevated to a height of 921 m above sea level. It is located only 29 km from Imphal, the capital city of Manipur. It is a peaceful place gifted with picturesque location.

Kangla: Kangla is situated close to the banks of the Imphal River. The Kangla fort or Kangla palace is a symbol of Manipur's glory. Kangla was the ancient capital of Manipur and a number of Meitei monarchs have ruled the destination from this fort.

Singola: Singola is situated at a distance of about 16 kilometers, west of Imphal. Singola located at a height of 921 meters above sea level. It overlooks an artificial lake and the Manipur valley. Singola dam is a multipurpose project which is constructed at the Singola river in Kangchus.

Khongjom: The Khongjom is the historical place of Manipur. It is situated about 10 kms to the south of Thoubal on the Indo-Myanmar Road. It is here that Major General Poona Brajabashi, one of the great warriors of Manipur proved his valor against the Superior force of the invading British Army in 1891.

Koubru hill: Koubru hill is the highest peak in Manipur. It is located in Senapati district just twenty five km away from Imphal. National Highway No. 39, the main life line of the State is running through the foot hill of Koubru. Ngun River, the biggest river in the region is running down from Kangpokpi till Motbung through its foot hill.

There are two ponds on the hill top located in opposite direction. The two ponds are believed to be the abode of python/Lairenbi. So, the Hindu mountaineers used to worship the ponds. Just before reaching the top, there is a hole called Kulung in Kuki which is believed to be the road leading to the home of sprites.

Shri Shri Govindajee Temple: This temple adjacent to the palace of the former rulers of Manipur, is a sacred center for Vaisnavites. It is a simple and beautiful structure with twin gold domes, a paved courtyard and a large congregation hall. The presiding deity, Radha Govinda is flanked by idols of Balaram and Krishna on one and Jagannath, Balabhadra and Subhadra on the other.

Saheed Minar: The imposing Minar of Bir Tikendrajit park standing tall in the eastern side of the Imphal Pologround of the state's capital commemorates the indomitable spirit of Manipur martyrs who sacrificed their lives while fighting against the British in 1891. The eye-catching Minar also serves as an ideal background for photo shoots.

War Cemetery: The British and the Indian Army Cemeteries commemorating those who died in the Second World War are serene and well maintained with little stone markers and bronze plaques recording brief accounts of their anguish and sacrifice. These graves are maintained by the Commonwealth War Graves commission.

Khwairamband Bazar or IMA Market: A unique all women's market, having 3000 "Imas" or mothers who run the stalls. This is a large crowded market at the heart of Imphal city. The market is exclusive in the sense that all the stalls are managed by women.

Manipur Zoological Garden: About 6 kms from Imphal towards the west, lies the Zoological Garden at Iroishemba, hidden half-a-mile from the Imphal-Kangchup road. Graceful brow-antlered deer (Sangai), one of the rarest species in the world, can be seen there in sylvan surroundings. A trip to this garden at the foot of pine-covered hillocks in the western-most corner of Lamphelpat will be an affair to remember.

Manipur State Museum: This interesting museum near the Polo Ground has a fairly good display of Manipur's tribal heritage and a collection of portraits of Manipur's former rulers. Particularly interesting items are costumes, arms & weapons, relics and historical documents.

Khonghampat Orchidarium: Seven kilometres from Imphal on Highway No. 39 is the Central Orchidarium, which covers 200 acres and houses over 110 rare varieties of orchids, which include almost a dozen endemic species. The peak blooming season of this orchidarium is March-April.

Singda: At an altitude of 921 metres, Singda is a beautiful picnic spot 16 kms away from Imphal. The scenery is inviting. There is an Inspection Bunglow to convenience visitors. Greeted by a breeze-ruffled artificial lake, every visitor is tempted to revisit the spot.

Kangchup is a beautiful health resorts on the hills overlooking the Manipur Valley. The site is picturesque and worth seeing. With the construction of Singda Dam at Kangchup, the place has become one of the important picnic spots.

Langthabal: It is 6 kms from Imphal on the Indo-Myanmar road. Langthabal is a small hillock rich in the relics of an old historical place, well-planned tempted to attract the tourists.

Red Hill (Maibam Lokpa Ching): It is a hillock about 17 kms South of Imphal City on Tiddim Road. The place was an action-packed location where a fierce battle took place between the Allied Forces and the Japanese Forces in World War II. Japanese war veterans constructed a monument at the foot of this hill and it was significantly named "India Peace Memorial"

Bishnupur: Bishnupur is 27 kms away from Imphal City on Tiddim Road. Here stands the conical temple of lord Vishnu built in 1467 during the region of King Kyamba.

Loukoipat: It is a hot-favourite tourist spot in Bishnupur district lying just in the outskirts of the district headquarters. A small but aesthetically satiating lake surrounded on all sides by green foliage-rich hillocks, is the main attraction of the spot. Boating facility is also provided to the tourists. A cool greenery-hedged IB built on an elevated site overlooking the lake awaits to host visitors on the look-out for a night's stay.

Phubala: A charming resort on the western fringes of the Loktak lake is situated 40 kms south of Imphal. It is joined to the mainland by a low causeway. From there, life in and around the gigantic expanse of the Loktak lake can be viewed vividly.

Moirang: Moirang is located 45 kms away from Imphal city on Tiddim Road. The ancient temple of the pre-Hindu deity, Lord Thangjing stands there. Every May, men and women in bright traditional costumes sing and dance in honour of the lord there in an eventful festival called Moirang Lai Haraoba.

Keibul Lamjao National Park: The Park is located in the south western part of the Loktak lake. This is the last natural habitat of the marsh-friendly brow-antlered deer (Sangai) of Manipur. Keibul Lamjao National Park is the only floating park in the world.

Andro: Andro lies 27 kms east of the state capital Imphal. The small town is an ancient Scheduled Caste village of the state. A cultural complex was established there by the Mutua Museum, Imphal. It exhibited potteries of the North-eastern region of India. There also is a Doll-house wherein dolls of recognized Tribes of the State are displayed.

Churachandpur: It is the second biggest town of the state spreading out on both sides of the Tiddim Road, 60 kms away from Imphal. It exhibited potteries of the North-Eastern region of India.

Tengnoupal: 69 kms away from Imphal on the Indo-Myanmar highway, one comes across the highest point in altitude on the way to Moreh, the border town with Myanmar. Over there, one is at advantage point to have a full view of the valley portion of the state. To stay at or pass through the elevated peak of a village, warm clothes are needed in any part of the year. You'll feel as if you are put inside a fridge. As in Ooty, summer is gone from Tengnoupal.

Moreh: The international border town is located on the Indo-Myanmar Road 110 kms south east of Imphal. Being a commercial town, it attracts a large number of people away from Tamu, its Myanmarese counterpart which was of late given face lift.

Ukhrul: The district headquarters of Ukhrul district is situated 83 kms away from Imphal in the east. Undoubtedly, one of the highest hill stations of the state, Ukhrul is famous for a peculiar type of terrestrial Lily, the Siroy Lily (Lilium macklinae sealy) which is grown on the Siroy Hill. Khangkhui Lime Caves are interesting places for excursion. Ukhrul wears gay and festive appearance during Christmas. Known for the natural hospitality of its people, it is the place where pioneer missionary, William Pettigrew was first offered a foothold.

Tamenglong: It's the district headquaters of Tamenglong district situated 156 kms from Imphal. The region is known for its deep gorges, mysterious caves, refreshing waterfalls, exotic orchids and oranges. The Tharon Caves, Booming Meadow, Zeilad Lake and Barak waterfalls are interesting tourist spots in Tamenglong district. There's nothing to beat the Tamenglong brand of oranges and cane-mats.

Waithout Lake: 16 kms on Indo-Myanmar Road a picturesque site famous for its pineapple slopes. A tourist lodge at the fringe of the lake.

Khoupum Valley: It is a very beautiful small valley with flat land of about 8 sq. miles (20.72 sq. kms). It is situated on the Old Cachar Road, roughly half way between Bishenpur and Jirighat.

Langol: It is scenic spot situated in the north-western part of Imphal town. The sprawling game villages with the overlooking ranges of hill is worth visiting. Temples of Thongak Lairembi, Langol Lairembi, Viswanath Mandir, Nature care Hospital, Shija Hospital etc. are located here.

Nupee Lal Memorial & Complex: It is built to perpetuate the memory of Nupeelal (women uprings). It is located by the side of Imphal Head post office. One can see photographs, records of the events displayed in this splendor memorial buildings.

Kanchup: It is a serene place lying on some enchanting hills with much beautiful scenary. The scheme of water works at it is quite enthralling to witness.

MAJOR TOURIST PLACES : AT A GLANCE

❖ **RELIGIOUS :** 1. Koubru Leikha,   2. Andro, 3. Shree Shree Govindajee Temple, 4. Kaina
❖ **HISTORICAL :** 1. INA Memorial (Moirang),   2. Khongjom, 3. Andro, 4. War Cemetery (Indian and British), 5. Shaheed Minar, 6. Bishnupur, 7. Canchipur, 8. Langthabal, 9. Red Hill
❖ **HILL STATION :** 1. Tamenglong, 2. Mao, 3. Tengnoupal, 4. Ukhrul
❖ **IMPORTANT TOWN :** 1. Churachandpur, 2. Imphal, 3. Moreh
❖ **WILDLIFE :** 1. Keibul Lamjao National Park, 2. Manipur Zoological Garden
❖ **SCENIC :** 1. Loukoipat, 2. Phubala, 3. Khonghampat Orchidarium, 4. Khangkhui cave, 5. Loktak lake and its isles, 6. Waithou lake, 7. Kangchup and Singda dam
❖ **MUSEUM :** 1. INA Museum, 2. Sekta Archaeological Living Museum, 3. Manipur State Museum, 4. Andro

● ● ●

Sports

Dating back to the history of Manipur, the tradition of sports is a history of small kingdoms. These kingdoms had the greatest and deepest desire to organise competitions with one another in past.

Some of the indigenous Manipuri games & sports are given below:

Sagol Kangjei (Manipuri Polo)

The Sagol Kangjei has been adapted and adopted by the international enthusiasts of the game as Polo and now it's now being played worldwide. Today, the world has accepted that the game of Polo originated from Manipur. The Manipuri Polo is played with seven players (in each side) who mount and ride ponies, which are usually 4/5 feet in height. Each player is fitted with Polo-stick made of bamboo root. The mounted player gallop after the ball to hit it straight into the goal. Extremely masculine and vigour-taxing, the exhilarating game is now played in two styles—the pana or original Manipur style and the international style i.e. Polo. It is heart-cheering to see Manipuri players in their sixties and even seventies riding ponies at full gallop playing Sagol Kangjei (polo) with gusto. The ponies are also decorated fully with various guards of protecting the eyes, forehead, flanks etc.

Khong Kangjei (Manipuri Hockey)

It is also a very popular Manipuri game. The game is played with seven players on either side and each player is equipped with a bamboo stick about 4 feet in length which is bended at the lower tip like the modern hockey stick. The ball is started with a throw of the bamboo-root-made ball in a field of 200 × 80 yards. A player may carry the ball in any manner towards the goal but he shall have to score a goal only by hitting the ball with his stick. There are no goal posts. A goal is scored when the ball crosses the goal-line fully. A player often encounters an opponent in his attempt at carrying or hitting the ball toward the goal. The encounter may develop into a tussling trial of strength which is indigenously known as Mukna. The game is actually an admixture of football, hockey, rugby and wrestling.

Yubi Lakpi (Manipuri Rugby)

"Yubi" in Manipur means coconut and "Lakpi" means snatching. The oriental game is played on the lush green turf of the palace ground or at the Bijoy Govinda Temple ground. Each side has 7 players in a field that is about 45 × 18 metres in area one side of which forms the central portion of the goal line. The coconut serves the purpose of a ball and is offered to the king or the judges who sit just beyond the goal line.

Hiyang Tannaba (Boat Race)

It is generally held in the month of November at Thangapat(Moat). The boats called Hiyang Hiren are regarded to be invested with spiritual powers and the game is associated with religious rites. The Meiteis believe that worship of the Hiyang Hiren will prevent one from evil omens. The rowers wear traditional dresses and head-gears. The game is also conducted during spells of natural calamity.

Kaang

Played on the mud floor of a big out house fixed targets hit with "Kang" which is a flat and oblong instrument made of either ivory or lac. Normally each team has 7 male partners. The game is also played as a mixed doubles contest. Played strictly during the period between 'Cheiraoba' (Manipuri New Year's day) and the Rath Yatra festival. Manipuri religiously adhere to its time-frame as popular belief holds that if the game is played beyond its given limit, evil spirits invade the mind of players and spectators.

Thang-Ta & Sarit Sarat

These are the forms of Manipuri Martial Arts, the traditions of which had been passed down over the centuries. They are energy-consuming and skill demanding arts of fighting. The indigenous martial art-forms were meant to hone one's battle-craft during peace times in the olden days when Manipuri war warrior required to serve his country at war-times. A martial-artist has to undergo strenuous pratice sessions. Only the brave and the athletic could excel. The art, as seen today, observes elaborate rituals and rules, which are strictly followed by the participants.

Mukna (Manipuri Wrestling)

It is also a very popular oldest game of Manipuri's. Mukna has been in vogue since the existence of Manipuri society. It is a trial of strength using sheer physical force. The game is part of a ceremonial function and enjoyed due patronage in the olden days. The game requires enduring physical stamina, speed and agility. In the olden days, players excelling in the game received royal favours and prizes. Whereas, it is survival of the fattest in Japanese Sumo-wrestling, it is survival of the fittest for Mukna.

Besides these, there are some other interesting games like Lamjel (foot-race), Mangjong (broad jump), Uraobi (Manipuri Kabbadi), Seboti (aerobic game style), Chenjong, Phibulhabi and Amangoi etc.

OLYMPIANS FROM MANIPUR

Since 1984, Manipur has consistently been a part of Indian Olympic squad. Some of the well-known Olympians from Manipur are:

Neel Komol Singh

He was the first Manipuri's Olympian, participated in Los Angeles, 1984 as a goal keeper of Indian Hockey team.

Thoiba Sing

Thoiba was a skilled forward hockey player. He participated in the 1988 Olympics at Seoul, South Korea.

Sanamacha Chanu

A weightlifter from Manipur who got the 6th position in 2000 Sydney Olympics. She also represented the state and nation in Athens Olympics, 2004.

Brojeshwori Devi

She was another Manipuri girl participated in Sydney games In 2000. She was the only women Judo player participant of India and reached upto 3rd round.

N. Dingko Singh

Boxer from Manipur participated in Sydney Olympics. Dingko Singh was also an Asian gold medalist.

N. Kunjarani Devi

Weightlifter, got the 4th position in Athens Olympics, 2004. She had also won the Gold medal in 2006, Melbourne Commonwealth Games.

M.C. Mary Kom

Women boxer from Manipur who won the bronze medal in 2012 London Olympics. She has also won the Gold medal in 2014, Incheon Asian Games and 2018 Gold Coast Commonwealth Games. She claimed her 6th title in the World women's boxing championships on November 24, 2018.

Important Personalities

CHAPTER 19

JUBRAJ TIKENDRAJIT (1858-1891)

Jubraj Tikendrajit Singh was the son of Maharaja Chandrakirti Singh and his mother's name was Chongtham Chanu Kouseswari Devi. During the reign of his father (Maharaja Chandrakirti), he was Kotwal, Senapati (during the period of Surachandra) and Jubraj (during the period of Kullachandra).

In his individiual capacity, he deposed Surachandra, the reigning king in the year 1890 and installed Kullachandra as the king of Manipur. During the battle with the British, the Manipuris fought very bravely under the direction of Tikendrajit. But it was all in vain against the superior mite and arms of the British.

GENERAL THANGAL

General Thangal was one of the most prominent heroes of the Anglo-Manipur war 1891. His father's name was Kangabam Kshetri Singh, and his mother's name was Thokchom Chanu Puinu.

He became popular since the period of Maharaja Gambhir Singh. But during the period of Chandrakirti Maharaja, Thangal Major was the most powerful member of the Durbar.

NIRANJAN SUBADAR

Niranjan Subadar was a Gurkha who was in the service of the British Army. He left the Britishers and joined the native force of Manipur and later appointed as Subadar by the Tikendrajit Jubraj.

He was tried by the chief Political Officer, Manipur Field Force and was sentenced to be hanged for assisting the Manipuris against the British. He was hanged on 8th June, 1891.

RANI GAIDINLIU

Rani Gaidinliu from Manipur was a fearless Indian freedom fighter who joined the agitation at the age of 13 and headed the movement against the British in the Manipur and Naga belts. The government of India honoured her with the prestigious Padma Bhushan in 1993.

JADONANG

Haipou Jadonang was a Rangnei Naga spiritual leader and political activist from Manipur. He established the Heraka religious movement, and declared himself to be the 'messiahking' of the Nagas. His movement was widespread in the Zeliangrong territory before the switch to christianity. He also envisaged an independent Naga Kingdom, which brought him in conflict with the British rules of India. He was hanged by British in 1931, and succeeded by his cousin Rani Gaidinliu.

M.C. MARY KOM

Mary Kom is an Indian boxer who got a chance to represent India in the 2012 Olympics at London and won bronze medal in the women's flyweight category in that. She has won World Boxing Championship five times successfully. She ranks fourth in the world in 51 kg women's category. For the fifth time consecutively, she won the World Boxing Championship title on 18th September 2010. She became the only woman boxer from India to be qualified for 2012 Summer Olympics. She was able to get this chance by reaching up to quarter final in 2012 AIBA Women's World Boxing Championships. In Olympics in flyweight category, she was outpunched by Nicola Adams of Britain and had to quit with semifinals and had to settle down for bronze medal, the first ever Olympic medal won by a woman boxer in India.

She has won international titles at Women's World Amateur Boxing Championships, Witch Cup, Asian Women's Championships, Venus Women's Box Cup, Asian Games, Asian Indoor Games and Asian Women's Cup. In recognition of her talents, she was given Arjuna Award in 2004, Padma Shree award in 2006 and Rajiv Gandhi Khel Ratna Award in 2009. At present she is nominated member of Rajya Sabha. She has also won gold medal in 2018 Gold Coast Commonwealth Games. She claimed her 6th title in the World women's boxing championships on November 24, 2018.

GURU BIPIN SINGHA

Guru Bipin Singha is reckoned as the pioneer of Manipuri dance. He is one of the prominent names among them, who made the place of Manipuri dance on the world stage, with great artist sense, Guru Bipin Singha created a fine mesh of popularity throughout the North-eastern part of the subcontinent including Bangladesh. The contribution of Guru Bipin Singha in Manipuri dance is rightly justified by addressing him as the "Father of Manipuri Dance and Style".

KUNJARANI DEVI

Kunjarani Devi is an Indian weightlifter who has won a number of medals in national and international weightlifting competitions. She was born on 1st March 1968 in Kairang Mayai Leikai in Imphal in Manipur. She took an interest in sports from her younger days.

She started her medal hunt from 1985 in the National Weightlifting Championships in 44 kg, 46 kg and 48 kg category and made two new National Records in the year 1987 in the event held at Thiruvananthapuram. She won a gold medal in Pune in the year 1994. In the event held at Manipur in 1998, she contested in the 48 kg category and could win only silver medal.

In 1989 she got her first World Women's Weightlifting Championship held in Manchester. She was motivated by the three silver medals that she won in the event. She set a record by participating in the world champions for seven times continuously except the one held in Melbourne in the year 1993. She won the gold medal at the 2006 Commonwealth Games at Melbourne in 48 kg category.

LAISHRAM SARITA DEVI

Laishram Sarita Devi is a successful lady boxer from Manipur. A National Champion, she won World Champion in the lightweight class in 2010 defeating Alexandra Kuleshova of Russia. She won it in the 51 weight category. Prior to it she was awarded with Arjuna Award in 2009 for her contributions to Indian sports.

Before she was awarded Arjuna award in 2009, she had already earned seven gold medals in various international events. She was 24 years old when she was given sports' most prestigious honour. She won gold at the 2006 World Championships in New Delhi. In 2014 Commonwealth Games in Glasgow she won a silver medal and in 2014 Asian Games in Incheon, South Korea, she finished with a bronze.

IROM CHANU SHARMILA

Irom Chanu Sharmila, better known as Irom Sharmila is a civil rights activist from Manipur, popular in news headlines for the hunger strike she started in the year 2000 against Indian government demanding complete repeal of the AFSPA from Manipur and other northeast states. She states that AFSPA is the cause of violence in north east states. She is regarded as one of the powerful Indian women in the recent times and most recently on the occasion of International Women's Day, 2014 she was voted the top woman icon of India by MSN Poll. Started the hunger strike in 2000, she has completed 500 weeks and is regarded as world's longest hunger striker. She has been arrested and released several times charging "attempts to commit suicide". But she states that it's non-violence principle of Mahatma Gandhi to fight against injustice. Every time she gets arrested nasogastric intubation was forced on her to keep her alive. She ended her hunger strike on 9 August 2016, after 16 years of fasting.

Till now she has been supported by many political parties and leaders like Anna Hazare and Mamata Banerjee as well as many social activists worldwide. She has also been honoured with many awards and honours globally and now she is regarded as "Iron Lady of Manipur" or "Mengoubi". This powerful lady is also a noted poet.

BOMBAYALA DEVI

Bombayla Devi Laishram is an Indian archer who represented India at the 2008 Beijing Olympics and 2012 London Olympics in the women's individual event and team events. However she could not enter the finals in any of these matches.

She was the first women to qualify for the Olympics 2008 after exhibiting her talents at the 2007 World Archery Championship at Leipzig in Germany. Her team won silver medal at the 46th World Archery Championship in Turin in Italy in July 2011.

She started her career in archery in 1996 and after ten years, in 2006, she became the member of the Indian team. She won gold at the recurve team event at 2010 Commonwealth Games held at New Delhi and this is one of her glorious moments.

She won Gold medal in the team recurve event of the World Cup Stage IV at Shanghai in China in 2011 and Bronze medal in the 17th Asian Archery Championship in Iran in 2011.

ASHANGBAM MINAKETAN SINGH

Ashangbam Minaketan Singh is regarded as the founder of Modern Manipuri literature. He lived in the 20th century, with a fruitful long 89 years witnessing every historic moment of Manipur. He has given contributions to every genre of Manipuri literature. He published 25 books on different branches of literature including poetry, prose, essays, translations, mythology, biography, autobiography and criticism. He is amongst the pioneer poets of Manipuri literature. Basanta Sheireng (1928) and Asheibagi Nityaipod (1976) are his poetry works. Asheibagi Sheirol (1977), Tonu Laijinglembi (Play), Bharatki Lonsingi Marakta (Essay) and Meitei Upanyas (Criticism) are his other works. Soviet Land Nehru Award (1977) and Sahitya Academy Award for Asheibagi Nityaipod (Poetry) the same year are the major awards received by him.

His words were noted for impressive power of imagination by lines. Apart from contributing a lot to Manipuri literature, he has also served in advisory board of many state committees. He passed away in 1995, living almost a century. In 2006, Ashangbam Minaketan State Level Celebration Committee, Imphal observed the 100th birth anniversary of Ashangbam.

BALA HIJAM

Bala Hijam, also known as Surjabala Hijam is a young actress from Manipur and has many Manipuri hits in her credit. She is a Manipuri actress who has a huge fan following crowd after her debut Malayalam flick, *Neelakasham Pachakadal Chuvanna Bhoomi* directed by Sameer Thahir. This highly acclaimed Malayalam movie is a thriller road movie; she played the role an engineering student Assi and Dulquer Salmaan's love interest. 

Her Bollywood debut - Zindagi on the Rocks. In 2011 she received Special Jury award for Manipuri from FAM. She is the only pan-Indian film star who played the female lead in movies from places as far apart as Manipur, Kerala and the Hindi-Urdu belt.

● ● ●

Administration and Governance

The government in Manipur is formed on the same lines as in other states of the country. Manipur has 2 seats in the Lok Sabha and 1 seat in Rajya Sabha. Like all other states of India, the head of the state is the Governor, appointed by the President of India. His or her post is largely ceremonial. The Chief Minister is headed by a group of ministers with independent power.

HISTORICAL PERSPECTIVE

The Maharaja

During the British regime, the Maharaja used to appoint the functionaries of the state. The Rules of Management of the State of Manipur, enforced on September 14, 1935, empowered the Maharaja to appoint the members of the Durbar, while a British Officer acted as the President of the Durbar. After independence, for a brief period, the Manipur State Constituent Act 1947 provided for the formation of a Manipur State Appointment Board to be the "final authority" in all matters of appointments and promotions.

The Chief Commissioner

Following merger into the Indian Union on October 15, 1949, Manipur became a centrally administered area, and remained so till October 31, 1956. During this period, the Chief Commissioner appointed the functionaries of Manipur, subject to the control of the Central Government.

Territorial Council

Manipur became a Union Territory under the States' Re-Organisation Act 1956 and Constitution (Seventh Amendment) Act 1956. Under the Territorial Council Act 1956 Manipur was allowed to constitute the Territorial Council with limited administrative powers over transferred subjects and appointment of officials thereto. The Chief Commissioner, however, continued to function as the Chief appointing authority of the territory. Subsequently the Territorial Council was abolished, and Manipur was placed under the Chief Commissioner from May 11, 1963 onwards with a Territorial Legislative Assembly and a Council of Ministers to assist him. Manipur attained statehood on January 21, 1972 under the North-East Area (Re-organisation) Act 1971.

THE GOVERNOR

The Constitution provides for the post of the Governor as the Head of a State in India. He is appointed by the President of India. He is both the constitutional Head of a State and an agent of the Central Government in a State.

The Governor is appointed for a term of five years. But before the expiry of his full term, the President can dismiss him from office. The Governor may also resign on his own. His term of office may be extended and he may be transferred to another State. However, the State Government cannot remove the Governor from his post.

To be the Governor, a person must be a citizen of India and should complete 35 years of age. And he cannot be a member of the Parliament or the State legislature. He should not hold any office of profit.

Powers and Functions

The Governor is the Chief Executive in a State. All the executive powers of the State Government are vested in him and decisions are taken in his name. He appoints the Chief Minister and his Council of Ministers. He may dismiss the members of the Council of Ministers on the advice of the Chief Minister. The Governor distributes the portfolios among the members of the Council of Ministers.

The Governor makes some important appointments of the State Government, such as, the Advocate general, Chairman and members of the State Public Service Commission and others.

The Governor may call for information from the Chief Minister regarding the activities of the State Government. He sends reports to the President about the situation of the State. The President imposes emergency in a State under Article 356 on the basis of the report of the Governor. The Governor also acts as the Chancellor of State Universities.

The Governor is an integral part of the State legislature, though he is not a member of either house of it. He summons and prorogues the sessions of the State legislature and he can dissolve the Legislative

Assembly. He addresses the members of the legislature and may send messages. Without the Governor's assent, no bill can become a law after it is passed by the legislature.

Money bills can be introduced in the State Legislative Assembly only with the permission of the Governor. The Governor may promulgate ordinances during the period when the Legislative Assembly or both the Houses of the legislature (when there are two Houses) are not in session.

The Governor may nominate one member of the Anglo- India Community to the Legislative Assembly if there are Anglo- Indian people in a State and they are not duly represented in the State legislature. He may also nominate 1/6 members of the Legislature Council (where they are from among persons who are experts in the fields of science, literature, arts, social service and co-operative movement).

The Governor makes the reports of various agencies placed on the floor of the State legislature. The annual budget of the State Government is laid before the legislature with the approval of the Governor. The Governor must give his assent to money bills. The Contingency fund of the State is also placed at the disposal of the Governor.

The powers of the governor, in actual practice, are exercised by the Council of Ministers headed by the Chief Minister. The State Council of Ministers is the real executive in a State.

Still, the Governor has some discretionary powers which can be exercised by him independently. He may send any bill passed by the Sate legislature for the consideration of the President. He can appoint any member of the State legislature as the Chief Minister if no political party secures absolute majority in the Legislative Assembly. During emergency, the Governor of a state can exercise his powers independently.

A Governor of state can be given additional duty of the Governor of the neighboring states by the President.

Position of the Governor

The position of the Governor of a State is compared to the President of India as a nominal executive. But the Governor is not always a nominal executive. He can exercise his powers in the real sense on some occasions.

According to the Article 161-Power of governor to grant pardons, etc. and to suspend, remit or commute sentences in certain cases, the Governor of a State have the power to grant pardons, reprieves, respites or remissions of punishment or to suspend, remit or commute the sentence of any person convicted of any offence against any law relating to a matter to which the executive power of the State extends.

He acts as an agent of the Central Government in a State. Therefore, he is responsible for maintaining relation between the Central Government and the State Government. The Governor may advise the Council of Ministers when it faces some difficult situations.

The Governor takes independent decisions while exercising discretionary powers. He may seek information from the Council of Ministers regarding various activities of the Government. He cannot be ignored by the Council of Ministers. He may even influence the decisions of the Council of Ministers in many ways as the Head of State.

According to the Article 361—The Governor of a State shall not be answerable to any Court for the exercise and performance of the powers and duties of his office or for any act done or purporting to be done by him in the exercise and performance of those powers and duties.

No criminal proceedings, whatsoever, shall be instituted, or continued against the President, or the Governor of a State, in any Court during his term of office.

While appointing the Governor, the President acts as per the advice of the Union Cabinet. The State Government is also consulted when the appointment is to be made. Generally, a person is not appointed Governor in his own State.

COUNCIL OF MINISTERS

The Governor appoints the State Council of Ministers. He appoints the leader of the majority party in the Legislative Assembly as the Chief Minister. On the advice of the Chief Minister, he appoints the other Ministers of the Council of Ministers. In the State Council of Ministers like that of the Union Council of Ministers, there are three categories of ministers- Cabinet Ministers, Ministers of States and Deputy Ministers.

All the Ministers, including the Chief Minister must be the members of the State legislature. If a Minister is not a member of the State legislature at the time of his appointment, he must be so within a period of six months from the date of his taking over charge as Minister.

The Chief Minister and Ministers heading individual departments of the government constitute the State Cabinet. It is the most powerful authority in State administration. All the important decisions of the State administration are taken by the Cabinet. The decisions of the Cabinet are binding upon the Council of Ministers

The Council of Ministers has no fixed term of office. The term of the Council of Ministers depends on the support of the majority members of the Legislative Assembly. If it loses majority support in the legislative Assembly, it has to resign. The Governor may also remove a Minister from the council of Ministers on the advice of the Chief Minister.

The council of Ministers headed by the Chief Minister exercises all the powers and functions of the Governor of the State. Therefore, it is called the real executive of a State. However, it can not exercise the discretionary powers of the Governor. The Council of Ministers remains responsible to the Legislative Assembly for carrying on the administration of the State.

Powers and Functions

The State Council of Ministers formulates the policies for State administration. The Council of Ministers also implements the directives given by the Central Government. It has to work in conformity with the national policies of the Central Government.

The Council of Ministers prepares proposals for legislation. It has also to take measures so that the legislations are passed in the legislature.

The Council of Ministers is responsible for maintaining law and order in the state. It is the real executive in the state. It is responsible for running the administration of a state according to the principles of the Constitution.

The Council of Ministers makes policies regarding recruitment, appointment, transfer, promotion, etc. of the Public Services in the state. It even advises the Governor for the appointment of important functionaries like the Chairman and members of the Public Service Commission Advocate General, etc..

It prepares the annual budget of the State government. The Minister for Finance presents the budget in the Legislative Assembly. It is responsible for maintaining sound financial condition in the state. The Council of Ministers advises the Governor regarding the date and time of summoning and proroguing the sessions of the legislature. It also advises the Governor to dissolve the Legislative Assembly.

The social, economic and political condition of a State is dependent upon the performance of the Council of Ministers. If the ministers are efficient and dedicated, then the State will definitely work better. It also depends on how the Chief Minister is leading the Council of Ministers.

CHIEF MINISTER

The Chief Minister is appointed by the governor, Art. 163 of the Constitution provides that there shall be a Council of Ministers with the Chief Minister at its head to aid and advise the governor. Once the election to the

Legislative Assembly is over the task of forming the government begins. The party with the Majority in the Legislative Assembly (Vidhan Sabha) is entitled to form the government.

However, some of the important powers and functions of the Chief Minister are as under:

To Aid and Advice the Governor

The Chief Minister is the link between the Cabinet and the Governor. It is he who communicates to the Governor all decisions of the Council of Ministers. He has to furnish such information relating to the administration of the State as the Governor may call for.

The Governor can submit to the consideration of the Council of Ministers any matter on which decision has been taken by a Minister but which has not been considered by the Council of Ministers.

Head of the Council of Ministers

As Head of the State Cabinet, the Chief Minister enjoys the following powers:

(i) **Formation of the Ministry:** The other Ministers are appointed by the Governor on the advice of the Chief Minister. The Chief Minister has a free hand in preparing the list of his colleagues. The Governor may suggest the names of the persons to be included in the Ministry, but he cannot insist upon any person to be included in the Ministry. Assigning departments or portfolios to the Ministers is done by the Governor on the advice of the Chief Minister.

(ii) **Removal of Ministers:** The Ministers hold office during the pleasure of the Governor. This, however, does not mean that the Governor can dismiss his Ministers at his will. The Government is in fact dependent on the Chief Minister. Therefore, the Chief Minister can reconstruct his Ministry as and when he likes. He may ask anyone of his colleagues to resign. If he declines, he will be dismissed by the Governor.

(iii) **Presiding over the Meetings:** As Chairman of the Cabinet, the Chief Minister has a position which enables him to impose his decision. It is he who controls the agenda for the Cabinet meetings. It is for the Chief Minister to accept or reject proposals for Cabinet discussion.

(iv) **Co-ordinates the Working of Various Departments:** The Chief Minister supervises and co-ordinates policies of the several Ministers and Departments. Several ministries are involved in the formulation and implementation of a policy.

Leader of the House

The Chief Minister is the leader of the State Legislative Assembly. All principal announcements of policy are made by him. The Chief Minister intervenes in debates of general importance. He can appease an angry House by promising immediate relief or concessions when needed.

Position of the Chief Minister

The Chief Minister's position is pre-eminent in the State governmental system. In practice, his position will be strong only when his party commands a clear majority in the State Legislature.

When it is a coalition government, it becomes difficult to safeguard the principle of collective responsibility. Much of the time and energy of the Chief Minister will be wasted on keeping his team united and sufficiently disciplined.

LEGISLATIVE ASSEMBLY

The first Manipur State Assembly was elected on adult franchise in July 1948 - the first of its kind in India. "The representative returnable from General, Hill and Mohammedan constituencies were in the ratios of 30:18:3 respectively with an additional two seats for the representatives of Educational and Commercial interests".

The whole valley of Manipur was divided into 29 constituencies. Three of them were plural constituencies. That is each voter had two votes, one for the Mohammedans and the other for the non-Mohammedans. "The special constituencies from which one Muslim and one Hindu were returned were Lilong, Mayang Imphal and Yairipok".

The Jiribam (Rajbari) (Hill area) was allotted a general seat. The whole hill area of Manipur was divided into 18 single member constituencies. The hill man residing in the valley demanded that one seat should be allotted to them in one of the valley constituencies.

Accordingly, "Moirang constituency was made a special constituency from which one Hill representative and one valley representative were elected". Therefore, the Manipur Legislative Assembly consisted of 53 seats. The State Assembly was, however, dissolved after Manipur was merged with the Dominion Government of India on 15th of October 1949. Manipur became a Part C State and the State continued to be administered by the President through a Chief Commissioner or a Lieutenant Governor who acted as his agent.

There was an Advisory Council appointed by the President in consultation with the Chief Commissioner. The Council met once in three months presided over by the Chief Commissioner. The Council was an advisory body and as such its advice was not necessarily binding on the Chief Commissioner.

On November 1, 1956 Manipur ceased to be a Part C State. Manipur became a Union Territory under the Union Territorial Council Act, 1956. The Territorial Council consisting of 30 elected Members and 2 nominated Members was constituted on 16.8.1957. The Territorial Council was later converted into the Territorial Legislative Assembly in June 1963.

The Territorial Legislative Assembly consisting of 30 elected Members and 2 nominated Members started to function from 23.7.1963. With the enactment of the North-Eastern Areas (Re-organization) Act, 1971 by the Indian Parliament Manipur was conferred full statehood on 21st January 1972 with a 60 Member Legislative Assembly.

The normal tenure of the Assembly is five years, unless sooner dissolved. There are 13 Standing Committees in the Assembly. In India, the State Legislature consists of the Governor and one or two houses. The lower house is called the Legislative Assembly or Vidhan Sabha while the upper house is called the Legislative Council or Vidhan Parishad.

Legislative Powers

The main function of the Legislative Assembly is to make laws. But its power to make laws is confined to the State List and the Concurrent List. However, the Parliament has also jurisdiction over the Concurrent List.

Where a law made by the state legislature on a matter listed in the Concurrent List conflicts with law made by the Parliament on the same matter, the latter will prevail, if the state law has not received the assent of the President.

Normally the Parliament has no jurisdiction over the State List. But during Emergency the Parliament can make laws on the State List. Even in normal times the Parliament shall be competent to make laws on the State List if the Council of States (Rajya Sabha), by two-third majority adopts a resolution urging the Parliament to make laws, in national interest, on subjects listed in the State List.

Further, the Governor has discretion to reserve some bills, passed by the state legislature, for the assent of the President of India. If such a bill, returned by the President for reconsideration by the state legislature, is again sent to the President by the state legislature for his assent, he is not bound to give assent to it. He may or may not give his assent to the bill. If the President does not give his assent second time, the bill is rejected. Thus the President can veto, if he desires, some bills passed by the state legislature.

Two things now stand clear. First, the lawmaking power of the state legislature is not absolute; it is limited. Secondly, the lawmaking power is shared by the Legislative Assembly and the Legislative Council in a state having a bicameral legislature. However, in respect of lawmaking, the Legislative Assembly has stronger voice than the Legislative Council.

Financial Powers

The Money Bill can be introduced only in the Legislative Assembly. It cannot be introduced in the Legislative Council.

The Council can detain a Money Bill at the maximum for 14 days. The Legislative Assembly is required to pass the demand for grants (authorizing expenditures) and tax-raising proposals.

Without authorization by the Legislative Assembly, no money can be spent from the State Treasury. In financial matters, the Legislative Assembly is clearly more powerful than the Legislative Council.

Control over Executive

The Ministers are collectively responsible to the Legislative Assembly and not to the Legislative Council. They will be forced to resign if a no-confidence motion is passed by the Legislative Assembly. Further, if the Money Bill is defeated in the Legislative Assembly the Ministers resign.

The members of the Assembly can control the government by other means like asking questions and moving cut motions and adjournment motions. The Assembly has thus better control over the government than the Council.

Constituent Power

In the United States of America, both the Congress and the state legislatures can propose amendments of the constitution. But in India it is only the Parliament which can propose amendment.

The state legislatures cannot propose amendments. However, some amendments, relating to federal provisions, require ratification by at least one-half of state legislatures.

If a state has a bicameral legislature, then the amendment bill has to be ratified by both Houses - Legislative Assembly and Legislative Council.

Thus, the state legislatures have limited powers in relation to the amendment of the constitution.

Electoral Functions

(i) The elected members of the Legislative Assembly form part of the Electoral College which elects the President of India. This means that the members of Legislative Council have no role in the election of the President of India.

(ii) The members of Rajya Sabha representing the state are elected by the Legislative Assembly.

(iii) In case of a State having a bicameral legislature, one-third of the members of the Legislative Council are elected by the Legislative Assembly.

(iv) The Speaker and the Deputy Speaker are also elected by the members of the Legislative Assembly.

Miscellaneous Functions

(a) The Legislative Assembly can punish anybody for its contempt.

(b) It selects some of the members of University Senate (s).

(c) It considers the reports of the Public Service Commission and the Auditor General.

(d) It appoints different Committees of the House.

(e) It sends delegations to the Union Government to press the demands of the state.

MANIPUR HIGH COURT

Finally the long cherished dream of the people of Manipur, particularly the legal fraternity, has been fulfilled with Chief Justice of India Altamas Kabir inaugurating the Manipur High Court on March 25, 2013. Former Chief Justice of Chhattishgarh AM Sapre has already been sworn in as the first Chief Justice of Manipur High Court on March 23, 2013. Justice Sapre, is the first Chief Justice of the newly-set up Manipur High Court. The court will have three judges including Justice Sapre in the beginning. Judge of Guwahati High Court N. Koteswar has been appointed as a judge of Manipur High Court. The inaugural function held at the newly constructed High Court complex at Chingmeirong was attended by former Union Law Minister Dr. Ashwini Kumar, Chief Minister O. Ibobi, Gauhati High Court Chief Justice A.K. Goyal and two Supreme Court Judges. Manipur was within the jurisdiction of the Imphal Bench of Gauhati High Court till March 25, 2013. Earlier, the Imphal Bench of Gauhati High Court came into existence on 21st January 1972, the day Manipur attained its statehood.

SUBORDINATE JUDICIARY

The courts of Manipur are divided into two divisions, viz Manipur East and Manipur West. Manipur East comprises of Imphal East, Imphal West and Ukhrul whereas Manipur West comprises of Bishnupur, Thoubal, Churachandpur, Tamenglong, Senapati and Chandel. There are two District courts & two Session Courts in Manipur headed by one District and Sessions Judge each. A number of subordinate Courts at the District and subordinate level come under these District Courts.

District Court

The code of Civil Procedure, 1908 regulates procedures of conduct of cases by all Civil Courts and it came into force since 1st January, 1909. The District Court is subordinate to the High Court and every Civil Court of a grade inferior to that of a district Court and every Court of small causes is subordinate to the High Court and District Court. It is headed by a District Judge appointed by the Manipur High Court, Imphal. Other subordinate courts like Additional District Court, Senior Division and Junior Division are lower hierarchies next to the Manipur High Court, Imphal. Each of these courts were established under different sections directed by Supreme Court which was passed by the Parliament from time to time.

Criminal Court

The code of Criminal Procedure 1973 has come into effect from April 1, 1974. The Courts for Criminal cases are established in accordance with the provisions of the code of Criminal Procedure 1974. The Criminal Procedure code is mainly an adjective law of procedure. The object of the code of Criminal Procedure is to provide a machinery for the punishment of offenders against the substantive Criminal law such as the Indian Penal code. The Sessions Court is the highest criminal court subordinate to the High Court and the subordinate Courts of the Chief Judicial Magistrate, the Additional Chief Judicial Magistrate and the Judicial Magistrate first class.

Special Courts

NDPS

The Government of Manipur established a special Court under section 36 of the Narcotic Drugs and Psychotropic Substances Act, 1985 namely the special (ND & PS) Court, Manipur located at Uripok Courts Complex, Imphal. Its main purpose is for speedy trial of offences relating to narcotic drugs & phychotropic substances.

Family Courts

Established under the family Courts Act 1984. It deals with family disputes, maintainence, claims, judicial seperation and divorce. There is only one family court located at Lamphel Courts Complex.

Fast Tract Courts

Established on October 5, 2001. At present, it is located at Uripok Courts Complex and is headed by an Additional District Judge. Long pending cases more than two years at District and Sessions Courts level are transferred to the Fast Tract Courts for quick disposal.

Like courts, not exactly similar, Government of Manipur sets up other offices for adjudication of quasi-judicial nature of cases viz Tribunals, Commissions and Forums etc.

Tribunals

The Tribunal functions as a Revenue Tribunal under the MLR and LR Act 1960, as a Motor Accident Claims under the Motor Vehicles Act, 1988 and as an Industrial Tribunal under the Industrial Disputes Act 1948. The Government of Manipur established the said Tribunal to function as a Tribunal as and when required under any law.

Commission

Manipur Human Rights Commission, Lamphelpat was established on 27th June 1998 under the Protection of Human Rights Act, 1993. The main purpose is for protection of human rights and prevention of violation of human rights. A person can make a complaint for violation of human rights to the State Commission. The Commission at present consists of four members headed by one chairperson.

LOCAL SELF GOVERNMENT

The institutions of local government have been functioning in India since time immemorial. The village elder's council or Village Panchayat as they were popularly called, were ancient institutions and were themselves functioning like a republic system of government.

They exercised power in various spheres such as village court, administrative units, civic maintenance, religious function etc. Thus India in spite of being a vast country, the administrative political organisation has been well functioning right from the grass root level since ancient days and in the political history of India, this local governance system has a distinct place, without which political system in India would have no authenticity in itself.

Panchayati Raj System

Manipur came under British rule as a princely state in 1891. The Manipur Constitution Act, 1947, established a democratic form of government with the 'Maharajah' (King) as the executive head and a legislature constituted by election based on adult franchise.

The Legislative Assembly so constituted was dissolved after the integration of the state with the Dominion of India in October 1949. It became as a part 'C' state under the Indian Constitution with effect from 26-1-1950. Manipur achieved full statehood on January 21, 1972.

Manipur is geographically divided into the hills and valley. The Hill areas are inhabited predominantly by the Nagas, Kukis, Paites, Gangtes etc. with a sprinkling of the Nepalese in the immediate neighbourhood of the valley.

The valley is inhabited by Meiteis (Manipuri Hindus), Pangals (Manipuri Muslims), the Nepalese, and the Business communities like Marwaris, Punjabis, Biharis and so on. The Barak basin is inhabited by the Meiteis and the Bengalis.

The Panchayati Raj institutions were functioning only in the valley districts and Jiribam sub-division. In the hill districts, there were village authorities, almost similar to village Panchayats, functioning under the provisions of the 1956 Manipur (Village Authorities in Hill Areas) Act.

Evolution of Panchayats

Traditional form of Panchayats had been existing both in the valley and hill areas of Manipur from time immemorial. In the villages of valley there were institution viz, Singlup or wood clubs, resembling the Panchayats of Bengal, under the 'Sardar' or head of village. Besides generally controlling village affairs, these singlups used to adjudicate petty disputes in the villages.

In December 1896, the singlups were replaced by Panchayats. These Panchayats were constituted with five members. These Panchayats had the power to impose fines up to fifty rupees, and of deciding civil suits upto value of fifty rupees or less.

The apex Panchayat at Imphal, known as Sadar Panchayat, adjudicated in civil cases of appeals from the village Panchayats besides looking after the civil cases of the Imphal area.

Under the Manipur State Courts Act, 1947, Village Panchayats were conferred powers of the lowest court for the administration of Justice in criminal and civil cases.

Modern Panchayat System

The Panchayat system in Manipur was introduced in 1960 under the provisions of the United Provinces Panchayat Raj Act, 1947, which was extended to the state. Under the Act, a two-tier system was introduced in the state.

The state government enacted the Manipur Panchayati Raj Act in 1975 which provided a three tier system of Panchayat in the state comprising Gram Panchayats at the Gram Sabha level, Panchayat Samities at the block level and Zilla Parishads at the district levels, besides Nyaya Panchayats for judicial purposes.

Post 73rd Amendment Developments

In conformity with the 73rd constitutional Amendment Act of 1992, the Manipur Panchayati Raj Act 1994 was passed on 23rd April, 1994 by repealing the Act of 1975.

The new Act has provided for the constitution of a two-tier Panchayati Raj in the valley areas, the Gram Sabha at the village level and Zilla Parishad at the district level.

The Act of 1994 was amended substantially in 1996 to accommodate gram sabha at the village level having population of not less than 3,000 and not more than 6,000. The last elections took place in 2001.

The state government has not devolved a number of the subjects to the Panchayats and elected members went on strike, demanding reinstatement of their rights.

Autonomous District Council

The Manipur (Hill Areas) District Council Act, 1971, an Act passed by the Parliament paved the way for establishment of six Autonomous District Councils in Manipur. In accordance with the powers vested on the Governor of Manipur, following six Autonomous Districts Councils were constituted on 14th February, 1972–

1. Churachandpur ADC
2. Chandel ADC

3. Senapati ADC

4. Sadar Hills ADC

5. Tamenglong ADC

6. Ukhrul ADC

The first election to the autonomous district councils was held in 1973.

Amendments to the Act: So far the 1971 Act has been amended thrice:

1975–The first amendment to the Act envisaged removal of the Chairman of the District Council by the Government for reasons to be recorded in writing upon passing of a resolution by the District Council by a simple majority of the total membership of the Council.

2006–The second amendment envisaged the following features:

- Notifying areas as urban areas for the purpose of development plan and to execute the works;

- Allotment/transfer/lease of land by a resolution passed by the District Council.

2008–The third amendment to the Act envisaged the following:

- Increase in membership from 18 to 24.

- Election Commission of the State to be entrusted election to HDC;

- Constitution of Executive Committee.

- Addition of 9 entries to the list of powers of the autonomous Hill Districts.

Municipal Councils

The Municipal Councils of Manipur are responsible for the overall development of the state. The Municipal councils of the state take several measures to achieve a balanced development of the state.

In Manipur there are 09 Municipal councils which are headed by the Municipality Commission.

1. Imphal Municipal Council

2. Thoubal Muc (TBL)

3. Kakching Muc (TBL)

4. Mayang Imphal Muc (I/W)

5. Nambol Muc (BPR)

6. Moirang Muc (BPR)

7. Ningthoukhong Muc (BPR)
8. Bishnupur Muc (BPR)
9. Jiribam Muc (I/E)

Nagar Panchayats

There are 18 Nagar Panchayat in the state. These are given below:

1. Lilong Thoubal NP (TBL)
2. Samurou NP (I/W)
3. Thongkhong Laxmi Bazar NP (I/W)
4. Lilong NP (I/W)
5. Kakching Khunou NP (TBL)
6. Andro NP (I/E)
7. Yairipok NP (TBL)
8. Kwakta NP (BPR)
9. Kumbi NP (TBL)
10. Wangoi NP (I/W)
11. Wangjing NP (TBL)
12. Lamshang NP (I/W)
13. Oinam NP (BPR)
14. Shikhong Sekmai NP (TBL)
15. Sugnu NP (TBL)
16. Sekmai NP (I/W)
17. Lamlai NP (I/E)
18. Heirok NP (TBL).

● ● ●

Districts

The Jewel of India in its wide territory of 22,327 sq.km. includes 16 districts named as Imphal-East, Imphal-West, Senapati, Tamenglong, Thoubal, Ukhrul, Bishnupur, Chandel, Churachandpur, Jiribam, Kangpokpi, Kakching, Tengnoupal, Kamjong, Noney and Pherzawl. Each of these districts has its own colourful culture, wide flora and fauna and many other specialities.

IMPHAL EAST

Introduction

Imphal East District came into existence on June 18, 1997. The District is situated in two separate valleys of the state namely Central Valley and Jiribam Valley. The District is situated at an altitude 790 metres above the M.S. Level. The climate of the District is salubrious and Monsoon is tropical. The minimum temperature goes down to 0.6 degree Celsius in winter and 41 degree Celsius in summer. It has no rail network and hence communication is entirely dependent on roads except Jiribam Sub-Division bordering Cachar District of Assam where there is a railhead. The District is connected with NH-39, NH-53 and NH-150.

District Profile

There are four Revenue Sub-Divisions in the district namely:- (1) Porompat Sub-Division; (2) Sawombung Sub-Division; (3) Keirao Bitra Sub-Division and (4) Jiribam Sub-Division. The total number of SDC Revenue Circles in the district is 9 (nine). There are 237 Revenue villages in the district. The total number of urban local bodies is 4 (four) comprising of 2 (two) Municipalities and 2 (two) Nagar Panchayats. The 2 Municipalities are Imphal Municipal Council and Jiribam Municipal Council whereas the 2 (two) Nagar Panchayats are Andro Nagar Panchayat and Lamlai Nagar Panchayat.

IMPHAL WEST

Introduction

The Imphal West District falls in the Category of Manipur valley region. It is a tiny plain at the centre of Manipur surrounded by Senapati District on the north, on the east by Imphal East and Thoubal districts, on the south by Thoubal and Bishnupur Districts, and on the west by Senapati and Bishnupur Districts. Imphal City, the State Capital is the nodal functional centre of this District.

Geographical Features

Climate

The district enjoys comfortable temperature throughout the year; not very hot in summer and not very cold in winter. Over all the climatic condition of the district is salubrious and monsoon tropical. The whole district is under the influence of the monsoons characterised by hot and humid rainy seasons during the summer, and cool and dry seasons during the winter. Temperature ranges from minimum of 0°C to maximum of 36°C. The district gets rainfall from the South-West monsoon.

Soil

The valley area of Imphal West district is fertile land and is mainly made up of alluvial soil of recent origin.

Rivers

Main rivers draining Imphal West plain are Imphal river, Nambul river and their tributaries.

Special Attractions

Shree Shree Govindajee Temple

A historic Vaishnavite center, adjoining the Royal palace of Manipur's former Maharajas, the Govindajee temple is a simple yet beautiful structure. Twin domes, a pave courtyard, and a large raised congregation hall form a perfect backdrop for priest who descend the steps, to accept offerings from devotees in the courtyard. The shrines of Krishna and Balaram and Jagannath flank the two sides of the presiding deity.

Women's Market or Ima Keithel

A unique all women's market, having 3000 "Imas" or mothers who run the stalls, it is split into two sections on either side of road. Vegetables, fruits, fish and household groceries are sold on one side and exquisite handlooms and household tools on the other. Not far away is a street where beautiful wicker works and basketry are sold.

War Cemeteries

Commemorating the memories of British and Indian soldiers who died during the Second World War, these cemeteries are managed by the Commonwealth War Graves Commission. Serene and well maintained, the graves carry little stone markers and bronze plaques recording the sacrifice of those gallant soldiers.

Manipur Zoological Gardens

6 km to west of Imphal city, at the foot of the pine growing hillocks at Iroisemba on the Imphal-Kanchup Road are the Zoological Gardens.

Manipur State Museum

This interesting museum near the polo ground has a fairly good display of Manipur's tribal heritage and a collection of portraits of Manipur's former rulers. Particularly interesting items are costumes, arms and weapons, relics and historical documents.

The District is under humid subtropical climate. The soil is moderately fertile with clay loam soil with little patches of clay and loam. The temperature ranges from a minimum of 3.36°C to a maximum of 34.14°C. The annual rainfall ranges from 671 mm to 1454 mm. There are about 110 watersheds each of geographical size ranging from 2000 to 3000 hectares, which are drained finally at about 5 major rivers /streams of different aspects and sources.

Special Attractions

Mao

Mao is one of the oldest Hill Stations of Manipur bordering Nagaland located midway between Dimapur and Imphal on the National Highway 39 at an altitude of 5762.02 feet above sea level. The Mao Inspection Bungalow built by the Royal Military Engineers in 1897 is a hundred years old. The cultural mosaic of Manipur is not complete without the colourful Mao Naga Dance.

Makhel

Makhel is the historical place of Naga dispersal and the legendary place of common origin of the Meiteis and Nagas. Makhel has the oldest pear tree, memorial to the dispersal, Dzukou valley with its pristine beauty blooms with a rare lily between May and July.

Geographical Features

Out of the state's nine districts, Tamenglong is located along the western boundary of the state. The land was believed to have been formed due to orogenic movement during cretaceous and Eocene period. The main rock formations are sandstone, shale, schist. Due to weak and fragile nature of rocks and high gradient of the hill slopes, landslide is a common phenomenon in the whole district in rainy season.

People and Culture

Tamenglong is inhabited by majority Zeliangrong Naga tribe (comprising of Rongmei, Liangmei, Zemei and Pumei) and Kukis, besides minority Hmars, Chirus and Khasis. Racially or physically and linguistically Zeliangrongs are Tibeto-Burman (Indo-Mongoloid) of Sino-Tibetan family of the Mongolian race. Based on history it is assumed that Mongoloid groups including Zeliangrong Nagas were inhabiting the upper course of the Yangtze and Howang Ho rivers in China in the prehistoric times.

The Zeliangrong belongs to patriarchal social system. Each clan enjoys equal status. Clan exogamy is strictly observed. Cross-cousin marriage is most preferred but parallel cross-cousin is seldom. Besides following many other normal customs of a Naga-tribe, they also have some strange and fearful customs. Some of them are as below:

Nasitheimei or Nathitheimei

If a woman die in childbirth the child is not permitted to live but buried with the dead mother.

Mandu (Bone money)

Mandu is the bone price of wife. Patrilineal relatives of the wife demand this. On the death of a wife her father demands Mandu from the husband, or if he be dead, the late husband's nearest relative. Mandu ensures that every care will be taken both of wife and offspring.

Flora and Fauna

Tamenglong District is blessed with virgin forests, exotic orchids, rare and endangered plants, and wildlife. The forests can be grouped as Tropical-Ever-green forest, Sub-tropical forest and Bamboo brakes. The dense tropical Evergreen Forests are located along both the sides of rivers flowing in the district, varieties of ground flora, creepers, herbs and grasses are found here. These forest are the main source of timbers. Cane brakes are found in and around water bodies. The Sub-tropical forests are found on the highest altitudes. Varieties of orchids are found in this zone of forests. In the degraded forest areas the bamboo brakes are found in plenty.

The forests are rich in wildlife. Pheasants, peafowl, jungle fowls are important birds of this area. The Sambar, deer, hog deer, bear, fox, hyena, wild pig, wild dogs, slow loris, serow are reported. Leopard and Tiger are also reported from Barak valley area and Tousem area. Migrated herds of elephants are sighted in Tousem during winter. Krait, Cobra, Viper and Python are found inside the forest. Large tortoises are found in the Zeilad lake. Varieties of cranes, ducks and teal are seen in the Zeilad lake.

European Kestrel, Falco tinnunculus, or Lesser Kestrel, Falco naumanni (local name is Akhoipuna / Kiuhoipuna), the migratory bird visits Tamenglong during the early winter till the last week of November.

Tamenglong is called as the land of the Hornbill. Great pied Hornbill and Indian pied Hornbill species are found here. A number of exquisite orchids are found. They are epiphytic, lithophytic and terrestrial in nature.

The Dendrobium, Vanda, Cymbidium, Cattleya and Lycaste are found in abundance. The Phius tunkervels, a rare terrestrial orchid is found in the Barak valley. Thunia alba which is known as bamboo orchid is found around Taobam village. Paphiopedilum is found in Leimatak area.

Special Attractions

Tamenglong district of Manipur is blessed with a topography of irregular undulation. It has in its small area most of the awesome features that nature mould to a hilly terrain. Turbulent waters, roaring waterfall, pitching dark caves, enchanting lakes of the wilderness, rocks chiseled to wondrous form and yet the thick blanket of dense tropical forest most part of which are still virgin.

Some of the popular tourist places of Tamenglong district are:

   (i) Along the river Barak there are seven waterfalls in series at close range.

(ii) The famous Tharon cave is located at about 27 kms from the district HQ. The map of the entire cave is engraved and painted on a stone at the main entrance. Archaeological excavation of the cave shows affinities with Hobinian culture of North Vietnam.

(iii) The legendary Zeilad lake at Makoi (Atengba) is associated with a number of pythons, fishes and water birds. There are six other lakes nearby Guiphop Zei, Nrou Zei, Nap-sam Zei etc.

(iv) The Buning (N-piulong) meadow is located on the western side of the picturesque Tamei town. A number of well-groomed uneven small mounts, numerous glittering brooks studded the stretch. Come June the meadow is coloured with enchanting groud orchids and various wild lilies. Cry of Hoolock gibbon, howling of foxes, melodious chirping of birds altogether form a big family of the wildlife evoking wonder and admiration of many who have witnessed the meadow.

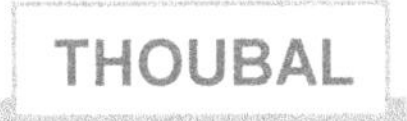

History

The district came into existence in May, 1983 through a notification of the Government of Manipur, under the Manipur Land Revenue and Land Reforms Act 1960. By the said notification, Thoubal sub-division of the erstwhile Manipur Central District (now Imphal district) with all its administrative units was transferred to form a new district under the name of Thoubal with its head quarters at Thoubal. Later, in November, 1983, Thoubal was bifurcated into Thoubal and Kakching sub-divisions comprising of Kakching and Waikhong Tahsils.

Although little is known about its ancient history, the district has in recent past, seen many bloody and disgraceful battles. Through the district runs an international road that leads to Myanmar (Burma) via Moreh and Tammu and this road is, in the days before the independence of India, the route of many military expeditions and counter-expeditions by the forces of Manipur and Burma, and later on, by that of the British Government. It is in this district, at Khongjom, that the last battle of the independence of Manipur was fought in April, 1891 by a few and ill-equipped soldiers of Manipur against the might of the British empire where the sun does not set, as the saying goes. It is not just an irony of the fate that Major Paona Brajabashi and others would meet their last days in this battle. The battle symbolizes the honourable deed of an extreme sacrifice for his motherland, knowing fully well that the fight would mean sure defeat.

Geographical Features

Rivers: Important rivers that flow through the district are the Imphal and the Thoubal. The Thoubal river originates in the hill ranges of Ukhrul and is an important tributary of the Imphal river. On its course, it passes through Yairipok and Thoubal before joining the Imphal at Irong near Mayang Imphal. The Imphal river rises in the hills of Senapati district and flows south. It forms the boundary demarcating line of Thoubal district on its north and the west. During the dry seasons these rivers are lean and thin but, during the rainy monsoon periods these rivers are very wild and frequent floods occur causing widespread damage to the paddy fields, property and life. These rivers were once good means of transport for valuable merchandise. Other rivers in the district are the Wangjing, the Arong and the Sekmai. These rivers originate in the hills of Ukhrul district. The Arong river flows through Khangabok and falls into Kharung Pat. The Wangjing river flows west via Heirok and Wangjing before joining the Loushi Pat.

Lakes: The south-western portion of the district is a low-land forming a part of the Loktak Lake region and this area has a number of shallow and rain fed lakes, the important ones being Kharung, Ikop, Pumlen, Lousi and Ngangou. On the northern portion there is Waithou lake form by the drainage waters sandwiched between Waithou hill on the west and the villages and paddy fields on the east. Due to constant siltation and reclamation of vast areas for agricultural purposes the lakes are gradually shrinking in size and at present some of them are only in name. These lakes drain into the Imphal river. They provided very good fishing ground for a variety of fishes in the recent past.

Hills: The district is dotted by a few hillocks and hills of low heights. Some of them are Mantak, Kwarok and Thongam Mondum-Punam. Of these, Punam hill has an elevation of 3310 ft. above sea level. Geologically, Khekman range belongs to the Brail Series and Simsang formation. Good vegetation once covered these hills. But constant deforestation have made them barren and unattractive.

Roads

The district has a fairly developed system of road transport. All towns and important villages in the district are connected either by the National or State or district or village roads. It is the only district in the state where the road length per km. is almost at per with the area per sq. km. of area against the state, average of only 19.17 km. The National Highway No. 39—Indo-Burma Road, passes through the heart of the district and connects Lilong with Pallel via Thoubal. From Thoubal an important district road goes east to Sikhong Sekmai via Yairipok. On the southern portion, the state highway connects Kakching, Wabagai and Sugnu with Imphal via Mayang Imphal. The widening of the district and state highways, construction of a number of bridges and culverts and metalling of kaccha roads will go a long way in further improving the road transport systems in the district.

Fair and Festivals

The district is mainly inhabated by the Meiteis, the majority of whom have professed Hinduism about 500 years ago and the important fair and festivals observed in the district are a mixture of Hindu culture and the age-old traditions and local beliefs. The biggest festival is the Dol Jatra (Yaosang in local Manipur langauge). Rath Yatra (Kang) is another important festival.

Introduction

Ukhrul District, the land of the colourful Tangkhuls was marked out first a Sub-Division in 1919 during the British Raj. Then in November 1969 it was upgraded to a full-fledged district, bearing the nomenclature of Manipur East District. The area of the district was 8,200 sq.km. according to the CSI Publication 1976. Later Tengnoupal District, now called Chandel District was carved out from this district on 15th July, 1983 and the area of the then Manipur East District was sliced down to 4,544 sq.km. and the title of the district was changed into Ukhrul District in 1983. Ukhrul is the District HQ, which, now, is extended down to Hundung.

Geographical Features

Ukhrul District is bounded by Myanmar in the east, Chandel District in the south, Imphal East and Senapati Districts in the west and Nagaland State in the north. The terrain of the district is hilly with a varying heights of 913 m to 3114 m (MSL). The district HQ Ukhrul is linked with Imphal, the state capital by a NH 150 about 84 km.

The climate of the district is of temperate nature with a minimum and maximum temperature of 3°C to 33°C. The average annual rainfall is about 1,763.7 mm. The exact location of the district in the globe is 24°N - 25.41°N and 94°E - 94.47°E. The rainy season in the district is from May to beginning of October broadly but Winter is chilly.

The highest peak is the Khayang peak-3114 m (MSL), though the more popularly known peak is the Shirui Kashung Peak - 2,835 m (MSL). Ukhrul, the District HQ is 2,020 m (MSL). Most of the major rivers originate from the crevices and slopes of this Shirui Peak.

The terrain of the district is rippled with small ranges and striped by few rivers. Somrah-Angkoching range, striped by Sanalok and Namba Lok; Shangshak-Phungyar range adjacent to which is the Shokvao - Mapithel - Kasom range striped by Tuyungbi and Taret Lok in the middle and Thoubal river in the West and Kachai-Hoome-Tampak Ngashan (Mahadev) range, striped by the tributaries of Thoubal river in Eastern side and Iril River in the Western side.

Administrative Set-up

Ukhrul District was first marked out as a Sub-Division in 1919 by the then British-India. Later it was upgraded to a District in the year 1969 by the Govt. of India. The District now has 5(five) Sub-Divisions which are co-terminus with the 5(five) Development Blocks. In addition to these administrative units the District has 4(four) Sub-Deputy Collectors Offices.

Flora and Fauna

Ukhrul District is best introduced by its beautiful Shirui Lily, Lilium Mackleanae Sealy, grown only on the peak of Shirui Kashung, some 18 km. east of the district HQ Ukhrul. This world famous Shirui Lily, which belongs to the lilium family was discovered by Frank Kingdon Ward in 1946 when he came to Manipur Hills for botanical collection on behalf of the New York Botanical Garden. The rareness and the uniqueness of this Lily is that, it has seven colours when examined through a microscope. Later, Frank won the prestigious prize of the Royal Horticulture Society Award, London in 1948. This Lily plant is 2ft. to 3ft. tall, consisting of a hard stem around which lanceolate leaves are spirally arranged.

The District is gifted with rich flora and fauna. There are hundreds of varieties of trees, barderian flowering plants, orchids of enumerable hues and kinds, Epiphetic ferns, varied species of plants and shrubs. Some of the known species of plants and trees are: Alder (Alnus nepalensis), Prunus cirosirdes, Symingtonia, Acacia auriculifornis, Parkia javanica, Paraserrianthes falcotaria, Michelia oblanga, Cmilina arborea, pinus kerya, robinea psedudoacacia, besides various iris species, wild roses, red and white rhododendrons etc.

Some of the important species of fish found in the district are; Golden Mhaseer (Tore Putitora) locally known as Ngara, Snow trout (schizothorax), locally known as khainguila, Barilius guteltus, locally called ngapaila,

Mastcembelus, locally known as chipang, Botia species, locally known as masengla, Naemecheilus species, locally known as hangkorkhai, Chana species, locally known as khaiva, Pontius species, locally known as khaiwonla and khaipukla, Esomus species, locally known as wonsangla, Gara species, cyprinio semiplotus, glyptothorax plailigopanoide, botisdorio, xenden cacila etc.

History

The original name of Bishnupur was Lumlangdong (now Lamangdong). As soon as Kyamba ascended the throne of Manipur in 1467 A.D he conquered Kyang, which was a Shan kingdom in the Kabow Valley. Then he assumed the name of Kyamba which means the conquerer of Kyang. There always had been a good relation between the Pongs and the Meities. During the reign of Kyamba there was good relations between Kyamba and the Pong King Khe-Khomba. Actually it was the good foreign policy of King Kyamba that he was able to have a good relation with the neighbouring countries.

Kyamba wanted to conquer Kyang. So around the thirds of his reign he attacked Kyang along with Chaopha Khe Khomba, the king of Pong. After the battle was won, the conquered areas were divided between the two kings, they dined together in golden vessels and drank in join made of gold. They also exchanged servants and scholars. It is said that an image of Vishnu was given by the Pong king along with the fruit pong "hei" ton (guava) and the ponghawai (a kind of dal), Kyamba kept the given "Vishnu" image at Lumlangdong which also came to be known as Bishnupur i.e. abode of Vishnu. Perhaps, it was during the reign of Kyamba that Vishnu worship started in Manipur. This Bishnupur is the very place where king and Brahmins conserved the lord "Vishnu". Manu Brahmins also immigrated to Manipur. King Kyamba requisitioned the service of one such Brahmins and began the regular worshiper of Vishnu here at Bishnupur.

He built Vishnu Temple, the Temple of brick, at Bishnupur which has now become a protected historical monument under the Ministry of HRD (Archaeology), Government of India. It is now standing as a symbol of the remains of ancient times. And the statue got by Kyamba from the Pong king is very important since it gives us the idea of the religious beliefs of those days and the very name that it had given.

Another remarkable feature of Bishnupur is worth mentioning. During the reign of King Bheigyachandra, there was an interesting story regarding the installation of the statue of Shri Shri Govindajee which was performed in 1780 A.D. It is also said that one night Lord Krishna appeared in his dream and asked him to find an image of the Lord. Bheigyachandra answered the command of the Lord and founded the statue of Govindajee. Along with this statue, another six statues were made from the same jackfruit tree. They are Bijoy Govinda (now at Sagolband, Imphal); Gopinath (at Ningthoukhong); Nityainanda (at Imphal); Madan Mohan (at Imphal); Anuprabhu (at Nabadwip, West Bengal) and Abdeitya, now enshrined at Bishnupur.

The installation ceremony of the statue of Abdeitya enshrined in Bishnupur in the Vishnu temple took place in the year 1793 A.D. Since then, a number of pilgrims and saints have been visiting this temple.

Special Attractions

Keibul Lamjao National Park: Keibul Lamjao National Park is situated 53 km from Imphal on the fringes of Loktak Lake. The only floating National Park in the World, on the Loktak Lake is the last natural habitat of "Sangai"—the dancing deer of Manipur. A glimpse of the deer in this unique wetland ecosystem is a must for any wildlife enthusiast. Other wildlife like Hog Deer, Otter and a host of water fowls and migratory birds can also be sighted during November to March. The Forest Department maintains watch towers and two rest houses within the park.

Loktak Lake And Sendra Island: Loktak Lake is a largest fresh water lake in the North-Eastern region located 48 km from Imphal. Loktak Lake is a huge and beautiful stretch of water spread upto 312 sq. km. area and looks like a miniature island sea. From the Tourist Bungalow set atop Sendra Island, visitors get a birds eye view of life on the Lake. The Sendra Tourist Home with an attached Cafeteria in the middle of the lake is an ideal tourist spot, boating and other water sports can also be enjoyed here. Fishermen and their families who live near the shores of lake in neat huts also build their houses on island of floating weed that dirt around the lake. A myriad hues grace the lake from the warm golden glow of dawn to the peach, pinksand greys of the day and the absolute silver of high noon.

Phubala: Phubala resort is a virgin land 40 km south of Imphal. The marshy islands of Loktak actually float. Besides the human inhabitants of the lake, there are other life forms here too. Living along the reedy marshes and swamps bordering the lake is the kingdom of Manipur's endangered Brow Antlered Deer or Tkamin. They live in small herds, lying up in cover during the day and feeding in the mornings and evenings. There are very few of them left here, because their delicately balanced eco-system has been endangered by progress. Captive colonies of them, however, have been relocated in safer areas and they are thriving awaiting their return to beautiful Loktak.

INA Memorial—Moirang: 45 kms from Imphal, the town is one of the main centres of early Meitei folk culture with the ancient temple of the pre-Hindu deity Lord Thangjing, situated here. Every year a ritual dance festival "Lai Haraoba" held here in the month of May, when men and women, dressed in colourful traditional costumes sing and dance in honour of the Lord at the Moirang.

The town also has a special place in the history of the Indian Freedom Struggle. It was at Moirang that the flag of the Indian National Army was first unfurled on April 14,1944. The INA Museum containing letters, photograghs, badges of ranks and other memorabilia reminds the visitor of the noble sacrifices made by the INA under the charismatic leadership of Netaji Subhash Chandra Bose.

Loukoipat Ecological Park: Under the Ecological Development plan of the Government of Manipur, the Management Committee was constituted of the District Level Officers and public leaders of the Bishnupur for establishment and management of an Ecological park at Bishnupur. Accordingly the Ecological park at Loukoipat, Bishnupur was established in the early part of 1992.

To have a better tourist attraction, the Management Committee of the Ecological Park hired 4 Pedalos (Pedal Rowing Boat) from the Directorate of Tourism, Government of Manipur. The said boats were put into service at Loukoipat lake within the Ecological Park, Bishnupur.

Geographical Features

The Chandel District (formerly known as Tengnoupal District) came into existance on May 13, 1974. The District lies in the south-eastern part of Manipur. It is the border district of the state. Its neighbors are Myanmar (erstwhile Burma) on the south and the east, Churachandpur district on the south and west, and Thoubal district on north. It is about 64 km away from Imphal. The National Highway No. 39 passes through this District.

The District is inhabited by several communities. It is sparsely inhabited by about 20 different tribes. Prominent tribes in the district are Anal,

Lamkang, Kukis, Moyon, Monsang, Chothe, Thadou, Paite, and Maring etc. There are also other communities like Meiteis, and Muslims in small numbers as compared to the tribes. Non-Manipuris like the Tamils, Bengalis, Punjabis, and Biharis are also settled in this district.

The Moreh town, the international trade center of the state lies on the southernmost part of the District. When the Trans-Asian Super Highway comes into existence, Chandel district will be one of the gateways to the Asian countries.

Even though considered as one of the backward districts, Chandel is not left behind when the safety of the nation comes.

Special Attractions

Tengnoupal: It is about 20 km from Chandel. The highest point on the Indo-Myanmar Road, from here one can enjoy a full view of the valley of Manipur. When a visitor passed along the road, he will find himself above the clouds but in natural surroundings.

Moreh: This border town is located on the Indo-Myanmar Road, about 70 km from Chandel. Being a commercial town it attracts a large number of people from neighbouring places. Moreh is only 5 km from Tamu town, its Myanmar counterpart. Opening of the Border Trade turns Moreh into an important centre in the Northeast.

CHURACHANDPUR

Introduction

The Statehood in 1972 saw Manipur divided into five districts, simply called Central, West, East, North and South Districts. The Central District comprised of the whole of the Imphal Valley and Jiribam Sub-Division, which in the 1980s was further divided into the three valley districts of Imphal, Bishnupur and Thoubal.

The East, West, North and South Districts later became the hill districts of Ukhrul, Tamenglong, Senapati and Churachandpur respectively. A fifth hill district, Chandel, was carved out from the erstwhile East and South Districts.

Among the hill districts, the fastest growing district headquaters and hill-town is that of Churachandpur. It is truly an island of peace, tranquility, prosperity and progress. Here all the communities of Manipur live happily in small but noticeable sizes amongst the more populous tribal folk belonging to Chin, Kuki, Mizo, Naga and Zomi ethnic groups—a mosaic of tribes, well laid out and glowing with life.

Churachandpur, which the locals call "Lamka"—meaning roads meeting at a mouth—possesses an air of fledging cosmopolitanism and can appropriately be dubbed 'The Cosmopolitan Hill Town of Manipur.'

Churachandpur / Lamka is a mini-India, living, thriving yet trying to find its feet. It is colourful, dynamic and vibrant; a well laid out mosaic, bright and attractive; a beautifully woven and patterned fabric of a God-fearing society. Two ethnic classes—the Kuki-Naga(1992) and Kuki-Zomi(1997)—tore at the long and painstakingly-woven fabric of tribal co-existence. But with changing times and advent of the new millennium, and the rips in the fabric is being mended in the able and loving hands of weaver-craftsfolk, the tribal themselves who have learnt through pain.

SEVEN NEW DISTRICTS CREATED

The Governor of Manipur on December 8, 2016 (No. 16/20/2016-R) ordered the creation of 7 new districts by bifurcating the following existing districts:

Sl. No.	Existing Districts	New Districts	Sub-division under the newly created districts
1.	Imphal East	1. Imphal East	Porompat, Keirao Bitra & Sawombung
		2. Jiribam	Jiribam & Borobekra
2.	Senapati	3. Senapati	Tadubi, Paomata, Purul, Willong, Chilival Phaibung, Tuijang Waichong, Song-Song & Lairouching
		4. Kangpokpi	Kangpokpi, Champhai, Saitu Gamphazol, Kangchup Geljang, Saikul, Lungtin, Island & Bungte Chiru
3.	Thoubal	5. Thoubal	Thoubai & Lilong
		6. Kakching	Kakohirig & Waikhong
4.	Chandel	7. Chandel	Chandel, Chakpikarong & Khengjoy
		8. Tengnoupal	Machi, Moreh & Tengnoupal
5.	Ukhrul	9. Ukhrul	Ukhrui, Lungchong-Maiphai, Chingai & Jessami
		10. Kamjong	Kamjong, Sahamphung, Kasom Khuilen & Phungyar
6.	Churachandpur	11. Churachandpur	Churachandpur, Sangaikot, Tuibuong, Mualnuam, Singngat, Henglep, Kangvai, Samulamlan, Saikot
		12. Pherzawl	Pherzawl, Thanlon, Parbung-Tipaimukh & Vangai Range
7.	Tamenglong	13. Tamenglong	Tamenglong, Tamei & Tousem
		14. Noney	Nungba, Khoupum, Longmei (Noney) & Haochong

Note: *The detailed information of seven newly created districts are not available. The data of these districts are included in those districts from which they are created.*

● ● ●

CHAPTER 22

The People

The people of Manipur are grouped into three main ethnic communities - Meiteis those inhabiting the valley and 29 major tribes in the hills dividing into two main ethno-denominations, namely Nagas and Kuki-Chins. Under the Meiteis, Bamon and Meitei Pangans are also included. All speak Meiteilon or otherwise known as Manipuri to the outsiders. In addition to Meiteis, the valley is also inhabited by Nepalis, Bengalis, Marwaris and other Indian communities. At present several people from the hill have also migrated and settled in the valley. The Naga group consists of Zeliangrong (composed of three related tribes, namely, Rongmei or Kabui, and Liangmei and Zemei or Kacha Nagas), Tangkhul, Mao, Maram, Maring and Tarao. The Chin-Kuki group consists of Gangte, Hmar, Paite, Thadou, Vaiphei, Zou, Aimol, Chiru, Koireng, Kom, Anal, Chothe, Lamgang, Koirao, Thangal, Moyon and Monsang. In recent times, several Chin-Kuki communities have identified themselves as Nagas *e.g.*, Anal, Kom, Thangal, etc. depending on socio-economic and geo-political advantages to the tribes. The term Chin is used for the people in the neighboring Chin state of Myanmar whereas Chins are called Kukis in the Indian side. Other groups like Paite, Zou, Gangte, and Vaiphei identify themselves as Zomi and have distanced themselves from the name, Kuki. Thadous remain the major Kuki population in this Chin-Kuki group while Hmar identify closer to the Mizo or Lushei group.

One needs to examine the different communities of Manipur individually in order to bring out an understanding and to start a meaningful dialogue among themselves.

Aimol

The aimols are a scheduled tribe of Manipur. They settled at Aimol Khullen at Chandel District and at Kha-Aimol near Loktak lake and other places in the Senapati district. It is also believed that some migrated in Mizoram and Tripura. Thus, their legend believes that they came out of mountain like the mountain crabs. They practice both wet and shifting paddy cultivation in the hill. Some of the crops other than paddy are sesamum, maize, soyabean, pumpkin, gourd, ginger, tomato, chilly and groundnut. Kakching and Pallel are the two important towns for marketing and trading. Most of the Aimols are now converted to Christianity and identify with the Nagas although they may be related to the Chin-Kuki group.

Anal

The Anals are also a scheduled tribe settled in the Southern Manipur hills at Tengnoupal district. They are known as Pakan among themselves. During migration, they were splitted to Anal, Lamkang, Moyon, and Monsang tribes. Anal is considered to be one of the oldest Chin-Kuki tribes of Manipur and belong to the Tibeto-Burman family of tribes. Their cultural life is rich and preserved in traditional folklores and folksongs.

Chiru

They are concentrated in Senapati, Tamenglong and Bishnupur districts of Manipur. Their manners, customs, and language appear to identify with Kuki origin but their physique, habits, hairstyle, and bachelors' quarters are Naga way of life. The word Chiru means the seed of a plant. Women play an important role in agricultural work, collection of firewood, and fetching water for drinking and household uses. They practise both shifting and wet cultivation.

Gangte

The Paite, Vaiphei and Thadou call them Gangte but Mizos call them Rangte. Their origin is traced in a cave called *khul* somewhere in the extreme north. They settle mostly in the Southern part of Churachandpur district. Apeasement of the village deity was an annual feature before they converted to Christianity. They share folksongs, folktales and dances with other communities like Paite, Zou, Thadou, Vaiphei and vice versa.

Hmar

They speak Hmar language and converse well in Meiteilon. They also have populations in Cachar, North Cachar and Aizwal district of Mizoram. They are one of the highly educated Christian communities of Manipur tribes. They enjoy zu, home brewed rice bear, but Christianity has restricted it and replaced with tea in rituals. Earlier Hmars worshiped spirits, the mountains, the rocks and rivers.

Koirao

Koiraos inhabit the mountain ranges in the south of the Mao and Maram but they accept themselves by the name Thangal. They are concentrated in the Sadar hills of Senapati district. They believe that children are a gift of God and the village maibi will pronounce the birth of a child by saying *Haiguiye* while holding a dagger in her hand. *Khullakpa* is the chief of the village council known as *Katammi*. Favorite festival is *Linhut tangnit* (Seed sowing festival), along with Christian festivals.

Koireng

The Koirengs believe that they originated from a cave. Pathian is believed to be their supreme God before Christianity. They live in small villlages on the hills to the north of Imphal valley in Senapati district. Imphal, Iril, and Maklang rivers run through their villages. The status of women is relatively high due to their taking part in economic activities. A woman member is also represented in the village council. They cultivate paddy, maize, sesame, potato, arum and ginger and traded with the Meiteis.

Kom

The Koms believe that thier ancestors came out of a hole in the earth or Kom. Their language is to an extent recognised by the Aimol, Koireng and Chiru. They also have close relationship with the Hmar. The Koms are easily identified by their way of dressing. They wear a black shawl embroidered in the border. Koms believe in Pathen, the supreme god and goddess, Lengjai. They are omnipresent and believe to live in the heaven.

Kukis

The Kukis are also called Khongjois. They are distributed widely in Manipur, occupying the south-western, south and south-eastern hills which spread in the district of Churachandpur, Tangnoupal district and Sadar hills in the north Manipur. There are different beliefs about their origin. Some of the Kukis believe their origin is in the north at a place Maikel. Some traces the Kukis links with Zomi, who migrated from China. The term Zomi is an ancient and historical name of the Zo ethnic groups (Zo means cold region and Mi means men). With the reference to the alpine climate the people living on the hills could be named as Kuki. The Kukis who came to Manipur during 1830 and 1840 were a nomadic race. Some authorities consider them having traces to Malaya peninsula. There are different groups among Kukis. Those who migrated from Mizoram are called Mizos and are educationally advanced. Another group of those migrated from Burma side in 1830 is like the Paite. Manipuris consider Kukis to be of two groups, old Kuki and new Kuki. The new group of Kukis is the group comprising those who migrated to Manipur during the region of Raja Nar Singh. The old Kukis of Manipur are the Thadao and Vaipei.

Langang

The Lamgang dialect is quite similar to Anal, Moyon and Monsang of the Kuki-Chin group of languages of the Tibeto-Burman family. They speak Meiteilon while talking to others. They address themselves as Kasen.

Lois

The Lois consider themselves as the oldest inhabitants. Lois means 'slaves or dependent'. These small tribals inhabit the valley of Manipur. They are called Singmei, Undro and Chairel. All of them speak different dialects but with a considerable mixture of Manipuri words.

Mao

The Maos inhibit the hill ranges to the extreme north of Manipur on Highway 39. The Mao as such is the village or place and the people are Maomei or Imemei. The Angamis of Kohima call them as Shipfumei. The literacy rate among tribes in the Mao area are high.

Maring

It is said that they had close relationship with the Meitei Kings and their name derived from mei (fire) and ring (start or produce). Meitei kings depended on them during wars with neighbors. There are three mains groups of Marings who identify themselves with different colors in their clothings: Black, Red, and Red and Black on the border. They participate actively in the State politics. If provided adequate road and communication infrastructure, they will be a very progressive group of tribes.

Meiteis

The Meiteis are distributed throughout the Manipur valley. By rule, any Meitei is not allowed to own land in the hills while the people of the hill can live anywhere in Manipur. The Meiteis make up about 60% of the total population of Manipur. Among the Meitei-fold are included the Bamons (Brahmins), Pangans (muslims), and other schedule caste groups like the Chakpas (previously called lois) and Thoubal Khunous (previously, Yaithibis). A large number of Meiteis also follow the traditional Sanamahi religion at present after the revival of the old Sannamahi faith. Even the Bamons and Hindu Meiteis worship Sanamahi inside their houses. The Vaishnavite culture of Meiteis and the Ras Lila Dance is known widely in India and other countries.

The Meiteis are also primarily agriculturalists. Rice is the staple food. Fish is a favorite meat for Hindu Meiteis. But, the younger generation tastes all kinds of meat available in the market. Fruits such as pineapple, mango, orange, lemon, guava, jackfruit are also cultivated. Produces like peas, potatoes, cabbage, cauliflower, carrot, etc. are abundant.

Monsang

The name Monsang is derived from the name of the village called Mosang by the Meiteis and others whereas they themselves called *sirti* or southerners. They live mostly in the Chandel District in five villages namely Liwachaning, Heibunglok, Liwa Sarei, Japhou, and Monsang Pantha. They speak a similar language with the Anals.

Moyon

The Moyon themselves are known as Bujuur. Their legend indicates that they originated from a cave located at Sijjur. Their sowing festival is known as *Sachii ichii* and harvest festival is *Buren limpeh*. They also believe that they originated from a cave, known as Khur or Khul. The Moyons attach considerable importance to education and every village has at one primary school. They converse and read Meiteilon (Manipuri) very well.

Naga

The Nagas occupy the northern, north-eastern, and north-western hills of Manipur. The different groups of Nagas are Thangkhuls, Mao, Muram Nagas, Tadubi, Kolya, Khoiras or Mayang Khong, Kabuis, Koirengs, Chirus and Marings. There are several stories about the origin of different groups of Nagas. It is believed that Nagas and Meiteis have common ancestors.

Paite

They live in Churachandpur district in Southern Manipur. Along with Thadou, Vaiphei, Gangte, Hmar and others they were refered to as Chin-Kuki group in the past. Jhum cultivation is their main occupation on the slopes near the villages.

Tangkhul

They live in the Ukhrul district in the east. According to their legend, two groups led by two brothers went out to seek suitable places for settlement. They believe they migrated from Mekhel village in Senapati destrict like other Naga tribes.

Tarao

They are a minor community in the Chandel district. They speak Taraotrong but speak Meiteilon well with others. The Taraos were also referred to as Kuki in earlier ethnographic studies but now they identify with the Nagas. It is said that Maharaja Chingthang Khomba had an orchard at a place near Pallel and his orange trees were looked after by the Taraos at Komlathabi. They are concentrated at four villages. They are involved in planting fruits like banana, lemon, pineapple, papaya, etc. Their land is considered to be the driest place in Manipur.

Thadou

The Thadou are a schedule tribe of Manipur. They are classifed as an Old Kuki Group by anthropologists. Their communities are dispersed in several districts of Manipur. The history of this community is found in oral traditions including folklore and folktales. Their origin traces like other tribes of Manipur to a cave at the origin of Gunn river (Imphal river). They can be identified by the traditional design of the shawls, which are marked in black with a few stripes of red.

Vaiphei

Their dialect is Vaiphei and slightly different from the Gangte, Zou and Paite. Their speech is closer to Gangte but spell similar to Paite. They use Roman characters. The major economic source is the jhum cultivation from paddy and depend on forest products.

Zeliangrong

The Zeliangrong is a composite group of three related tribes inhabiting in the Tamenglong district of Western Manipur. The three groups are Rongmei (Kabuis), Liangmei and Zemei (also called Kacha Nagas). Many Kabui villages are also found in the plains of Manipur, Assam and few settlements in Nagaland.

Zou

Zous live close to the Paites and have close similarities. They share many oral traditions, folklore, dance and music with Paites. They also claim to have originated from a cave or *khul* somewhere in the extreme north. Their number is about 11,251 in 1981. The village administration is at the hands of the village chief. Their economy is low and mostly depend on agriculture and labor for small wages.

Muslims

Muslims are living in several villages at Mayang, Imphal, Yaripok, Lylong, Thoubal etc. Their main occupation is agriculture. Some educated ones also seek official jobs in state and central government service. They are intelligent and hard-working persons. They have mixed characters of Mongoloid and Aryans in their features. They follows all norms of the Muslim society.

Sikhs

The Sikhs settled in Manipur are of Punjab origin but most of them have come from Burma where they had gone from Punjab in earlier times. Some of them entered Manipur after the Second World War and some others after the Burmese government disallowed them the citizenship. They have Gurudwaras at Imphal and Moreh. At these two places only they are largely concentrated. All Sikhs keep beard and wear turban. They are strict in keeping the five "ks", the kesha, kangha, kripan, kara, kachha i.e. to grow hair, keep comb, keep sword, keep armlet and wear shorts. All Sikhs are businessmen dealing in transport, cloths and contracts etc. They are pioneer transporters in Manipur. Salwar-kurta or sari-blouse is the common dress among Sikh women. They speak Punjabi among themselves but are also fluent in Meitei and even tribal languages. The Sikhs of Moreh also speak Burmese. They are an adaptable society. They keep their culture and are very particular about their faith and the ritualistic performances in the Gurudwaras and their homes. Sikhs believe in the gurus, the great religious teachers who got the inspirations from the God and taught the masses to follow the right path. For the Sikhs the guru is the guide to the religious path.

Nepalis

The Nepalis are the old settlers in Manipur. The contribution of Nepalis to the Manipuri society is valuable. Most of the Nepalis entered Manipur as servants and labourers and settled here. Some started cultivation of the tribal chief's land as tenants with sufficient share of the crops. They were known for cattle rearing. Most of the settlers started dairies along with their agriculture. Nepalis have scattered into small valleys in Mao, Maram, Karong and Kangpokpi areas. This is the main belt of Nepalis and they have improved agriculture and crops in Kangpokpi, Tomei-Tamenglong areas. Their thick population is between Tomei and Kangpokpi. The greatest contribution of the Nepalis is to transform the habitat to their advantage.

Bishnupuris

Some people of lower caste entered Manipur and they got good promises for their labour and jobs. Safaiwalas, cobblers, watermen, gardeners, washermen etc. were not available. Manipur being a casteless society was unmindful of these requirements. In Manipur these jobs are done by all. There are some Sudra Manipuris who are supposed to be the descendants of immigrants who married Manipuri women. This is also a degraded class called Kalacheiya or Bishnupuris which consists of descendants of Doms and other Bengalis of low castes. They have played an important role in the society. In Manipuri society they are respected. There is no concept of untouchability. Those who are declared bonafide citizens of Manipur get the reservation benefits.

Biharis

Most of the labour class comprises people of Bihar and Uttar Pradesh. They have come here to earn their bread. They are fluent in Meitei as well as in Tribal dialects. They have established themselves throughout the valley on all routes. Biharis speak their Hindustani and also learn tribal dialects. This linguistic exchange is a great social advantage to both sides. The Biharis have maintained their culture. Their Hindustani dress will never change. They are all Hindus. Some are from upper castes and some from scheduled castes. Some Muhamadans have also migrated from Bihar in search of jobs or to run shops in Manipur. The curious character of Biharis is that they get adapted to any society. They are very good at business. They give due respect to the tribal and Meitei social custom and take part in the social ceremonies. The Biharis help each other and they are known for their unity.

Punjabis

There are some non-Sikh Punjabi traders settled at Imphal. Their contribution to Punjabi culture is worth mentioning. Their dishes are very tasty. They retain their habit of speaking Punjabi amongst themselves. They speak in a hilarious and jubilant mood. Their women wear salwar-kurta, sari and are very fond of cosmetics. Inside Punjabi house one finds several items of furniture and comfort. They believe in decent living and eating.

Marwaris

Marwaris are the dominating business community in the north-eastern region. They deal in big business and wholesale trade. Their concentrations are only in the established old towns and business centres like Imphal,

Churachandpur and Moreh. They have entered Manipur in the late nineteenth and early twentieth century. They migrated from Rajasthan. Their religion is Hinduism, some observe Jainism and some Sanatan Dharm. Some have adopted Vaishnavite sect. They marry within their community. Generally they live as joint family. Their food habits are very simple. They are vegetarian and refrain from meat, egg, chicken and alcoholic drinks. Their dress is unique. They wear white kurta pyjama without turban or with white turban. Their women wear sari and choli. During Hindu festival their women are dressed in costly saris. Their marriage parties are the occasions to display their rich clothes they wear. Their greatest contribution to Manipuri society is business mobilization in this isolated state. They have created a vital business line between Moreh, Imphal and Dimapur. There are Jains among Marwaris and also from Uttar Pradesh and other parts of the country.

South Indians

Moreh town of Manipur is the real settlement of Tamils and Keralites. Most of them are refugees from Burma. They have introduced Idli and Dosa, the famous snack dishes of South Indians to the Meiteis and tribals. The men dress in lungi and shirt. Office goers wear pants and shirts. The women wear sari and blouse. They are all Hindus and a few Christians may also be there. Moreh Tamils are all Hindus and have established several temples of Kali, Durga and Shiva in the town. They also celebrate their festivals with great pomp and show.

Bengalis

The Bengalis are the old settlers in Manipur. Due to the geographical closeness with Bengal the land has experienced a lot in respect of socio-cultural and socio-religious interaction between the two societies. The contribution of Bengalis to the Manipuri society is valuable. Bengalis are one of the most advanced and intellectually superb ethnical group of India. Bengali dress of the men is dhoti, kurta, shawl and turban which is same as of a Meitei man. The women wear sari and blouse. The food habits resembles those of Meiteis. Bengalis are rice eaters and fish is the main dish at every evening meal. They take keen interest in celebrations of Hindu festivals. They have maintained their Bengali culture with its finest heritage. They speak Bengali. Bengalis in Manipur are in almost all government offices, business and in teaching profession. Some of them have married Meitei girls.

Thus, Manipur is having all kinds of people and the society gets status of a cosmopolitan society and all groups are in harmonious relations.

Govt. Recognised Tribes

The Government of Manipur has recognised 32 tribes in the state. These are as follows:

1. Aimol	9. Anal	17. Angami	25. Chiru
2. Chothe	10. Gangte	18. Hmar	26. Kabui
3. Kacha Naga	11. Kharam	19. Koirao	27. Koireng
4. Kom	12. Lamgang	20. Lusai Tribes	28. Maram
5. Maring	13. Mao	21. Monsang	29. Mayon
6. Paite	14. Poumi Naga	22. Purum	30. Ralte
7. Sema	15. Simte	23. Sahlte	31. Tangkhul
8. Tarao	16. Thadou	24. Vaiphei	32. Zou

● ● ●

Manipur GK
MULTIPLE CHOICE QUESTIONS

1. The first Chief Minister of Manipur State was:
   A. Rishang Keishing
   B. R.K. Dorendro Singh
   C. M.K. Priyobrata Singh
   D. O. Ibobi Singh

2. The shrine at Kaina in Manipur was built during the reign of which king?
   A. Shri Jai Singh Maharaja
   B. Maharaja Bhagyachandra
   C. Meidingu Nongdaa Lairen Paakhangba
   D. Maharaja Pamheiba

3. Which of the following is/are true with regard to Forest Survey of India Report 2017:
   1. The forest and tree cover of Manipur is 77.69% of its geographical area.
   2. There is a decrease in forest cover of Manipur compared to 2015 assessment.
   3. There is an increase in forest cover of Manipur compared to 2015 assessment.
   4. The Main reason for change in forest cover in Manipur is shifting cultivation.
   Codes:
   A. 1 only
   B. 1, 2 and 4
   C. 3 and 4
   D. 1 and 3

4. National Waterways 6 is a proposed waterway announced in Budget 2013-2014. It is planned to integrate the waterways in the
   A. North eastern states
   B. Vidarbha region of Maharashtra
   C. Bundelkhand region of Uttar Pradesh and Madhya Pradesh
   D. Kalahandi region of Odisha

5. Locate Senapati District on this Map of Manipur

   A. A
   B. B
   C. C
   D. D

6. The Manipur State Durbar was established in 1907
   A. to assist the Maharaja in the administration of Manipur
   B. to assist the British in the administration of Manipur

   C. to assist the Government of India in the administration of Manipur
   D. None of the above

7. In Manipuri history, Jadonang who was hanged in August, 1931 was
   A. a great Meitei leader
   B. a great Zeliangrong leader
   C. a great Zomi leader
   D. a great Naga leader

8. The Manipuri kings who got titles of KCSI are
   A. Chandrakriti and Budhachandra Maharaja
   B. Budhachandra and Surchandra Maharaja
   C. Surchandra and Churachand Maharaja
   D. Chandrakriti and Churachand Maharaja

9. Match the items in List-I with List-II and select the correct answer from the code given below:

List-I
(*a*) B.C. Allen
(*b*) Mrs. Ethel Grimwood
(*c*) James Johnstone
(*d*) William Shaw

List-II
1. *Gazetteer of Naga Hills and Manipur*
2. *My Experience in Manipur and Naga-Hills*
3. *My Three Years in Manipur*
4. *Notes on Thadou Kukis*

Code:

	(*a*)	(*b*)	(*c*)	(*d*)
A.	1	2	3	4
B.	2	1	4	3
C.	1	3	2	4
D.	2	1	3	4

10. The "mighty Vaishnava ruler and conqueror who styled himself as the refugee of the poor and in whose character is found the rare combination of a martial quality of a Kshatriya and the humility of a Vaishnava", refers to
   A. Khagemba
   B. Charairongba
   C. Garibniwaja
   D. None of these

11. According to 2011 Census total population of Manipur is
   A. 28,55,794
   B. 31,99,203
   C. 23,18,822
   D. None of these

12. According to 2011 Census, Sex ratio in Manipur is—
   A. 935   B. 948
   C. 985   D. 919

13. 'State Fish' of Manipur is—
   A. Hilsa   B. Pabda
   C. Karimeen   D. Pengba

14. In which year Manipuri (Meitei) language was included in 8th schedule?
   A. 1992   B. 1995
   C. 2001   D. 1990

15. Birth place of Polo game is—
   A. China
   B. Manipur
   C. Meghalaya
   D. Uttar Pradesh

16. 'Pung Cholom' is—
   A. a dance   B. a animal
   C. a bird   D. a tree

17. Who was the first governor of Manipur?
   A. Shri B.K. Nehru
   B. Shri L.P. Singh
   C. Shri Ved Marwah
   D. Shri Arvind Dave

18. How many Parliamentary Constituencies are in Manipur?
    A. 1   B. 2
    C. 3   D. 4

19. In which year the "Manipur Municipality Act" was introduced in the Urban areas of the State?
    A. 1976   B. 1977
    C. 1969   D. 1975

20. The first president of Manipur Pradesh congress was—
    A. E. Tompok
    B. M. Koireng
    C. R.K. Bhubonsana
    D. L. Jugeswer

21. In which festival of Manipur, long narrow boats are used—
    A. Cheiraoba
    B. Heikru Hindongba
    C. Ningol Chakouba
    D. None of these

22. If India adopts two time zones based on 75° E meridian for western India and 90° E meridian for eastern India, which one among the following states of eastern India will be benefited most?
    A. Manipur
    B. West Bengal
    C. Assam
    D. Bihar

23. The chief racial groups constituting India's population are the Dravidian, Aryans, and Mongoloids. Where do the Mongoloids live?
    A. Western India
    B. Southern India
    C. North-Eastern India
    D. South-Western India

24. Which is the largest producer of Pineapple in Manipur?
    A. Churachandpur
    B. Chandel
    C. Thoubal
    D. Senapati

25. Who introduced 'Boat Race' in Manipur?
    A. Thangbi Lanthabu
    B. Keiphaba Yanglon
    C. Ninthou Punshiba
    D. Gambhir Singhla

26. The Manipur Merger Agreement was signed in—
    A. Sept. 15, 1949
    B. Sept. 21, 1949
    C. Oct. 15, 1949
    D. Oct. 21, 1949

27. The total length of the border of Manipur is—
    A. 854 km
    B. 352 km
    C. 750 km
    D. None of these

28. How long Manipur has common border with Myanmar?
    A. 452 km
    B. 352 km
    C. 500 km
    D. None of these

29. Highest Peak of the Manipur is—
    A. Mt. Essau or Tenipu
    B. Mt. Everest
    C. Siroi
    D. Kala Nagar

30. 'Thoubal' is the important tributary of the river
    A. Imphal
    B. Barak
    C. Brahmaputra
    D. None of these

31. In Manipur proportion of tribal population is—
    A. 41.51%
    B. 51.51%
    C. 40.88%
    D. None of these

32. In Manipur, total Forest covered area is—
  A. 17,346 sq. km
  B. 12,481 sq. km
  C. 5,309 sq. km
  D. None of these

33. Jiri-Makru wildlife Sanctuary is located in
  A. Ukhrul district
  B. Candel district
  C. Tamenglong district
  D. None of these

34. What is the name of State Bird of Manipur?
  A. Crow
  B. Parrot
  C. Nongyeen
  D. None of these

35. Who is the author of the poetry collection, '*These Errors are Correct*' in English?
  A. Robin Mehta
  B. Jeet Thayil
  C. Peter Hawk
  D. V S Naipaul

36. Locate Tamenglong District on this Map of Manipur?

  A. A   B. B
  C. C   D. D

37. Which one of the following causes rainfall in the north-western parts of India during Winter Season?
  A. Cyclonic depression

B. Retreating monsoon
  C. Western disturbances
  D. South West monsoon

38. The first colour feature film in Manipur is—
  A. Matamgi Manipur
  B. Langlen Thadoi
  C. Imagee Ningthem
  D. None of these

39. Hilly area constitutes of the total geographical area of Manipur
  A. 89%   B. 88%
  C. 75%   D. 92%

40. Newly created district of Manipur is—
  A. Thoubal
  B. Imphal West
  C. Imphal East
  D. Noney

41. Locate Bishnupur district on this Map of Manipur

  A. A   B. B
  C. C   D. D

42. Which of the following districts of Manipur was maximum forest covered area?
  A. Churachandpur
  B. Ukhrul
  C. Tamenglong
  D. None of these

43. Locate Thoubal district on this map of Manipur

A. A   B. B
C. C   D. D

44. Which is the first Manipuri feature film
A. Ishanou
B. Khonjel
C. Saphabee
D. Matamgi Manipur

45. State animal of Manipur is
A. Sangai
B. Elephant
C. Cow
D. None of these

46. L. Sarita Devi is related with—
A. Weightlifting
B. Polo
C. Boxing
D. Hockey

47. Locate Imphal West district on this map of Manipur

A. A   B. B
C. C   D. D

48. Area of Chandel district is—
A. 4,391 sq. km
B. 3,313 sq. km
C. 4,544 sq. km
D. None of these

49. Per capita forest & tree cover in Manipur is—
A. 1.50 hect.
B. 2.50 hect.
C. 0.61 hect.
D. None of these

50. Chakpi river is the tributary of the river
A. Kongba
B. Dzuko
C. Imphal
D. None of these

51. Manipur State Gazette was first launched in the year—
A. 1932   B. 1923
C. 1934   D. 1944

52. First Manipur State Assembly was constituted on—
A. August 1948   B. July 1948
C. May 1948   D. July 1949

53. Manipur become a full-fledged state of India on:
A. 15th August, 1970
B. 26th January, 1971
C. 21st January, 1972
D. 15th August, 1972

54. Loktak lake is situated in—
A. Bishnupur district
B. Chandel district
C. Senapati district
D. None of these

55. Out of the 60 seats of Manipur Legislative Assembly how many are reserved for Schedule Tribe?
A. 15   B. 18
C. 19   D. 22

56. Manipur Science & Technology Council (MASTEC) was established in the year—
A. 1985
B. 1995
C. 1975
D. 1976

57. Locate Chandel district on this Map of Manipur?

A. A
B. B
C. C
D. D

58. Which of the following districts has common border with Myanmar?
A. Chandel
B. Bishnupur
C. Tamenglong
D. None of these

59. Khuga river is the tributary of river—
A. Chindiwin
B. Barak
C. Imphal
D. Kongba

60. Locate Churachandpur district on this Map of Manipur

A. A
B. B
C. C
D. D

61. Area of Manipur is—
A. 22,327 sq. km
B. 20,437 sq. km
C. 32,301 sq. km
D. None of these

62. Manipur University was established on—
A. June 10, 1990
B. June 5, 1980
C. July 5, 1980
D. None of these

63. Who was the first chairman of Manipur Public Service Commission?
A. Shri Laishram Gopal Singh
B. Shri G.B.K. Hooja
C. Shri Sibo Larho
D. None of these

64. In which year did Manipur become a Union Territory?
A. 1952
B. 1956
C. 1958
D. 1960

65. Mukna is a—
A. Fair
B. Festival
C. Game
D. None of these

66. In which year Manipur became the twentieth state of the Indian Union?
A. 1970
B. 1971
C. 1972
D. 1973

67. In which year revered king Pakhangba ascended the throne?
A. 30 A.D.
B. 31 A.D.
C. 32 A.D.
D. 33 A.D.

68. When was the Manipur Constitution Act passed?
A. 1947
B. 1948
C. 1949
D. 1950

69. In which year Nara Singha became the King of Manipur?
A. 1832   B. 1840
C. 1844   D. 1848

70. How many states touch the boundary of Manipur?
A. 3   B. 4
C. 5   D. 6

71. In which year was the Battle of Khongjom fought?
A. 1885   B. 1887
C. 1890   D. 1891

72. In which year did Manipur become a Union Territory?
A. 1950   B. 1955
C. 1956   D. 1960

73. When was Shillong Accord signed?
A. 15 Oct., 1949
B. 20 Sep., 1950
C. 25 Nov., 1952
D. 15 Aug., 1957

74. Who was the last King of Manipur?
A. Maharaja Gambhir Singh
B. Maharaja Tikendrajit Singh
C. Maharaja Ranjit Singh
D. Maharaja Purandar Singh

75. During the first world war, which King ruled over in Manipur?
A. Maharaja Nara Singha
B. Maharaja Garibniwaz
C. Maharaja Chandrakirti Singh
D. Maharaja Koineng Singh

76. During the reign of which King of Kangleipak was the title "Manipur" named after it?
A. Maharaja Churachand Singh
B. Maharaja Garibniwaz
C. Maharaja Bhagyachandra
D. Maharaja Chandrakirti Singh

77. What is the Capital of Manipur?
A. Imphal
B. Bishnupur
C. Churachandpur
D. Thoubal

78. What is the total population of Manipur as per the 2011 census?
A. 30,48,756   B. 28,55,794
C. 32,27,309   D. 22,18,960

79. When was the census started in Manipur?
A. 1750   B. 1752
C. 1757   D. 1760

80. When did Manipur come under the British rule?
A. 12 April, 1891
B. 12 March, 1890
C. 10 May, 1885
D. 5 June, 1860

81. How many District Councils are there in Manipur?
A. Five   B. Six
C. Seven   D. Eight

82. How many Legislative Assembly Constituencies are there in Manipur?
A. 50   B. 60
C. 70   D. 75

83. Which is the biggest river in Manipur?
A. Iril   B. Sekmai
C. Barrak   D. Nambul

84. Which one of the following is not a physical division of Manipur?
A. Churachandpur
B. Manipur Hills
C. Manipur Valley
D. Jiribam Plains

85. How many MLAs are elected from the Hill Districts to the Manipur Legislative Assembly?

   A. 20   B. 25
   C. 30   D. 35

86. On what date Martyr's Day is observed in Manipur?
  A. 10th August
  B. 13th August
  C. 15th August
  D. 18th August

87. In which District Khangkhui Caves are located?
  A. Chandel
  B. Ukhrul
  C. Senapati
  D. Tamenglong

88. Which is the first Manipuri colour feature film?
  A. Imagee Ningthem
  B. Brojendrogi Luhongba
  C. Langlen Thadai
  D. Matamgi Manipur

89. Who is the first Manipuri to win the Arjuna Award?
  A. Dingko Singh
  B. N. Kunjarani Devi
  C. M.C. Mary Kom
  D. Suraj Lata Devi

90. Who is the first Manipuri to win the Sahitya Academy Award?
  A. Pacha Meeitei
  B. N. Kunjamohan Singh
  C. L. Samarendra Singh
  D. A. Minaketan Singh

91. Who was the first woman MLA (Member of Legislative Assembly)?
  A. Kim Gangte
  B. W. Leima Devi
  C. Hangmila Shaija
  D. None of these

92. Who was the first Lok Sabha member from the Inner Parliamentary Constituency of Manipur?
  A. L. Jugeswar Singh
  B. L. Achaw Singh
  C. S. Tombi Singh
  D. M. Meghachandra

93. Who was the first Lok Sabha member from the outer Parliamentary Constituency of Manipur?
  A. Rungsung Suisa
  B. Rishang Keishing
  C. Paokai Haokip
  D. Yangmaso Shaiza

94. Heikru Hitongba festival was introduced in Manipur in :
  A. 1778   B. 1775
  C. 1779   D. 1772

95. Who was the first Governor of Manipur?
  A. L.P. Singh
  B. S.M.H. Burney
  C. K.V. Krishna Rao
  D. B.K. Nehru

96. Who was the first Rajya Sabha M.P. from Manipur?
  A. Ng. Tompok Singh
  B. L. Lalit Madhob Sharma
  C. S. Krishnamohan Singh
  D. Salam Tombi Singh

97. How many members represent Manipur in the Rajya Sabha?
  A. 1   B. 2
  C. 3   D. 4

98. How many members represent Manipur in the Lok Sabha?
  A. 2   B. 4
  C. 5   D. 7

99. When did the Gauhati High Court come into existence in Manipur?
  A. 21-1-1972   B. 21-4-1970
  C. 21-4-1971   D. 21-4-1973

100. In which of the following rivers does the Imphal river fall?

    A. The Iril river
    B. The Loktak lake
    C. The Brahmaputra
    D. The Chindwin river

101. In which year Imphal District was divided?
    A. 1995   B. 1996
    C. 1997   D. 1998

102. When was the "Khongjom War" fought in Manipur?
    A. 23-7-1891   B. 23-6-1891
    C. 23-4-1891   D. 16-9-1890

103. Who is the first olympian from Manipur?
    A. P. Nilkamal Singh
    B. N. Kunjarani Devi
    C. H.L. Tangkhul
    D. Thoiba Singh

104. 'Nongyeen' was declared as the State Bird of Manipur in the year :
    A. 1986   B. 1987
    C. 1988   D. 1989

105. The first Legislative Assembly was inaugurated in Manipur in:
    A. 1961   B. 1962
    C. 1963   D. 1964

106. In which lake the Sendra island is situated?
    A. Loukai lake
    B. Waithou lake
    C. Ikop lake
    D. Loktak lake

107. Who is the first sports person from Manipur to win a gold medal in the Asian Games?
    A. N. Kunjarani Devi
    B. Suraj Lata Devi
    C. M.C. Mary Kom
    D. Dingko Singh

108. In which year Manipuri language was included in the 8th schedule of the Indian Constitution?

    A. 1990   B. 1991
    C. 1992   D. 1993

109. Pamheiba was the most powerful kings of Manipur in whose reign the state reached the pinnacle as a powerful state. His original name was—
    A. Madhuchandra
    B. Churachand Singh
    C. Chandrakirti
    D. Garibniwaz

110. When did Doordarshan start in Manipur?
    A. 30 April, 1990
    B. 30 April, 1991
    C. 30 April, 1992
    D. 30 April, 1993

111. What is the percentage of land under the cultivation in Manipur to its area?
    A. Nearly 10%
    B. Nearly 20%
    C. Nearly 30%
    D. Nearly 40%

112. Who is the poet of "Dustbin Amagi Warri"?
    A. R. Constantine
    B. T.C. Hudson
    C. T. Ibopishak Singh
    D. Vedaja Sanjenbam

113. How many recognised Tribal communities are in Manipur?
    A. 30   B. 32
    C. 34   D. 36

114. How many years Manipur remained as a part state and Union Territory?
    A. Twenty
    B. Twenty one
    C. Twenty two
    D. Twenty four

115. During the reign of which King in Manipur the first Telegraph line and Telegraph office were established?
A. Maharaja Chandrakirti in 1886
B. Maharaja Madhuchandra in 1801
C. Maharaja Yumjaotaba in 1820
D. Maharaja Churachand Singh in 1891

116. Which period was known as the "Dark Period" in Manipur?
A. 1730 A.D. to 1750 A.D.
B. 1755 A.D. to 1826 A.D.
C. 1650 A.D. to 1726 A.D.
D. 1820 A.D. to 1850 A.D.

117. "Manipur is the Jewel of India and Switzerland of the East". Who said this quotation?
A. Jawaharlal Nehru
B. Mahatma Gandhi
C. Subhash Chandra Bose
D. M. Kaireng Singh

118. Who introduced Polo in Manipur?
A. Thayanthaba
B. Ebudhou Marjing
C. Garibniwaj
D. Koiremba

119. When did Hindu Priest Santidash Goshai come to Manipur?
A. 1550 A.D.　　B. 1600 A.D.
C. 1760 A.D.　　D. 1716 A.D.

120. When was Manipur State Film Festival started?
A. 1982　　B. 1983
C. 1984　　D. 1985

121. What is the state language of Manipur?
A. Manipuri
B. English
C. Hindi
D. None of these

122. In Manipuri week days 'Nongmaijing' is known as :
A. Monday
B. Sunday
C. Tuesday
D. Wednesday

123. In which year was 'Meitei Chanu' the first journal of Manipur published?
A. 1920　　B. 1922
C. 1924　　D. 1926

124. The number of Jila Parishads in Manipur is :
A. 4　　B. 3
C. 5　　D. 6

125. 'Chon Festival' is celebrated by which tribe of Manipur?
A. Aimol
B. Kabui Naga
C. Thadou
D. Kuki

126. How many alphabets were there in the original Meitei language?
A. 20　　B. 22
C. 25　　D. 27

127. When did Doordarshan's Metro Channel (DD2) start in Manipur?
A. December 23, 1995
B. December 23, 1990
C. December 23, 1991
D. December 23, 1992

128. The historic Kangla Fort Complex was formally handed back to the people of Manipur in the presence of the former Prime Minister Manmohan Singh on :
A. 20th November, 2004
B. 20th November, 2005
C. 20th November, 2006
D. 22nd November, 2006

129. When was the first "Nupi Lal" happened in Manipur?

A. 1904 A.D.   B. 1905 A.D.
C. 1906 A.D.   D. 1907 A.D.

130. In which district of Manipur can we find "DZUKU LILY"?
A. Imphal East   B. Chandel
C. Senapati   D. Thoubal

131. Who introduced the art of manufacturing paper in Manipur?
A. Sheikh Zunaid
B. Md. Sani
C. Nongsamei
D. Tribals

132. The founder of the Praja Sameleni was :
A. Hijam Irabat Singh
B. Lalita Madhop
C. Elangbam Tompok
D. Aaiga Bankabihari

133. Who is the author of the book 'Labangalata'?
A. Lucy Zehol
B. Khwairakpam Chaoba
C. M.K. Singh
D. E.W. Dun

134. The Sangai Deer is found at which National Park/wild life sanctuary in Manipur?
A. Sirohi
B. Keilam
C. Keibul Lamjao
D. Yaingangpokpi Lakchao

135. Tharon caves are located in which district of Manipur?
A. Chandel   B. Thoubal
C. Tamenglong   D. Senapati

136. What is the state tree of Manipur?
A. Teak
B. Pine
C. Parkia Javanica
D. Uningthou

137. Who become the first woman minister in Manipur?

A. R. Apabi Devi
B. Kh. Thoibi Devi
C. Kim Gangte
D. Khaidem Sakhi Devi

138. The state of Manipur lies between .... and .... east Longitude.
A. 80°20′ and 84°35′
B. 92°58′ and 94°45′
C. 75°10′ and 60°20′
D. 96°20′ and 99°13′

139. In which year Manipur Olympic Association was formed?
A. 1947   B. 1948
C. 1949   D. 1950

140. Who was the founder President of the Manipur Olympic Association?
A. Churachand Singh
B. R.K. Madhuryajit Singh
C. Kalachandra
D. Debendra Singh

141. Who was the founder of the "Ningthouja Dynasty" in Manipur?
A. Nongdalairen Pakhangba
B. Atom Yairemba
C. Keiphaba Yanglon
D. Nongchup Lamgaingamba

142. Who gave the popular title Garibniwaz (Benefactor of the Poor) to king Pamheiba (1709-1748 AD)?
A. Meitei community
B. Bengali Muslims
C. Muslim Saints
D. Tribal community

143. Who was the first British Political Agent of Manipur?
A. George Gordon
B. Grimwood
C. Captain William
D. James Hednic

144. Who introduced "Bell metal currency" in Manipur?

    A. Kyamba Maharaj
    B. Maramba Maharaj
    C. Khagemba Maharaj
    D. Labanyachandra Maharaj

145. Porompat, Keirao Bitra, Sawombung and Jiribam are the sub-divisions of which district?
    A. Churachandpur
    B. Chandel
    C. Imphal West
    D. Imphal East

146. Who was the first Chief-Minister of Manipuri?
    A. Md. Alimuddin
    B. M.K. Priyobrata Singh
    C. F.F. Pearson
    D. Braj Kumar Nehru

147. Who introduced 'Vaishnavism' as a state Religion?
    A. King Chingthangkhomba
    B. King Koiremba
    C. King Bhagyachandra
    D. King Bharatsai

148. Who may be given the title of the "First Modern Political Leader of Manipur?
    A. Hijam Irabat Singh
    B. L. Jugeswar Singh
    C. Paokai Haokip
    D. Ng. Tompok Singh

149. The first English Journal of Manipur 'Meitei Leirang' was published in :
    A. 1965   B. 1969
    C. 1972   D. 1975

150. Which is the first Health Journal of Manipur?
    A. Chingtam
    B. Sanaleibak
    C. Meeyam
    D. Meitei Maiba

151. Who was the first speaker of Manipur Legislative Assembly?

    A. T.C. Tiankham
    B. Sibo Larho
    C. M. Koireng Singh
    D. Tombi Singh

152. What is the literacy rate of Manipur as per the 2011 census?
    A. 65.36 per cent
    B. 72.16 per cent
    C. 76.94 per cent
    D. 75.24 per cent

153. What is the density of population in Manipur as per the 2011 census?
    A. 128   B. 110
    C. 132   D. 120

154. Who is the first Manipuri girl to become Miss East India?
    A. Aparna Jhaveri
    B. Bonnie Gurumayum
    C. Gayatri Heisnam
    D. Priyanka Kokila

155. The number of Universities in Manipur is:
    A. 2   B. 3
    C. 4   D. 5

156. Manipur University was established in:
    A. 1977   B. 1978
    C. 1979   D. 1980

157. Board of Secondary Education, Manipur was established in :
    A. 1972-73   B. 1974-75
    C. 1976-77   D. 1978-79

158. Script of the Grand Prix award winning film 'Imagee Ningthem' is written by :
    A. N. Kunjamohan
    B. M.K. Binodini
    C. A.K. Paul
    D. L.R. Singh

159. 'Seven Years Devastation' (Chahi Taret Khuntakpa) covers the period from :

A. 1810 to 1816
B. 1819 to 1825
C. 1829 to 1835
D. 1827 to 1833

160. When did the Manipur State Archives set up?
A. 1980   B. 1982
C. 1985   D. 1988

161. Who described Manipur as "An oasis of comparative civilization amidst the Barbarians?"
A. James Hotten
B. William Ban
C. Alfred Lyll
D. George Linde

162. Who is known as Queen of Boxing in Manipur?
A. M.C. Meri Kom
B. N. Kunjarani Devi
C. Suraj Lata Devi
D. Brojeswari Devi

163. During the reign of which King of Manipur the "Scout Movement" was started in the state?
A. Maharaja Chalamba Singh
B. Maharaja Chura Chand Singh
C. Maharaja Bharatsai Singh
D. Maharaja Ching Thang Khomba Singh

164. What is the area of Kangla, the ancient palace of Manipur?
A. 240.56 acres
B. 350.16 acres
C. 237.62 acres
D. 290.48 acres

165. Who is the first chairman of Hill Area Committee?
A. P.K. Mohan
B. P.C. Mathew
C. E.P. Moon Jan
D. S.P. Henry

166. When was the first Community Development Block established in Manipur?
A. 1952   B. 1953
C. 1954   D. 1955

167. Keilam Wildlife Sanctuary is located in which district?
A. Churachandpur
B. Senapati
C. Thoubal
D. Ukhrul

168. How many airports are there in Manipur?
A. 1   B. 2
C. 3   D. 4

169. Which is the first railway station of Manipur?
A. Dimapur Railway Station
B. Jiribam Railway Station
C. Toubal Railway Station
D. Karong Railway Station

170. Where is airport of Manipur located?
A. Churachandpur
B. Tamenglong
C. Imphal
D. Chandel

171. What is the 'State Game' of Manipur?
A. Thang Yannaba
B. Mangjong
C. Lamjel
D. Sagol Kangjei

172. In which year 'Manipur Hockey Association' was formed?
A. 1976   B. 1977
C. 1978   D. 1979

173. The author of the book 'Bir Tikendrajit Road' is :
A. T.C. Hudson
B. Hijam Guno
C. Nilima Roy
D. Lal Dena

174. Who is the first Manipuri to appear on postage stamp?
A. Laishram Memma
B. Jugeswori Devi
C. Rani Gaidenlilu
D. Rashi Devi

175. Who is the first person from Manipur to receive the 'Padma Shree'?
A. N. Kunjarani Devi
B. Irom Leikhendra
C. P. Neelkamal
D. Atombapu Sharma

176. The number of Industrial Training Institutes in Manipur is :
A. Four   B. Five
C. Six   D. Eleven

177. Manipur Handloom and Handicrafts Development Corporation was set-up in :
A. 1972   B. 1976
C. 1980   D. 1982

178. In which year was the Manipur State Museum established?
A. 1965   B. 1969
C. 1975   D. 1979

179. What is Manipuri Polo called :
A. Yubi Lakpi
B. Khong Kangjei
C. Mukna Kangjei
D. Sagol Kangjei

180. Who was the first Deputy Chief Minister of Manipur?
A. L. Jugeshwar Singh
B. M. Koireng Singh
C. Irengbam Tompok Singh
D. Yangmasho Shaiza

181. When was the 'Patriot Day'' observed at the first time in Manipur?
A. 1965   B. 1966
C. 1968   D. 1969

182. Which religious community introduced the tool called Pangandem (throw shuttle) for weaving in Manipur?
A. Tribal community
B. Meitei community
C. Manipuri Muslim
D. Bengali Muslim

183. During the period of Khagemba's reign (1597-1652 AD), who principally looked after the affairs of whole Muslim community in Manipur?
A. Maulvi Qazi Wali-Ullah
B. Sheikh Zunaid
C. Muhammad Sani
D. None of the above

184. When was the first "District Library established in Manipur?
A. 1950   B. 1952
C. 1955   D. 1958

185. R.K. Chandrajit Singh is related to:
A. painting   B. writing
C. music   D. sport

186. In which district of Manipur the highest hill mount Tenipu is situated?
A. Senapati
B. Imphal East
C. Thoubal
D. Bishnupur

187. 'Manipur Film Society' was established in :
A. 1955   B. 1960
C. 1962   D. 1966

188. Which is the first Manipuri documentary film?
A. Maipak – the Son of Manipur
B. Meitei Pung
C. Chatldo Eidi
D. Yellhou Jagai

189. Who is the director of first Manipuri documentary film?
A. M.A. Singh
B. Aribam Shyam Sharma
C. Devkumar Bose
D. Oken Amakcham

190. The Number of National Highway passes through Manipur is :
A. 3
B. 4
C. 5
D. 6

191. When was the Jiribam Railway Station inaugurated?
A. 1990
B. 1982
C. 1987
D. 1992

192. The number of Post Offices in Manipur is :
A. 600
B. 1394
C. 700
D. 725

193. Which is the largest export-oriented agricultural product of Manipur?
A. Maize
B. Rice
C. Cotton
D. Wheat

194. Manipur State Kala Academy was established in :
A. 1965
B. 1970
C. 1972
D. 1975

195. What is the average height of Imphal valley above MSL (mean sea level)?
A. 790 metres
B. 850 metres
C. 990 metres
D. 1050 metres

196. Who started the festival of Kang-Chingba (Ratha Yatra) in Manipur?
A. Maharaja Jai Singh
B. Maharaja Madhuchandra
C. Maharaja Churachand Singh
D. Maharaja Gambhir Singh

197. The Meities were converted into Hinduism during the reign of which king?
A. King Garibniwaz
B. King Maramba
C. King Marjit
D. King Kyamba

198. When was the last independent war of Manipur fought against British?

A. 20th March 1875 to 25th June 1875
B. 24th March 1891 to 27th April 1891
C. 15th January 1890 to 25th February 1890
D. 10th May 1879 to 27 July 1879

199. What is the serial number of Manipuri as it is listed in the Eight schedule to the constitution of India?
A. 9th
B. 10th
C. 11th
D. 12th

200. The judges of Manipur High Court are appointed by :
A. The Chief Justice of India
B. The President of India
C. The Chief Minister of Manipur
D. The Governor of Manipur

201. The language spoken by the largest number of people in the Manipur is :
A. English
B. Bengali
C. Hindi
D. Manipuri

202. What was the old name of Senapati district?
A. Manipur East
B. Manipur West
C. Manipur North
D. Manipur South

203. Who was the most influential contemporary of L. Dhananjoy Singh (popularly known as Nongsamei) who usually paid attention and acted as the chief Qazi for the entire Muslim community in the history of Manipur during the reign of king Khagemba?
A. Munan Khan
B. Kourif Sheikh
C. Abdus Salam
D. Muhammad Sani

204. The ornament, which is worn around the neck by the Manipuri women, is called :
A. Khonanakpi   B. Khuji
C. Khorau   D. Kanberi

205. In which year Manipur was included on the Indian Railway Map?
A. 1989   B. 1990
C. 1991   D. 1992

206. As per the 2011 census what is the sex ratio in Manipur?
A. 985   B. 980
C. 975   D. 995

207. Loktak Project was commissioned in:
A. 1983   B. 1984
C. 1985   D. 1986

208. In which district of Manipur Zoological Garden is located?
A. Tamenglong
B. Imphal
C. Churachandpur
D. Bishnupur

209. Manipur Agro-Industries Corporation was set-up in:
A. 1989   B. 1990
C. 1991   D. 1992

210. The last Lieutenant Governor of Manipur was :
A. J.M. Raina
B. P.C. Mathew
C. D.R. Kohil
D. Baleshwar Prasad

211. Which King introduced Kwak Tomba religious ceremony in Manipur?
A. Khuiyoi Tompok
B. Keiphaba Yanglon
C. Khui Ningngomba
D. Chingthang Lanthaba

212. During the reign of which King in Manipur the game Yubi Lakpi first played?
A. King Thawanthaba
B. King Chingthangkhomba
C. King Lanthaba
D. King Ayangba

213. In which district of Manipur Khagemba's old palace was situated?
A. Bishnupur
B. Churachandpur
C. Chandel
D. Ukhrul

214. Jhaveri sisters are famous for:
A. Odissi Dance
B. Kathak
C. Manipuri Dance
D. Bharat Natyam

215. Manipur Theological college is located at :
A. Thoubal   B. Ukhrul
C. Imphal   D. Chandel

216. In Manipur INA Museum is located at :
A. Moirang   B. Nambal
C. Kakching   D. Lilong

217. Where is the state Museum of Manipur situated?
A. Chandel
B. Senapati
C. Imphal
D. Tamenglong

218. Who was Manipur's first MBBS Doctor?
A. Dr. Nanda Babu Roy
B. Dr. P.K. Rana
C. Dr. J.C. Arya
D. Dr. C.L. Mohan

219. Who was Manipur's first lady medical Doctor?
A. Manorama Devi

B. Thangjam Ongbi Bedamani Devi
C. N. Chidambara
D. Payal Ghosh

220. When was the first Operation Theatre opened in Manipur?
A. 1920   B. 1926
C. 1930   D. 1935

221. When was the first Hospital ward opened in Manipur?
A. 1925   B. 1928
C. 1930   D. 1931

222. Who was first Mr. Manipur?
A. P. Jugol
B. Irom Leikhendra
C. R. Shyam
D. Ranabir Meitei

223. Who is the Manipur's first Mr. India?
A. M. Gopal Sharma
B. K. Dilip Singh
C. Nongthongbam Maipak
D. M. Phanjoubam

224. Who is the author of the book "Manipur: The Jewel of India"?
A. E. Ishwarjit Singh
B. S.C. Joshi
C. L.R. Singh
D. H. Guno Singh

225. Who is the author of the book "Madhabi"?
A. Kh. Chaoba
B. R.K. Shitaljit
C. Dr. Komal Singh
D. Lal Dena

226. Who is the author of the book 'Mao : The Naga Tribe of Manipur?
A. Lorho Mary Maheo
B. Naorem Sanajaoba
C. R. Constantine
D. H. Bhuban Singh

227. Where is Nupee Lal Memorial Complex is located in Manipur?
A. Imphal
B. Moirang
C. Churachandpur
D. Moreh

228. Ruins of Citadel was built during the reign of :
A. King Jai Singh
B. King Khagemba
C. King Marjit
D. King Chourjit

229. Ruins of Citadel was built in the year :
A. 1500 A.D.   B. 1550 A.D.
C. 1600 A.D.   D. 1611 A.D.

230. Where is Shree Shree Govindajee Temple located?
A. Bishnupur
B. Kongla Fort
C. Old Langthabal Palace
D. Ukhrul

231. Who is the first Manipuri Child to get the Best Child Actor Award?
A. Leikhendra Singh
B. Ranbir Goswami
C. Shyam Singha
D. K. Narsingha

232. A veteran freedom fighter and a great socio-religious leader, Rani Gaidenliu was a living goddess for the manipuri people. Name the great Prime Minister of India who described her as "the daughter of the hills and gave the title "Rani of her people".
A. Lal Bahadur Shastri
B. Pandit Jawaharlal Nehru
C. Smt. Indira Gandhi
D. Morarji Desai

233. Which is the first Manipuri magazine started in 1917-18?

A. Longtai   B. Wakhal
C. Meitei Leima   D. Athouba

234. Which was the first Manipuri book to be awarded with the Telem Ningol Atoibema Award in children's literature?
A. Sana Kakchao
B. Ithak Ipom
C. Jahira
D. Ima

235. Who is the first Manipuri to win the Sangeet Natak Akademi Award?
A. H. Atomba Singh
B. T. Amudon Sharma
C. Bipin Singh
D. M. Amubi Singh

236. Who is the first Manipuri to win a Gold Medal in Asian Games?
A. Ng. Dingko Singh
B. Sanamacha Chanu
C. N. Kunjarani Devi
D. M.C. Mary Kom

237. Who is the first Manipuri to become a Union Minister?
A. Ng. Tompok Singh
B. R.K. Jaichandra
C. R.K. Dorendra Singh
D. N. Gouzagin

238. Who is the first Manipuri Film Actor?
A. Leikhendra Singh
B. Robindro Sharma
C. Aribam Shyam Sharma
D. M.A. Singh

239. Who is the first Manipuri Film Actress?
A. Gita Devi
B. Manorama Devi
C. Rashi Devi
D. Rashmi Devi

240. Who is the first Manipuri to win Rajiv Gandhi Khel Ratna Award?

A. Ng. Dingko Singh
B. Thaiba Singh
C. M.C. Mary Kom
D. N. Kunjarani Devi

241. Who is the first Muslim Chief Minister of Manipur?
A. Md. Alimuddin Lilong Turel Ahanbi
B. Md. Abdul Qayum
C. Md. Ali Akbar
D. Javed Ahmed

242. Who is the first Manipuri Muslim Woman Advocate?
A. Noor Bano
B. Benazir Majumdar
C. Fatima Shaikh
D. Sabnam Noorani

243. What is the percentage of Muslim population as per 2011 census?
A. 22.40   B. 25.50
C. 8.40   D. 15.60

244. What is the area covered by the Manipuri Hockey field?
A. 200 × 20 Yards
B. 200 × 40 Yards
C. 200 × 60 Yards
D. 200 × 80 Yards

245. The historic 'International Polo Tournament' was held in Manipur in the year :
A. 1985   B. 1987
C. 1989   D. 1990

246. In which year Oak Tassar was introduced in Manipur?
A. 1973-74   B. 1975-86
C. 1977-78   D. 1980-81

247. Who built the famous Vishnu temple situated at Bishenpur?
A. King Kyamba
B. King Telheiba
C. King Tonaba
D. King Punsiba

248. Sirohi National Park of Manipur got its recognition by the government in the year :
A. 1990   B. 1998
C. 1999   D. 2000

249. In which year was Yaingangpokpi Lakchao Wildlife Sanctuary opened :
A. 1989   B. 1991
C. 1995   D. 1998

250. The Manipur State Museum was inaugurated by which Prime Minister of India?
A. J.L. Nehru
B. Indira Gandhi
C. Rajiv Gandhi
D. A.B. Vajpayee

251. In which year Manipur University was upgraded as a Central University?
A. 1990   B. 1992
C. 1994   D. 1998

252. Which is the largest and most important mineral resource of Manipur?
A. Chromite
B. Coal
C. Lignite
D. Limestone

253. What is the hydro-electricity potential of Manipur?
A. 1784 MW   B. 1700 MW
C. 1680 MW   D. 1480 MW

254. In which year the first Manipur Panchayati Raj Bill was passed?
A. 1972   B. 1975
C. 1978   D. 1980

255. In which year Manipur got its own High Court?
A. 2010   B. 2011
C. 2013   D. 2012

256. In which year the Indian Penal Code was first enacted in Manipur?
A. 1901   B. 1902
C. 1903   D. 1904

257. The number of Autonomous Hill District Councils in Manipur is :
A. 6   B. 9
C. 10   D. 12

258. The area covered by the Jiribam Rubber Farm is:
A. 800 hectares
B. 889 hectares
C. 900 hectares
D. 1050 hectares

259. How many districts are in Manipur?
A. 7   B. 8
C. 16   D. 10

260. Which river flows from Manipur to Assam?
A. Barrak   B. Thoubal
C. Iril   D. Makru

261. Which is the largest grown agricultural product of Manipur?
A. Wheat   B. Maize
C. Rice   D. Orange

262. When was the old Cachar road constructed in Manipur?
A. 1530   B. 1532
C. 1534   D. 1536

263. Who constructed the old Cachar road?
A. Meidingu-Kabomba
B. James Johnstone
C. Yengkham Deksan Singh
D. J. K. Rajan

264. In which district was Khagemba's old palace situated?
A. Senapati
B. Churachandpur
C. Tamenglong
D. Ukhrul

265. Who was the first chief commissioner of Manipur?
 A. Major General Rawal Amar Singh
 B. Himat Singh
 C. E. P. Moon Jan.
 D. P. C. Mathew

266. Who was the first Lieutenant Governor of Manipur?
 A. D. R. Kohli
 B. Baleswar Prasad
 C. J. M. Raina
 D. E. P. Moom

267. Loktak Lake is located in which district?
 A. Bishnupur
 B. Thoubal
 C. Ukhrul
 D. Tamenglong

268. Kachouphung Lake is located in which district?
 A. Ukhrul
 B. Bishnupur
 C. Thoubal
 D. Tamenglong

269. Barak waterfalls are located in which district?
 A. Tamenglong   B. Bishnupur
 C. Ukhrul   D. Senapati

270. Sangboo cave is located in :
 A. Chandel
 B. Ukhrul
 C. Churachandpur
 D. Imphal East

271. Height of Leikat Peak is :
 A. 2,832 m.   B. 2,760 m.
 C. 2,560 m.   D. 2,960m.

272. As per the 2011 census, the urban population of Manipur is :
 A. 8, 34, 154
 B. 9, 50, 325
 C. 7, 90, 660
 D. 10, 10, 548

273. As per the 2011 census, the rural population of Manipur is :
 A. 20, 18, 224
 B. 16, 20, 360
 C. 20, 21, 640
 D. 17, 10, 660

274. The State Emblem of Manipur is:
 A. Singda Dam
 B. Komgla Shaa
 C. Shree Govindajee Temple
 D. Khang Khui Cave

275. Who is the writer of novel 'Leikangla'?
 A. M. Borkamya
 B. K. Bira
 C. S. Biren
 D. N. Ibabi

276. As per the 2011 census which is the highly populated district in Manipur?
 A. Thoubal   B. Bishnupur
 C. Imphal West   D. Senapati

277. As per the 2011 census which is the less populated district in Manipur?
 A. Ukhrul
 B. Churachandpur
 C. Chandel
 D. Tamenglong

278. As per the 2011 census which is the most densely populated district in Manipur?
 A. Imphal West
 B. Thoubal
 C. Bishnupur
 D. Imphal East

279. As per the 2011 census which is the less densely populated district in Manipur?
 A. Ukhrul
 B. Tamenglong
 C. Chandel
 D. Churachandpur

280. What is the decadal growth rate (2001-11) of Manipur as per the 2011 census?
A. 20.01% B. 25.02%
C. 24.50% D. 32.03%

281. Which is the largest city in Manipur?
A. Kakching B. Thoubal
C. Lilong D. Imphal

282. Who is known as the "Lion of Manipur"?
A. Bir Tikendrajit
B. Hijam Irabat
C. Paona Brajabashi
D. Zilla Singh

283. Who is known as 'Mahakavi' in Manipur?
A. H. Guno Singh
B. Hijam Anganghal
C. Kh. Chaoba
D. Dr. Komal Singh

284. What is the hottest month in the State of Manipur?
A. July B. August
C. September D. June

285. Where is the headquarters of Imphal East district?
A. Porompat B. Kirao Bitra
C. Sawombung D. Jiribam

286. Where is the headquarters of Imphal West district?
A. Lamsang
B. Lamphelpat
C. Patsai
D. Wangai

287. How many Tribes are recognised by the Government of Manipur?
A. 30 B. 31
C. 32 D. 35

288. Manipur 'Statehood Day' is celebrated on :

A. 25th February
B. 13th August
C. 28th September
D. 21st January

289. 'Manipuri Language Day' is celebrated on:
A. 20th August
B. 28th September
C. 30th September
D. 12th September

290. 'Manipur Integrity Day' is celebrated on :
A. 25th September
B. 28th September
C. 23rd April
D. 25th February

291. When was the State Institute of Journalism established?
A. 15th May 1990
B. 16th June 1994
C. 19th October 1992
D. 20th July 1995

292. When was the Council of Higher Secondary Education, Manipur established?
A. 1990 B. 1991
C. 1992 D. 1993

293. Manipur Human Rights Commission, Lamphelpat was established on :
A. 20th June 1995
B. 27th June 1998
C. 11th May 1990
D. 15th June 1992

294. Bunning wildlife sanctuary is situated in which district?
A. Imphal East
B. Tamenglong
C. Chandel
D. Churachandpur

295. Which wildlife sanctuary has the largest area in Manipur?

A. Yaingoupokpi Lokchao
B. Keilam
C. Zeliad
D. Jiri Makru

296. Zeliad wildlife sanctuary is located in which district?
A. Chandel
B. Tamenglong
C. Bishnupur
D. Churachandpur

297. Which was the first English Journal of Manipur?
A. Meitei Leirang
B. Manipur Mail
C. Sangai Express
D. Manipur News

298. Who is the first Manipuri Film Producer?
A. Debkumar Bose
B. Karam Manmohan Singh
C. Kh. Pramodini
D. Aribam Shyam Sharma

299. Which was the first Manipuri Film to receive the President's Medal in the 20th National Film Festival?
A. Matamgi Manipur
B. Langlen Thadoi
C. Imagee Ningthem
D. None of these

300. First Arjuna and Rajiv Gandhi Khel Ratna Award winner for Manipur N. Kunjarani Devi is famous in which sport?
A. Cricket   B. Hockey
C. Weightlifting   D. Boxing

301. Suraj Lata Devi is related with which sport?
A. Hockey
B. Weightlifting
C. Boxing
D. Cricket

302. N. Dingko Singh is related with which sport?
A. Cricket   B. Football
C. Hockey   D. Boxing

303. Anita Chanu has fame in which sport?
A. Mountaineering
B. Football
C. Tennis
D. Cricket

304. The first National Games were held in Manipur in :
A. 1995   B. 1996
C. 1997   D. 1999

305. Who was the editor of the "Manipur Paojel" in 1939?
A. Keisham Kunjabihari Singh
B. George Gordon
C. Dr. Brown
D. Hijam Irabat

306. When was the "Clapped song" sung first time in Manipur?
A. 1830   B. 1847
C. 1857   D. 1870

307. Which jail in Manipur houses drug exclusively?
A. Shajiwa Jail
B. Imphal Jail
C. Jiribam Jail
D. None of these

308. When was the Manipur State Transport established?
A. 10th July, 1948
B. 15th August, 1949
C. 13th May, 1950
D. 20th April, 1952

309. When was the Manipur State Transport become a Corporation?
A. 20th July, 1972
B. 14th December, 1978
C. 27th March, 1976
D. 16th November, 1976

310. When does Manipur observe "Save Boundary Day"?
    A. August 4, 1987
    B. May 6, 1987
    C. July 4, 1987
    D. October 10, 1987

311. When did the King Gambhir Singh die?
    A. 1831   B. 1832
    C. 1833   D. 1834

312. When was the second "Nupi-Lal" (Women war against British) took place in Manipur?
    A. 1939   B. 1940
    C. 1941   D. 1942

313. Where is the Pony Breeding Project established in Manipur?
    A. Tamenglong District
    B. Senapati District
    C. Bishnupur District
    D. Chandel District

314. When was the first Bank opened in Manipur State?
    A. 1942   B. 1944
    C. 1946   D. 1948

315. Manipur State Bank was opened in :
    A. 1942   B. 1944
    C. 1945   D. 1947

316. Who was the editor of the weekly journal "Anouba Yug" in 1947?
    A. Hijam Irabat Singh
    B. George Gordon
    C. R.K. Bhubonsana
    D. Dr. Brown

317. During the reign of which king of Manipur the festival "Ningal Chackouba" was introduced?
    A. Maharaja Tangjama
    B. Maharaja Chandra-Kirti
    C. Maharaja Garibnivaj
    D. Maharaja Maramba

318. Who built the famous Lord Krishna temple situated in Imphal?
    A. Nara Singha
    B. King Surchandra
    C. King Charairongba
    D. King Kulachandra

319. When was the famous Lord Sanamahi temple built?
    A. 1880 A.D.   B. 1885 A.D.
    C. 1890 A.D.   D. 1891 A.D.

320. In which early part of the century Christianity came to Manipur?
    A. 17th century
    B. 18th century
    C. 19th century
    D. 20th century

321. Which song of Manipur is sung by only women?
    A. Nat Ishei   B. Nupi Pala
    C. Ougri   D. Pena Ishei

322. The creator of the Manipuri classical dance 'Ras Leela' was:
    A. King Bhagyachandra Singh
    B. King Chingthang Khomba
    C. King Ningthou Khomba
    D. King Madhuchandra

323. Nongthombam Maipak got the 'Mr. India' title in the year :
    A. 1967   B. 1968
    C. 1969   D. 1970

324. In which year Sougaijam Somorendra Singh became the first graduate from Manipur?
    A. 1920   B. 1925
    C. 1932   D. 1935

325. The Aimol, Purum, Kom, Koireng and Chiru are the sub-tribes of which tribe?
    A. Konrem   B. Mao
    C. Angami   D. Kacha Naga

326. Manipur Agro-Industries Corporation was set-up in :
    A. 1992   B. 1993
    C. 1994   D. 1995

327. What is the total area under

cultivation of different crops in Manipur?
A 2,50,000 hectares
B. 2,60,000 hectares
C. 2,85,000 hectares
D. 3,00,000 hectares

328. Which district is the largest producer of Sugarcane in Manipur?
A Chandel
B. Imphal west
C. Bishnupur
D. Thoubal

329. Yangmaso Shaiza was the first tribal :
A Chief Minister of Manipur
B. Chief Commissioner of Manipur
C. M.P. from Manipur
D. Governor of Manipur

330. How many seats are reserved for scheduled castes in Manipur?
A 1   B. 2
C. 3   D. 4

331. The total area covered by the Manipur Valley is :
A 1800 sq. kms.
B. 1843 sq. kms.
C. 1860 sq. kms.
D. 1875 sq. kms.

332. What is the height of Mount Tenipu?
A 2910 metres
B. 2950 metres
C. 2970 metres
D. 2994 metres

333. With which country Manipur shares an international border?
A Myanmar
B. China
C. Bangladesh
D. None of these

334. Mount Tenipu is located in which district of Manipur?

A Tamenglong   B. Senapati
C. Thoubal   D. Bishnupur

335. Who was the first footballer among the Manipuri Muslims?
A. Md. Hussain of Lilong Bazar
B. Md. Athar
C. Salim Khan
D. Md. Yaqub

336. The biggest source of the state income of Manipur is :
A Industry
B. Forest Resource
C. Agriculture
D. None of these

337. The State Anthem of Manipur was composed by :
A B. Jayanta Kumar
B. K. Kunjabihari
C. A. Thambou Singh
D. Sagolsem Indramani

338. L.M.S. Law college stands for :
A Lairenmayum Seibyasachi Law College
B. Lairenmayum Sobita Law College
C. Longjam Mani Singh Law College
D. Liberal Manipur Society Law College

339. Manipur's first eastern dam Khoupum Dam is situated on which river?
A Imphal river
B. Manchandui river
C. Iril river
D. Nambul river

340. In which district Khoupum Dam is located?
A Bishnupur
B. Thoubal
C. Ukhrul
D. Tamenglong

341. In which year was the Loktak

Hydel Project commissioned?
A. 1980   B. 1981
C. 1982   D. 1983

342. Manipur's premier college Dhana Manjuri College (D.M. College) was established in the year :
A. 1946   B. 1947
C. 1948   D. 1949

343. In which part of Manipur bamboo forests are abundantly grown?
A. Eastern Part
B. South western Part
C. South Northern Part
D. Northern Part

344. Who brought out the technological revolution of Agriculture and Weaving in Manipur?
A. Cachari Migrants
B. Assamese Muslims
C. Manipuri Muslims coming through military invasions and migrations
D. None of the above

345. Who was the author of the 18th century book called "Sana Manik"?
A. E. Sonamani Singh
B. R.K. Madhubir
C. Wahengbam Madharam
D. Sudhir Naoraibam

346. Who was the first Chief Minister when Manipur was a full-fledged state?
A. M. Koireng Singh
B. Md. Alimuddin
C. Yangmasho Shaiza
D. R. K. Dorendro Singh

347. Padmashree Award winner author who translated 'Mahabharata' book in Manipuri is:
A. Ch. Kalachand Shastri
B. Bircndrajit Naorem
C. Ningombam Sunita
D. N. Ibobi Singh

348. Luira is a festival of which tribe?
A. Thadou   B. Tangkhul
C. Kabui   D. Kuki

349. Which popular form of festival is observed by Kuki tribes?
A. Chumpha
B. Chavang Kut
C. Gan Ngai
D. None of these

350. Who was Manipur's first to get Lalit Kala Akademi Award?
A. T.A. Mudon Sharma
B. T. Kunja Kishore Singh
C. Th. Tombi Singh
D. Y. Gambhini Devi

351. Who was the name of the Chief Minister who categorically started observing the 13th August as 'The Patriots Day' in the history of Manipur?
A. Priyobrata Singh
B. Pearson
C. M. Koireng Singh
D. Md. Alimuddin

352. The game of 'Kong' flourished during the reign of :
A. King Ningthou Kongba
B. King Laitongba
C. King Keiphaba
D. King Khomba

353. R. K. Singhajit got Padmashree for his work in :
A. Dance   B. Literature
C. Drama   D. Education

354. As per the 2011 census which district have the highest literacy rate?
A. Imphal East
B. Imphal west
C. Bishnupur
D. Churachandpur

355. When was Manipur Human Rights Commission established?
A. 25th May 1995
B. 27th June 1999

C. 27th June 1998
D. 28th April 1996

356. As per the 2011 census what is the Males population of Manipur?
A 1,438,586   B. 1,105,680
C. 1,516,123   D. 1,315,219

357. As per the 2011 census what is the Females population of Manipur?
A 1,170,338
B. 1,417,208
C. 1,330,216
D. 1,175,670

358. The Kabaw Valley was handed over to Myanmar (Burma) in the year :
A 1830   B. 1834
C. 1838   D. 1840

359. When was the first English school established in Manipur?
A 1880   B. 1885
C. 1890   D. 1892

360. Who saved the life of king Khagemba (1597-1652 AD) for the territorial integrity of Manipur while fighting against the raids of tribal?
A Muhammad Sani and his troops
B. L. Dhananjoy Singh and his groups
C. Both B and C
D. None of the above

361. What is the full form of MOA?
A Manipur Olympic Association
B. Manipur Oil Association
C. Manipur Organisation of Adults
D. None of these

362. In which year was 'Manipur women's Football Association' formed?

A 1972   B. 1976
C. 1980   D. 1982

363. Who was the 'founder patron' of modern sports movement in Manipur?
A Charairongba
B. Keiphaba Yanglon
C. Sir Churachand Singh
D. Bhadra Singh

364. Who is the author of the book 'My Experience in Manipur'?
A Sir James Johnstone
B. Lucy Zehol
C. A.K. Paul
D. E.W. Dun

365. In Manipur 'Durga Puja' is locally known as:
A Heikru Hitongba
B. Kwak Yatra
C. Yaoshang
D. None of the above

366. What is the height of Saheed Minar?
A 45 feet   B. 50 feet
C. 55 feet   D. 60 feet

367. Who was the first Muslim Durbar Member of Manipur during the time of British?
A Maulvi Qazi Wali-Ullah
B. Maulana Baseruddin
C. Suleiman
D. Sheikh Zunaid

368. Ksh. Thouranisabi Devi got Padamshree for her work in :
A Nat Songkritan
B. Mountaineering
C. Cinema
D. Boxing

369. Where is Sainik School situated in Manipur?
A Imphal   B. Bishnupur
C. Senapati   D. Ukhrul

370. Who is known as the 'Melody

King' in Manipur?
A R.K. Bhogen
B. Nongmaithem Pahari
C. S. Devabrata Singh
D. L. Lakpati Singh

371. Who is known as the 'Melody Queen' in Manipur?
A Sabitri Heisnam
B. Y. Gambhini Devi
C. Laishram Mema Devi
D. Y. Ranjana Devi

372. Who is popularly known as the 'Jananeta' (leader of the people) in Manipur?
A L. Jugeswar Singh
B. N. Tombi Singh
C. Paokai Hao Kip
D. Hijam Irabat

373. Which is the biggest Temple in Manipur?
A Shree Shree Govindajee Temple
B. Vishnu Temple
C. Hanuman Thakur Temple
D. Radha Raman Temple

374. Which is the biggest cave in Manipur?
A Khu Kse
B. Khang Khui Cave
C. Sangboo
D. Tonglon

375. How many tribal dialects are recognised by the government of India in Manipur?
A 2   B. 4
C. 5   D. 6

376. Which is the highest rainfall area in Manipur?
A Thoubal   B. Ukhrul
C. Tamenglong   D. Chandel

377. Which is the lowest rainfall area in Manipur?
A Senapati

B. Imphal
C. Ukhrul
D. Churachandpur

378. Where is Orange Festival celebrated in Manipur?
A Tamenglong   B. Ukhrul
C. Senapati   D. Bishnupur

379. The present 10 + 2 + 3 system of education was started in Manipur from the academic session of:
A 1985-86   B. 1986-87
C. 1988-89   D. 1990-91

380. What is Jhum cultivation locally called in Manipur?
A Mono   B. Kamlou
C. Pamlou   D. Tuwalu

381. How many small Town committees are in Manipur?
A 20   B. 25
C. 33   D. 35

382. How many number of Municipalities are in the Urban areas of Manipur?
A 9   B. 12
C. 16   D. 18

383. "INAMPEILIN' is the annual festival of which tribe of Manipur?
A Maring   B. Tongkhul
C. Chothe   D. Tarao

384. It is reported that there were thirty two Manipuri Muslim women who involved and participated in the 1939 Second Nupi Lan. Name some of them.
A Noorjan, Tombi, Yaima, Jasmine and Safarjan
B. Noorjan, Tombi, Gulzan, Leiren and Safarjan
C. Safarjan, Noorjan, Leiren, Thanil and Basira
D. None of the above

385. When was the status of chief commissioner upgraded to

Lieutenant Governor in Manipur?
A. 1968   B. 1969
C. 1970   D. 1971

386. Who is the first Manipuri Women Film Producer?
A. Sabitri Heisnam
B. Y. Ranajana Devi
C. Khaidem Sakhi Devi
D. K. O. Thouranisabi Devi

387. Among the five hundred soldiers recruited in the Gambhir Singh's Levy, there were sixteen Manipuri Muslims in this soldier's recruitment. Who were the important soldiers?
A. Rafi Muhammad, Sheikh Rafi, Sheikh Salena and Sheikh Salam
B. Rafi Muhammad, Sheikh Rafi, Sheikh Salena and Sheikh Subol
C. Rafi Muhammad, Sheikh Rafi, Sheikh Salena and Sheikh Sirajur
D. None of the above

388. Who was the first Director of Education in Manipur?
A. M.S. Sharma (1960-61)
B. S.D. Bahuguna (1958-59)
C. C. Kirti Singh (1972-73)
D. K.C. Tongbra (1975-76)

389. Which lake is known as the "Kohinoor of Manipur"?
A. Zailad Lake
B. Kachouphung Lake
C. Loktak Lake
D. Kharung Lake

390. What is the oldest salt mine (brine) in Manipur?
A. Ningel salt mine
B. Sikhong salt mine
C. Chandrakhong salt mine
D. Waikhong salt mine

391. Where is rubber grown in Manipur?
A. Kakching B. Jiribam
C. Nambal   D. Machi

392. When does the "Manipur Plantation Crops" establish?
A. 1985-86 B. 1990-91
C. 1979-80 D. 1981-82

393. Where is the hottest place in Manipur?
A. Tengnoupal B. Moirang
C. Jiribam   D. Kakching

394. Who was the first person to set up NCC in Manipur?
A. L.H. Harnet
B. H. Tombi Singh
C. P.K. Suisy
D. P. K. Behring

395. Who is the first Manipuri Chief Justice ?
A. P. Jugal
B. R. K. Manisama Singh
C. Ranbir Meitei
D. K. Sanatomba

396. The district of Manipur which is known as the birth place of Christianity in the state is :
A. Thoubal B. Senapati
C. Ukhrul   D. Chandel

397. The Number of tea gardens in Manipur is :
A. 4   B. 6
C. 10   D. 12

398. In which year Oak Tassar Project was introduced in Manipur?
A. 1971-72 B. 1975-76
C. 1973-74 D. 1978-79

399. Bir Tikendrajit Singh's crusade was against the :
A. Chinese B. Japanese
C. Burmese D. Britishers

400. Takhel Khong (Tripura Canal) was Constructed by :
A. Khabomba B. Punsiba
C. Telheiba D. Bharatsai

401. N.I. Devi is related with—
A. Literature   B. Sports
C. Arts   D. Medicine

402. How many Nagar Panchayats are in Manipur?
A. 15   B. 16
C. 17   D. 18

403. When was the war of Independence or the Anglo-Manipur war held?
A. 1890   B. 1891
C. 1895   D. 1897

404. When did the Chandel district come into existence?
A. May 13, 1974
B. July 6, 1977
C. June 10, 1978
D. September 5, 1980

405. When was the 'Fast Tract Court' established in Manipur?
A. October 5, 2001
B. November 6, 2002
C. January 7, 2003
D. July 5, 2001

406. When did Manipur Sales Tax Act & Rules come into force?
A. December 10, 1990
B. June 5, 1980
C. May 20, 1985
D. August 6, 1995

407. Manipur Public Service Commission was formed in:
A. 1972   B. 1973
C. 1974   D. 1975

408. Who was the first chairman of the Manipur Public Service Commission?
A. S. K. Behring
B. G. B. K. Hooja
C. K. L. Sharma
D. P. Krishnamohan Singh

409. Who among the following sportpersons is nominated in Rajya Sabha in 2016?
A. N. Kunjarani Devi
B. Suranjoy Singh
C. N. Dingko Singh
D. M.C. Mary Kom

410. What is the total area of Manipur under forest cover?
A. 16000 sq km.
B. 16538 sq km.
C. 17346 sq km.
D. 17503 sq km.

411. How many Gram Panchayats are there in Manipur?
A. 150   B. 155
C. 161   D. 166

412. Jiribam is located in which district?
A. Imphal East
B. Imphal West
C. Senapati
D. Tamenglong

413. Who was the Muslim Minister during the Chief Minister ship of M.K. Priyobrata Singh (14th August 1947–15th October 1949)?
A. Maulvi Basiruddin Ahmed
B. Mustaq Ali
C. Nasir Hussain
D. None of these

414. Who was the lone Muslim who involved while making the "Manipur State Constitution Making Body" in 1946 during the reign of Maharaj Bodhachandra?
A. Maulvi Basiruddin Ahmed
B. Salim Ali
C. S.H. Raza
D. M.K. Khan

415. The book 'Ima' was written by :
A. L. Premchand
B. Hijam Angahal
C. Lucy Zehal
D. E. W. Dun

416. The book 'Sur Vigyan' recognised by the state government as a text

book for music in Manipur is written by :
A. H. Guno Singh
B. E. Nilakanta Singh
C. Laishram Memma
D. R. K. Madhubir

417. In Manipur who was popularly known as Bob?
A. Birendrajit Naorem
B. Aribam Shyam Sharma
C. M. A. Singh
D. Ralengnao Khaling

418. Name some Manipuri Muslims who fought courageously in the Anglo-Manipuri War of 1891 AD for the sake of territorial integrity of Manipur.
A. Shinga Dewan, Niyamattulah, Ajjur Rahman, and Yusuf Ali
B. Subedar Sang-gai, Rahmattullah, Umor Nongsaiba, and Sadhu Mia
C. Both A and B
D. None of the above

419. Who is honoured with the title 'Nritya Rani'?
A. L. Ibemhal Devi
B. Elam Indira Devi
C. H. Ngangbi Devi
D. Darshana Jhaveri

420. When was the Paddy Transplantation Method in Manipur called in Manipuri language as Lingthokpa not Punghul and Pamphel introduced?
A. Muslims during the reign of Garib Niwaz
B. Muslims during the reign of Charairongba

C. Assamese Muslims during the period of Paikhomba
D. Muslims during the reign of king Khagemba

421. Who was the Manipuri Muslim, popularly known as Japan Pitru, who fought bravely for the Britishers against the Japanese forces in the Second World War and came back alive?
A. Naqi Ahmed Choudhury
B. Ali Akbar
C. Alauddin Khan
D. Mehtab Ali

422. In the initial period of Muslim settlement in Manipur, Muslims followed the Shariat 'loosely'. Who was the first Maulana who brought the concept of strict rules and regulations of Shariat like purdah system in Manipur?
A. Ibadullah from Irong Chesaba
B. Abdul Jalil from Thoubal Moijing
C. Tonjou Maulvi from Irong
D. None of the above

423. Which was the first Madarsa of Manipur?
A. Madarsa Mazharul-uloom of Mayang Imphal
B. Kshetrigao Madarsa
C. Alia Madarsa Lilong Haoreibi
D. Darul Uloom Lilong Haoreibi

424. Who was the first Head Master of Churachand High School?
A. Maulvi Qazi Wali-Ullah
B. Hafiz Ali Khan
C. Jaan Nisaar
D. Javed Ali

ANSWERS

1	2	3	4	5	6	7	8	9	10
C	A	D	A	B	A	B	D	C	C

11	**12**	**13**	**14**	**15**	**16**	**17**	**18**	**19**	**20**
A	C	D	A	B	A	A	B	A	C
21	**22**	**23**	**24**	**25**	**26**	**27**	**28**	**29**	**30**
B	A	C	C	C	B	A	B	A	A
31	**32**	**33**	**34**	**35**	**36**	**37**	**38**	**39**	**40**
C	A	C	C	B	D	C	B	B	D
41	**42**	**43**	**44**	**45**	**46**	**47**	**48**	**49**	**50**
D	A	B	C	A	C	A	B	C	C
51	**52**	**53**	**54**	**55**	**56**	**57**	**58**	**59**	**60**
A	B	C	A	C	A	B	A	C	A
61	**62**	**63**	**64**	**65**	**66**	**67**	**68**	**69**	**70**
A	B	B	B	C	C	D	A	C	A
71	**72**	**73**	**74**	**75**	**76**	**77**	**78**	**79**	**80**
D	C	A	A	C	B	A	B	C	A
81	**82**	**83**	**84**	**85**	**86**	**87**	**88**	**89**	**90**
B	B	C	A	A	B	B	C	B	A
91	**92**	**93**	**94**	**95**	**96**	**97**	**98**	**99**	**100**
C	A	B	C	D	A	A	A	A	D
101	**102**	**103**	**104**	**105**	**106**	**107**	**108**	**109**	**110**
C	C	A	D	C	D	D	C	D	C
111	**112**	**113**	**114**	**115**	**116**	**117**	**118**	**119**	**120**
A	C	B	C	A	B	A	B	D	C
121	**122**	**123**	**124**	**125**	**126**	**127**	**128**	**129**	**130**
A	B	B	A	C	D	A	A	A	C
131	**132**	**133**	**134**	**135**	**136**	**137**	**138**	**139**	**140**
A	A	B	C	C	D	A	B	A	B
141	**142**	**143**	**144**	**145**	**146**	**147**	**148**	**149**	**150**
A	C	A	C	D	B	C	A	B	D
151	**152**	**153**	**154**	**155**	**156**	**157**	**158**	**159**	**160**
A	C	A	B	A	D	A	B	B	B
161	**162**	**163**	**164**	**165**	**166**	**167**	**168**	**169**	**170**
C	A	B	C	D	A	A	A	B	C
171	**172**	**173**	**174**	**175**	**176**	**177**	**178**	**179**	**180**
D	A	B	C	D	D	B	B	D	C
181	**182**	**183**	**184**	**185**	**186**	**187**	**188**	**189**	**190**
D	C	C	D	A	A	D	A	C	A
191	**192**	**193**	**194**	**195**	**196**	**197**	**198**	**199**	**200**
A	B	A	C	A	D	A	B	A	B
201	**202**	**203**	**204**	**205**	**206**	**207**	**208**	**209**	**210**
D	C	D	A	B	A	A	B	D	C
211	**212**	**213**	**214**	**215**	**216**	**217**	**218**	**219**	**220**
C	A	B	C	C	A	C	A	B	B

221	222	223	224	225	226	227	228	229	230
D	B	C	B	C	A	A	B	D	B
231	232	233	234	235	236	237	238	239	240
A	B	C	A	A	A	B	B	C	D
241	242	243	244	245	246	247	248	249	250
A	B	C	D	D	A	A	B	A	B
251	252	253	254	255	256	257	258	259	260
C	D	A	B	C	D	A	B	C	A
261	262	263	264	265	266	267	268	269	270
C	D	A	B	A	B	A	A	A	A
271	272	273	274	275	276	277	278	279	280
A	A	C	B	A	C	D	A	B	C
281	282	283	284	285	286	287	288	289	290
D	A	B	C	A	B	C	D	A	B
291	292	293	294	295	296	297	298	299	300
C	C	B	B	D	B	A	B	A	C
301	302	303	304	305	306	307	308	309	310
A	D	A	D	A	B	A	B	C	A
311	312	313	314	315	316	317	318	319	320
D	A	B	C	D	A	B	C	D	D
321	322	323	324	325	326	327	328	329	330
B	A	D	A	A	A	C	D	A	A
331	332	333	334	335	336	337	338	339	340
B	D	A	B	A	C	A	A	B	D
341	342	343	344	345	346	347	348	349	350
D	A	B	C	C	B	A	B	B	C
351	352	353	354	355	356	357	358	359	360
D	B	A	B	C	A	B	B	B	A
361	362	363	364	365	366	367	368	369	370
A	B	C	A	B	C	A	A	A	B
371	372	373	374	375	376	377	378	379	380
C	D	A	B	D	C	D	A	B	C
381	382	383	384	385	386	387	388	389	390
C	A	C	B	B	C	B	B	C	A
391	392	393	394	395	396	397	398	399	400
B	D	C	A	B	C	B	C	D	A
401	402	403	404	405	406	407	408	409	410
C	D	B	A	A	A	A	B	D	C
411	412	413	414	415	416	417	418	419	420
D	A	A	A	D	C	D	C	B	D
421	422	423	424						
A	A	A	A						

1901

www.ingramcontent.com/pod-product-compliance
Lightning Source LLC
Chambersburg PA
CBHW050324160726
48002CB00001B/178